GILMORE GIRLS

The Cultural History of Television

Series Editors: Bob Batchelor, M. Keith Booker, Kathleen M. Turner

Mad Men*: A Cultural History*, by M. Keith Booker and Bob Batchelor
Frasier*: A Cultural History*, by Joseph J. Darowski and Kate Darowski
Breaking Bad*: A Cultural History*, by Lara Stache
Star Trek*: A Cultural History*, by M. Keith Booker
The Simpsons*: A Cultural History*, by Moritz Fink
Cheers*: A Cultural History*, by Joseph J. Darowski and Kate Darowski
Gilmore Girls*: A Cultural History*, by Lara C. Stache and Rachel D. Davidson

GILMORE GIRLS

A Cultural History

Lara C. Stache
Rachel D. Davidson

ROWMAN & LITTLEFIELD
Lanham • Boulder • New York • London

Published by Rowman & Littlefield
An imprint of The Rowman & Littlefield Publishing Group, Inc.
4501 Forbes Boulevard, Suite 200, Lanham, Maryland 20706
www.rowman.com

6 Tinworth Street, London SE11 5AL

British Library Cataloguing in Publication Information Available

Library of Congress Cataloging-in-Publication Data

Names: Stache, Lara C., 1981- author. | Davidson, Rachel D., 1978- author.
Title: Gilmore girls : a cultural history / Lara C. Stache, Rachel Davidson.
Description: Lanham : Rowman & Littlefield, 2019. | Series: The cultural history of television | Includes bibliographical references and index.
Identifiers: LCCN 2019001931 (print) | LCCN 2019005459 (ebook) | ISBN 9781538112847 (electronic) | ISBN 9781538112830 (cloth)
Subjects: LCSH: Gilmore girls (Television program : 2000-2007)
Classification: LCC PN1992.77.G54 (ebook) | LCC PN1992.77.G54 S73 2019 (print) | DDC 791.45/72—dc23
LC record available at https://lccn.loc.gov/2019001931

For John Wayne, Carolina, and Ivy—my three desert stars. Where you lead, I will follow.
—R. D.

For R.O.C., as strong as Dwayne Johnson and Alcatraz combined.
—L. S.

CONTENTS

ACKNOWLEDGMENTS

Thank you to my friends and family who always give nothing but support and positive encouragement.

To a wonderful writing partner and fabulous friend, Rachel D. Davidson. I am so happy to have sat next to you on a panel all those years ago. To the Chase family, who loves *Gilmore Girls* as much as I do, and to Sheena Ozbolt and Christine O'Brien, who have discussed the series with me in depth over the years. You all are my Sookie, my Lane, and even my Paris combined.

Thank you to the series editors, Keith Booker, Bob Batchelor, and Kathleen Turner, for taking on the monumental task of a series that explores the cultural history and impact of television. Thanks especially to Stephen Ryan, senior editor at Rowman & Littlefield, for your patience, knowledge, and support.

To the Stache, Altwine, and Mangun families—your support is always felt one million times over.

To my incredible husband, a Gilmore guy by all rights, and the best writer I know, Rob Mangun. I love this car. To Ogden and Campbell—I hope you always want me to sing you the *Gilmore Girls* theme song at bedtime, and when you inevitably do not, if it sticks in your head anyway, my job will be complete. I love you.

—Lara C. Stache

Thank you to the series editors, Keith Booker, Bob Batchelor, and Kathleen Turner, for giving us the opportunity to contribute to this exciting book series. A special thanks to Stephen Ryan, senior editor at Rowman & Littlefield, for your guidance and support of our project.

To my collaborator, colleague, and dear friend, Lara Stache. You have been the most ideal writing partner—patient, reassuring, brilliant, and an expert on all things Gilmore. Thank you for forcing me to watch *Gilmore Girls*. You were right! It is life-changing and so smart—just like you.

Lauren Graham, thank you for your inspiration (#momgoals) and for your kitchen timer technique . . . it works!

To my biggest fan, my mom, for always cheering me on and championing my work. Your support means so much to me.

John, thank you for watching (and rewatching) every episode of *Gilmore Girls* with me. Carolina and Ivy, thank you for your enthusiasm, curiosity, and overall support of me while working on this book. I love you, family.

Finally, to everyone who asked about the book and allowed me to gush for a moment about this research—THANK YOU! I hope you enjoy the final product.

—Rachel D. Davidson

INTRODUCTION

We Had a Gilmore Girl, We Lost a Gilmore Girl . . .

Gilmore Girls (2000–2007) debuted in 2000 on the WB network and features seven seasons with young single mother, Lorelai Gilmore (Lauren Graham), and her daughter, Rory (Alexis Bledel). The series is especially distinctive for its rapid dialogue, "like some kind of party game for smarty pants, the Cool Girls verbal Twister, pitched right at us so we all can play,"[1] as well as the numerous popular-culture references sprinkled liberally throughout each episode. Nuggets of wisdom like, "You can't always control who you are attracted to, you know? I think the whole Angelina Jolie–Billy Bob Thornton thing really proves that," are par for the course (Episode 1.5, "Cinnamon's Wake"). The central premise to the show revolves around the uniquely close relationship of mother and daughter, who only have a sixteen-year age difference. In the premiere episode, a dimwitted dude, who tries to hit on both Lorelai and Rory, quips, "You do not look like a mother. And you do not look like a daughter" (Episode 1.1, "Pilot"). Mother and daughter laugh together as he hightails it out of Luke's diner after learning Rory is only sixteen (not even yet), and the audience is officially introduced to the Gilmore girls and the utopian town of Stars Hollow.

The idea for the series came from something creator "[Amy] Sherman-Palladino pitched to executives from the WB on a whim: a TV show about a mother and a daughter who are best friends. But that off-the-cuff pitch led to a show that was witty, big-hearted, and full of quirky characters."[2] Moved across various networks during its run, as well as suffering a major shake-up with the departure of creator and showrunner, Amy Sherman-Palladino, as well as her writing partner and co-showrunner, Daniel Palladino, before the final year, *Gilmore Girls* lasted seven seasons and continues to gain new viewers. Although not entirely without criticism, *Gilmore Girls* was a closet hit garnering a devoted fan base that watched weekly as the various relationships developed. The series picked up an even larger audience once episodes began streaming on Netflix, and more than ten years later Sherman-Palladino and the actors negotiated a "final season" revival of four episodes, *Gilmore Girls: A Year in the Life* (2016), exclusive to Netflix. The revival had five million viewers in the first three days of the launch, a number that speaks to the appeal of the original series and the desperate desire to reconnect with Stars Hollow and the gang.

Replete with love triangles, family communication struggles, and speedy dialogue loaded with pop-culture references and witty comebacks, why do some viewers fight the allure of *Gilmore Girls*? When recommending the show to those who have not yet experienced the magic of Sherman-Palladino's creation, the recommender is inevitably met with skepticism, resistance, and (dare we say it?) a condescending smirk. How could that rom-com in television form possibly be interesting, funny, and smart? Why should that silly show from the WB win out in the queue over binge-worthy quality shows like *Breaking Bad*, *Orange Is the New Black*, *Mad Men*, or literally anything else? Because of Emily and Richard; because of Sookie and Michel; because of Dean and Jess and, yes, even Logan (ugh). Because of Luke and Christopher and Max and Jason. Because of Taylor and Kirk and Miss Patty, Babette, the Independence Inn, the Dragonfly Inn, Weston's Bakery, and even Rune (aka "Boo Radley"). Because the characters of Lorelai and Rory are enviable, complex, and flawed and offer a fresh take on "mother/daughter" narratives. In full disclosure, one of the authors of this book (Rachel) initially resisted the request from the other author (Lara) to watch the series and give it a chance. Lara even insisted Rachel watch the first episode with her and guaranteed she would be hooked. After the viewing, Rachel kindly but firmly rebuffed Lara's offer to loan her all seven seasons on DVD (this was before Netflix had them all) and did not approach the series again for four (FOUR!) years, when she promptly fell in love with

A (limited) cast photo of Gilmore Girls: Michel Gerard (Yanic Truesdale), Miss Patty (Liz Torres), Emily Gilmore (Kelly Bishop), Richard Gilmore (Edward Herrmann), Sookie St. James (Melissa McCarthy), Luke Danes (Scott Patterson), Lane Kim (Keiko Agena), Lorelai Gilmore (Lauren Graham), and Rory Gilmore (Alexis Bledel). *The WB / Photofest © The WB, Photographer: Jeffrey Thurner.*

it. Lesson learned: It is never too late to give the girls a chance (and Rachel is very stubborn).

This book is for the fans of the series; those who come back to the show again and again; those who were (im)patiently waiting for the November 2016 reboot on Netflix to finally find out Sherman-Palladino's intended last four words; those who love the characters and can construct an impassioned argument in favor of Dean, Jess, or Logan. If you find yourself repeating any of the fabulous lines when exasperated ("Oy, with the poodles already!") or use one as a daily mantra ("If you're going to throw your life away, he better have a motorcycle!"), this book is for you. Our book unpacks the nuances of this unassumingly complex and smart narrative and attempts to answer what it is about this series that is so appealing.

CULTURAL SIGNIFICANCE AND GOOD TV

Good television is about surprising the audience with well-written dialogue and interesting characters that make a series both entertaining and thoughtful. This requires the writers to both create a new world that people want to visit and reflect something about the world the audience lives in that makes the struggles, tensions, and dialogue relatable. *Time*'s James Poniewozik chose *Gilmore Girls* for his All-TIME 100 TV Shows list due as much to the impressive linguistic gymnastics as to his connection to the characters.[3] Television critic Alan Sepinwall chose the series for his Best Comedies of '00s list because, "at its best, *Gilmore Girls* was pure, concentrated happiness."[4] Airing in the same year that Bush became president of the United States over Al Gore and funded by the Family Friendly Programming Forum, a group who in 2000 defined "family friendly" as "'uplifting' shows that won't embarrass or offend an 'average' viewer,"[5] *Gilmore Girls* is smart and poignant while also being fun. It is both family friendly and progressive: the unicorn combination of television appeal.

The stories we see on television are both a creation of society and a mirror reflecting society. Not only is the character of Lorelai Gilmore funny, quick-witted, and relatable, but she also offers a complicated and refreshingly representative success story for a single young mother in America. Stacia Fleegal writes that Lorelai's depiction on *Gilmore Girls* is significant because, "in television culture, single mothers have about as much of a chance of being written good, forward-thinking, feminist parts as mothers in Disney movies have of survival."[6] This is particularly true at the turn of the century when series like *The Sopranos* and *The Wire* were cultural hits. Television critic Joy Press reminds us that when *Gilmore Girls* aired in 2000, the "template for quality TV. . . equated depth and substance with troubled male-characters, roiling masculine energy, internecine power struggles, and regular eruptions of highly realistic violence."[7] Straying so far from the "good television" template, "*Gilmore Girls*'s immersion in the emotionally tangled lives of intelligent women" gave it "virtually no chance of being seen as an important show."[8] To make matters worse, *Gilmore Girls* aired in the coveted television spot of 8 p.m. on Thursdays but on the WB, which meant they would be up against NBC's *Friends*. Even Lauren Graham thought they were sunk before they started.[9] However, the series stayed afloat, and Sherman-Palladino, a former writer on both *Roseanne* and *Veronica's Closet*, created a distinctive voice with characters that intricately balance funny and touching. Daniel Palladino explains, "We actually tend to see a lot of our characters as tragic, and then we write them funny. . . . In *Gilmore Girls* it was Emily: she lost her daughter, and she never really got her back."[10] This balance lends depth to the series, making it a hidden gem, until it started streaming on Netflix and it became a much more visible, blinking-arrow-pointing-at-it, Rachel's-rhinestone-sweatshirt-at-the-rummage-sale gem.

The primary success of the series is the fact that, though *Gilmore Girls* is about mothers and daughters, it is not just about mother/daughter relationships. The Gilmore girls "can be seen as the same person separated by time/age and set on two different paths, with the fork in the road going Ivy League versus having a teen pregnancy,"[11] and yet Lorelai and Rory are distinctively different in many ways. The fork in their paths is exactly where the series starts, when Rory is about to turn sixteen. It is a series that "explores heredity and habit—the faults and defaults of our programming"[12] but in a way that relates to relationships and situations across gender, class, and race. This appeal was intentional with Sherman-Palladino telling her writers to create "girlfriend stories," not "mother-daughter stories."[13] Additionally, the mix of both low-brow and obscure popular-culture references that could come from an *US Weekly* (or at times from the 1940s) with high-brow guest appearances like Madeleine Albright and Christiane Amanpour is a reflection of a panache that no other series had at the time. They even got Norman Mailer to appear with his son Stephen, who was hesitant at first but said, "I felt better when I saw a couple of runs of the show. . . . It had taste. It was witty and well put together."[14]

Categorized as a dramedy, Sherman-Palladino heavily focused on overloading the dialogue instead of allowing time for emotional pauses. The language matters—how it is said is just as important as what is said—and it is the dialogue that makes the series a cultural icon, both in content and pace. The average television script runs "fifty to fifty-five pages . . . but the *Gilmore Girls* scripts run seventy-seven to seventy-eight pages."[15] The size of Sherman-Palladino's scripts barely made it past the network's review.[16] In fact, Sherman-Palladino argues that *Gilmore Girls* would not work on advertising-focused network television today because in "our best episodes . . . the last 30 seconds were our most emotional part of the show, and that would have been cut."[17] In contrast, Sherman-Palladino contends that Netflix emphasizes storytelling over marketing. The streaming format was destined to house *Gilmore Girls*, in all its iterations.

All that said, even a fantastic series has its flaws at times. Primarily, there are some issues with timing. We assume Rory is in honors or advanced placement classes, or maybe all classes are that caliber at Chilton. That requires a lot of homework. How do the Gilmore girls have time to do homework, order food or eat dinner at Luke's, and watch one to two movies in the same evening? That is a little sketchy. In one particularly oddly timed episode in the series, Rory and Lane are wearing different clothes during the same day with no indication that one of them went home to change, and in the same episode, Lane bleaches her dark black hair and dyes it purple and then back to black all in one afternoon/evening (Episode 3.4, "One's Got Class and the Other One Dyes"). These timing issues are not in keeping with Sherman-Palladino's reputation for being controlling with the set and scripts. Actors and writers remember how important it was to read exactly what was written in the script. Sherman-Palladino relayed a memory of when an exasperated Edward Herrmann, who played Richard Gilmore, yelled at her, "We are not puppets! We are not puppets!"[18] Another strange aspect of the series is the reuse of actors to play different characters. Some are either minor enough or wearing enough makeup that the double dipping is quirky and fun. For example,

Alex Borstein (originally cast as Sookie for the pilot episode) is both Drella the harpist from season 1 and the elderly stylist Miss Celine in later seasons. Comedienne and actor Riki Lindhome plays Logan's friend Juliet in seasons 5 and 6 but also played a girl at Career Day in the same episode where Lane bleaches her hair. Sherilyn Fenn plays two characters in a particularly egregious middle finger to fans because she is so noticeable. Short white-blonde hair as Jess's kind-of-stepmom did not keep us from noticing her as Luke's former flame and April's mom, Anna Nardini (although we appreciate the inclusion of actors from *Twin Peaks*, like Mädchen Amick, who played Sherry Tinsdale, and Ray Wise, who played Emily's friend Jack in the revival).

Additionally, it is annoying how much junk food the women consume while maintaining incredibly thin physiques (at the beginning of season 3, Alexis Bledel looks scary thin) and flawless skin, especially when it has been documented that the actresses never ate anything like that in real life. Lauren Graham says that between takes, sometimes she and Kelly Bishop would share a small bag of Cheetos together; we're guessing those are literally the little ones that go in kid's lunchboxes.[19] However, these are minor issues and we chose to ignore them for the most part to focus on what they do so well: writing subtly complex characters and witty, fast dialogue that makes the series not only immensely binge-able but also rewatchable.

The late success, moving from a cult hit to a mainstream love after launching on Netflix, limits the in-the-moment discussion about the characters, story line, and obsession with showrunners that has become commonplace in the past decade. When it comes to hit shows from the past few years, like *Breaking Bad*, critics and fans endlessly wanted to parse what was going on in Walter White's head as he made the decisions he did, but we don't have the same nuances of character discussion with *Gilmore Girls* during the time that it aired. Much of the discussion takes place after the series is over and especially in conjunction with the revival ten years later. This is partly due to the fact that the series was slightly on the bubble before actors and showrunners were expected to podcast their thought process and embrace social media to relate to fans, but also due to the fact that it was a cult hit at first and there simply was not media demand for more information. Our goal in this book is to put some of what we see in the narrative in context with what was going on outside of it and make sense of the choices made to move the story forward.

"THAT'LL DO, PIG"

This volume deals with the original seven seasons of the series, saving a short discussion about the four-episode Netflix revival for the conclusion of the book. We do this for two reasons: (1) The revival's cultural significance—as it is at the time of this writing only four episodes long—is more relevant to the existence of it rather than the content in it at this point in time; and (2) the series existed as a complete story at the time of its airing. It may not have been Sherman-Palladino's intended complete story, but it was all that the fans had for ten years, and we believe it should be understood as its own artifact, with a discussion of potential impacts from the revival saved primarily for the conclusion.

With that being said, we deal as little as possible with season 7. Showrunners do not always know where a series is going, and in fact, the argument has been made that trying out different possibilities is part of what makes a good writer.[20] But we were not fulfilled by season 7, fans and critics overwhelmingly hate season 7, and it definitely did not end with the four words that Amy Sherman-Palladino had intended, so who knows where she would have taken the women? Although season 7 showrunner David S. Rosenthal worked with Sherman-Palladino in previous seasons, "for viewers at home, it was like watching familiar bodies occupied by foreign spirits."[21] Even Lauren Graham argues that, in the seventh season, "we weren't sure where the show was heading, and we were starting to feel a bit uninspired," explaining why she and Alexis Bledel did not take the raises they were offered to continue to an eighth season.[22] Season 7 introduces long shots, as well as close-ups, and emotional moments of pause, which is a style that Sherman-Palladino fought the network on from day one. She argues that the WB was used to something different: "Their stuff was very soapy; it was angsty. . . . My pace freaked them out, and my style of shooting freaked them out because I don't like close-ups."[23] Season 7 is closer to the WB's style, but it also lacked the right-on-top-of-itself dialogue that made *Gilmore Girls* so enjoyable to watch. In our analysis of the series, we do not completely ignore it, but we do not make it shine—kind of like what the final season did for the series.

Our analysis of *Gilmore Girls* is at once a deep dive into a highly entertaining, witty, and charmed world and an exploration of what was happening outside of the story, occurring at the turn of the century. We make an argument for the cultural significance of the series by analyzing both the inside narrative and the outside context. To do so, this book has been laid out in two parts: part I of the book breaks out the different types of relationships featured in the series. The core of *Gilmore Girls* is about the "tangled bonds among these three generations of female Gilmores and the complex matrix of love, money, and familial duty."[24] In the first chapter, we analyze the mother/daughter bonds through all three Gilmore women. But we also get into the equally important and smartly written romantic relationships, friendships, and fatherhood in this section of the book. In chapter 2, we focus on the representation of fatherhood in the series, arguing that the portrayal of Rory's father figures highlights consequences, both positive and negative, of an alternative family structure. Chapter 3 is an exploration of the romantic relationships for the women, starting with the parallel dyads of Christopher and Logan, Luke and Dean, and then, to really get you intrigued, Lorelai and Jess. Much has been written about the Gilmore girls' dependence and lack thereof on romantic partners, and we analyze what the decisions in the narrative say about how we expect romance to work. In chapter 4, we give some attention to the friendships of Lorelai and Rory, arguing that, in many ways, they provide important representations of female friendship that are unique and culturally significant.

Digging into the cultural conversations that *Gilmore Girls* both mirrors and creates, part II focuses on themes of feminism, the value of popular culture, issues of class and social status, as well as the representation of small-town living. In chapter 5, we attempt to decipher the somewhat conflicting messages about female empowerment, feminism, and what the Gilmore women want, but we also suggest that the sometimes contradictory messages about empowerment from Lorelai and Rory are actually a reflection of the world around them. Chapter 6 explores the heavy use of popular culture in the dialogue, arguing that the pop-loaded banter reveals important lessons about life and love, in addition to creating an appeal for fans that is rivaled by few. The theme of social status and class is the focus for chapter 7, where we dissect how the series creates tension between Lorelai and her parents but also with Lorelai and Rory in regard to money and social expectations. In the final chapter, we pay tribute to the town of Stars Hollow and the lovely characters that make it look like heaven to live there.

We now take you with us, dear readers, on a journey back to the beauty and magic of Stars Hollow, where we provide as much nostalgia and love for the series as we do a challenge to some of the messages and narrative choices when we view them as both a reflection and creation of society. In omnia paratus!

Part I

Relationships: "My sister, my daughter."

Road trip to Harvard. ***The WB / Photofest © The WB.***

1

MOTHERS AND DAUGHTERS

"Vicious Trollop"

> No mother in the history of television was ever cooler than Lorelai Gilmore. . . . Rory's motivation was all internal; no one had to nudge her toward high SAT scores. Discipline wasn't an issue. As a result Lorelai's mothering seemed effortless, relieved as she was of the worries so many others must endure.
>
> —Ginia Bellafante[1]

> That Lorelai and Emily share an instinct for manipulating Rory into submission through displays of abundance (food in Lorelai's case, money in Emily's) robs them of their self-righteousness.
>
> —Lili Loofbourow[2]

When it comes to the series' representation of motherhood, and specifically the articulation of what a mother/daughter relationship should or could be, "the cultural significance of the show cannot be overstated. Nothing captured, or idealized, the new model of American parenthood—one based on friendship and shared tastes—quite like *Gilmore Girls*."[3] Emily's upper-class version of conservative role-model motherhood is actively juxtaposed with Lorelai's contemporary, I'm-a-friend-until-I-pull-the-mom-card approach (and that does not always come out in Lorelai's favor). Motherhood is an element of the show that *Gilmore Girls* consistently gets right, and one that makes the series fun to watch again and again.

Part of the series' success in its portrayals of mothers is that Lorelai's version of motherhood is not always perfect, revealing her as an unreliable narrator at times. Writer and blogger Mary Chase states, "I love how watching the show always makes me think about being a better mother or daughter and all the ways I will probably never be better because, well, patterns are hard to break."[4] The versions of motherhood in the series can be seen as these patterns, both resisted and maintained, which makes watching *Gilmore Girls* overwhelmingly relatable and interesting.

Deputy culture editor for *New Statesman* Anna Leszkiewicz astutely notes, "Sherman-Palladino's work is littered with confident, fast-talking, witty women struggling to deal with the immense amount of pressure they put on themselves: whether that's Rory's academic conscientiousness, [or] Lorelai's decision to raise a child totally alone."[5] Sherman-Palladino argues that this pressure is "not so much [about] perfectionism. . . . It's dealing with the expectations: especially of the times."[6] This chapter sets out to explore the pressures and expectations found within Lorelai's and Emily's versions of motherhood.

While the relationship between Lane and Mrs. Kim offers some distinct parallels to Emily and Lorelai (and remember when Michel's mother comes to visit and Lorelai ruins his perfect relationship? Episode 2.18, "Back in the Saddle Again"), we focus on the mother/daughter dyads of Emily/Lorelai and Lorelai/Rory. We first detail how motherhood is represented in the series, specifically in the dialogue between characters about what it means to be a "good" mother. In these conversations, the supposed differences in parenting reveal a specific mind-set from both Emily and Lorelai about what it means to be a mom. Then we explore Lorelai as an unreliable narrator, highlighting the similarities between the women and their mothering, which is something that Lorelai works so hard to distinguish herself against.

DIFFERENCES APLENTY

Lorelai's version of Emily as an overbearing mother is corroborated early in the series. Emily adds the stipulation of weekly dinners to the financial loan for Chilton (Episode 1.1, "Pilot") and inserts herself into the girls' lives by showing up on Rory's first day at Chilton, setting up a DSL installation at Lorelai's house without permission, and insisting on buying Rory more clothes for school (Episode 1.2, "The Lorelais' First Day at Chilton"). After Rory has a "quite" nice time at the club with Richard, Lorelai and Rory see a little girl reprimanded for not sitting still during a wedding reception at the inn (Episode 1.3, "Kill Me Now"). Lorelai comments that the scene reminds her of her childhood, and Rory thanks Lorelai "for not putting me in a dress like that." At this point in the first season, these moments are relatively innocuous and more on the periphery, but as the series progresses, the definitions about motherhood start to be articulated via the conversations between the Gilmore women.

After Lorelai feels hope that Emily is starting to think about who they are and what they want ("think pudding"), Lorelai is slapped in the face with a reminder of what it means to embarrass Emily in public (Episode 1.6, "Rory's Birthday Parties"). At the first sweet-sixteen birthday party, Rory yells at Emily in front of her guests, refusing to give a speech to the crowd filled with Rory's snobby classmates, many of whom Rory actively dislikes and who dislike her. The overbearing Gilmore expectations are put on full display when a horrified Emily turns on Lorelai and tells her, "Your daughter has no manners whatsoever. You should be ashamed of yourself." In this episode, viewers witness Emily's version of mothering. Emily is a woman who parents within the framework of upholding the Gilmore name.

A more blatant conversation that specifically defines "good" mothers and "bad" mothers comes when Rory makes another publicly embarrassing mistake of falling asleep at Miss Patty's with Dean after the Chilton formal (Episode 1.9, "Rory's Dance"). Emily yells at Lorelai, "I will not stand by and watch you allow that girl to ruin her life. . . . What kind of mother are you to allow this to happen to her?" To which Lorelai retorts, "I don't know, Mom. What kind of mother were you?" What is particularly devastating about this scene is that the night before, when Emily takes care of an injured Lorelai, she clearly longs for the mothering role that Lorelai has denied her. She makes Lorelai a mashed banana on toast, something that Emily claims was a childhood favorite of Lorelai's. The snack offers a moment of levity when both Emily and Lorelai agree it is "disgusting," but Emily is initially hurt that Lorelai does not remember it or, more likely, that Lorelai doesn't remember that Emily took care of her when she was sick as a little girl. Later in the evening, a high-on-pain-medication and half-asleep Lorelai says, "Thank you, Mommy," when Emily puts a blanket on her, and Emily smiles, clearly pleased with the use of the moniker. During the fight the next morning, Emily levels Lorelai with the threat, "You are going to lose her. Just like I lost you," and this comment in combination with the tender moments from the previous evening reveals the pain that Emily bears.

Richard again hints at the level of Emily's pain (and his) when Lorelai thanks him for sticking up for her to Christopher's parents, Straub and Francine, a gratitude that Richard balks at (Episode 1.15, "Christopher Returns").

> Richard: Lorelai, what are you going to take away from this? That everything that happened in the past is suddenly fine because I defended you?
>
> Lorelai: No.
>
> Richard: That the hell that you put your mother and me through for the past sixteen years is suddenly washed away? Well, it's not.
>
> Lorelai: We've all been through hell, Dad.
>
> Richard: I had to tell my friends, my colleagues, that my only daughter, the brightest in her class, was pregnant and was leaving school.
>
> Lorelai: That must have been devastating.
>
> Richard: And then you run away. And you treat us as lepers. Your mother couldn't get out of bed for a month, did you know that? Did you?

Lorelai seems genuinely shocked, and we start to see that, although Richard and Emily can be overbearing and oppressive, they love Lorelai and have suffered for her decisions. It is in moments like these that we start to understand Lorelai as an unreliable narrator. In another example, at dinner with Max, Lorelai becomes increasingly enraged at Emily's seemingly uninterested reaction to the news that she and Max are getting married (Episode 2.2, "Hammers and Veils"). She storms over to the Gilmore home with Max in tow and attempts to berate Emily, calling her out on her bad behavior. As it turns out, Lorelai is the one in the wrong.

Lorelai as the unreliable narrator is most clearly conveyed when we get a flashback of what happened when she left the Gilmore home for good (Episode 3.13, "Dear Emily and Richard"). What is important about this episode is that it is written in a way that makes it almost impossible to not feel Emily's pain when she reads a note saying that Lorelai has run away and to not question Lorelai's version of how she "escaped" from Hartford. Assumed from the title of the episode and previous comments in the series, Lorelai starts the letter to them using their first names, telling them that she is taking their granddaughter and not telling them where she is going. This particular flashback scene cuts to a present-day moment where Lorelai is doing something nice for Emily by buying her a DVD player. Lorelai says she will figure out how to set it up, and Emily argues she will burn the house down trying. In response, Lorelai sings "Easter Parade" by Judy Garland and bounces up the stairs, with a concerned Emily following her. This episode is lovely. It reminds us there are two sides to the story and reveals a complexity to their relationship that can only be conveyed via skillful writers. If Emily can be negative, overbearing, and annoying, Lorelai can be impetuous, thoughtless, and annoying as well. It also reminds us that the day Lorelai left the Gilmore home, Emily abruptly not only lost her daughter but also lost her identity as a mother (at least for a time).

Failure and loss as a mother are both consistent themes throughout the series. Emily has failed as a mother, in her estimation, not only because Lorelai got pregnant on her watch but also because she has lost her daughter. Later in the series, Emily reflects on her mothering "failure" when she tells Lorelai that she lost Rory, just like she lost Lorelai (Episode 6.9, "The Prodigal Daughter Returns"). Lorelai does her best to negate Emily's feelings of failure as she responds, "You didn't lose her like you lost me. . . . And you didn't lose me."

Many of the episodes reinforce a recurring theme in the series: Is Lorelai a good mom or a bad mom? Sherman-Palladino argues, "Lots of people told me a real mom wouldn't do the things Lorelai does. . . . I tell them there are lots of ways to be a good mom. Lorelai is a great parent who isn't completely defined by her kid."[7] *Gilmore Girls* says she can be both and in-between and we can still love her, but it also implicitly guides us to feel the same way about Emily. Case in point, after defending Rory to Emily after the dance, Lorelai whirls on Rory: "You're going on the pill" (Episode 1.9, "Rory's Dance"). A hurt Rory, who insists that nothing happened, demands to know where the trust has gone and levels Lorelai with "You are just mad because I screwed up and I did it in front of Grandma and she nailed you for it." Lorelai's hypocrisy in this moment suggests that perhaps a part of her shares Emily's fears about Rory making the same mistakes Lorelai did and that Emily is not just being conservative and overbearing. This moment also indicates the pressure Lorelai feels to be a "good" mom after making the decision to do it on her own. We have heard this anxiety in the form of a joke before. When Richard and Emily visit Stars Hollow for the first time during Rory's second sixteenth birthday party, Lorelai comments to Sookie that she's "cursed in front of them twice, and Miss Patty already tried to hit on my Dad, and I'm pretty sure my mom is going to call child protective services" (Episode 1.6, "Rory's Birthday Parties").

The most blatant verbalization of Lorelai questioning her quality of mothering is when Paul Anka, the dog, gets sick at the tail end of Lorelai and Rory's estrangement (Episode 6.8, "Let Me Hear Your Balalaikas Ringing Out"). Using the dog as a metaphor for her feelings about Rory, she says she's a "bad mother," even though she "tried so hard." She asks, "How could I have let this happen? How could I have not seen this coming?" Little does she know, she did the right thing with Rory, letting her have her space to figure it out on her own. Prior to this, when Richard comes to tell Lorelai he should have listened to her (which he never actually says to her, of course), he attempts to come up with financial rewards or conditions to get Rory back to Yale (Episode 6.7, "Twenty-One Is the Loneliest Number"). Lorelai tells him, "Rory can't be bought," and she wants "Rory to *want* to go back to school," and she is right. She knows Rory best.

What *Gilmore Girls* offers consistently is that a good mother is not a perfect mother. When Rory is furious with Lorelai for sleeping with Christopher and breaking off her engagement with Luke, it is Lane who helps put everything into context for her: Mothers don't have to be perfect (Episode 7.2, "That's What You Get, Folks, for Makin' Whoopie"). But this sentiment does not just apply to Lorelai. The series regularly sets up moments to understand Emily's perspective, even if we do not love the frequent manipulation that comes with her resolve to steer the girls on the "right" path.

FRIEND FIRST/MOTHER SECOND

Gilmore Girls contemplates a contemporary definition of motherhood, exploring the possibility of how mothering can also cultivate a friendship. Writer Pamela Hill Nettleton suggests "*Gilmore Girls'* Lorelai and Rory legitimize single mothers and their children as family . . . walking the fine line between best friend and dependable parent as she and Rory gossip, binge-watch old movies, and order massive amounts of unhealthy take-out."[8] Starting in season 1, Lorelai and Rory get along great because, in part, Rory is mature for sixteen, while Lorelai seems young for thirty-two. Sometimes, mother/daughter roles are flipped and this seems out of the ordinary given Rory is the teenager. As Bruce Fretts of *Entertainment Weekly* writes about one of Rory and Lorelai's mother/daughter arguments:

> Rory's swamped with work, but Lorelai keeps bugging her to take an ice cream break. Finally, Rory erupts: "Lorelai, go to your room!" It sounds like your average family dramedy scene, except for one thing: Rory (Alexis Bledel) is a serious-minded 16-year-old prep schooler, and Lorelai (Lauren Graham) is her free-spirited 32-year-old single mother.[9] (Episode 1.4, "The Deer Hunters")

The atypical dynamic is consistent from the first episode, when Rory is rude and Lorelai tells her, "Hey, I had dibs on being the bitch tonight" (Episode 1.1, "Pilot"). Lorelai gets jealous because Rory enjoyed her time with Richard (Episode 1.3, "Kill Me Now") and then gets jealous again when Rory doesn't tell her about the kiss with Dean at Doose's Market (Episode 1.7, "Kiss and Tell"). When Lorelai decides to break up with Max, she asks Rory to return Proust to him and then makes out with him in his classroom, much to Rory's embarrassment (Episode 1.11, "Paris Is Burning"). In all these instances, Lorelai is acting more (or at least as) immature than Rory, thus making it easier to see them as friends in addition to mother and daughter.

When Emily tricks Lorelai into going to a spa with her, after a disastrous end to what started out as a good dinner, she asks Lorelai, "Why can't we have what you and Rory have?" (Episode 2.16, "There's the Rub"). (Side note: Did you know you can get a Vicious Trollop lip balm in real life?[10]). It is clear in this episode that Emily is jealous of Lorelai and Rory's relationship. Lorelai responds, "We are best friends first and mother and daughter second. And you and I are mother and daughter always." Amy Sherman-Palladino "always said that her creation was about two best friends who happened to be mother and daughter."[11] While the friend-first/mother-second relationship is enviable to Emily, she is not a person who can be best friends with her daughter. Instead, she sees her role as the referee, goalie, and captain for both teams at times (this is the best we can do with what we think is a soccer metaphor but wanted to include something for all you sports fans out there). When lamenting the state of their relationship, in a rare open conversation between the two women, Emily tells Lorelai, "I wasn't taught to be best friends with my daughter. I was taught to be a role model for my daughter."

In Emily's world, her main goal as a mother was to raise a daughter who did not have sex before marriage and chose the proper partner based on the status of the Gilmore name. This version of motherhood is highlighted after Emily finds out Rory is having sex with Logan. Emily sneakily moves Rory out of the pool house and into the main house (in a bedroom conveniently next door to Richard and Emily's) by putting rentals in the space; then she has plans to fumigate and then check for mold, rats, carbon monoxide, and so on (Episode 6.7, "Twenty-One Is the Loneliest Number"). Richard says they have "lost" Rory—they have failed—but Emily says, "We haven't failed until that girl comes home pregnant." For Emily, it was not about establishing a pal relationship but rather about maintaining face status in front of the social world where she holds a coveted spot. In another episode, Richard explains this social status hierarchy with the tea situation when Lorelai refuses to go on a second date with Peyton from the auction (played by Jon Hamm) (Episode 3.5, "Eight O'Clock at the Oasis"). He tells Lorelai, "There is a certain protocol that must be followed" in Emily's world. Richard agrees the "prime tea spot" is "insane," but it is important to Emily and thus should be important to Lorelai. Embarrassment in the world of high society has repercussions for status in Emily's world. However, Emily's ambitions for her daughter are not just about avoiding embarrassment in front of her friends. In her world, networking and maintaining social status are signs of success, and Lorelai doing her own thing (all the time) is a reminder to Emily and all of those in her world that Emily did not bring up her daughter to appreciate the system.

Although Emily's strategy for mothering both Lorelai and Rory does not go well, Lorelai's friends-first approach is not exactly sunshine and roses all the time. In the premiere episode, Lorelai pulls the last-resort "mom card" telling a hesitating-because-of-a-boy Rory she's "going to Chilton, whether you want to or not" (Episode 1.1, "Pilot"). When Rory tells Emily about their termite issue and the need for a loan, it is Lorelai who ices Rory out, telling her that she had "no right" to tell Emily about their money issues (Episode 2.11, "Secrets and Loans"). Later, when Rory sleeps with a married Dean, Lorelai says she did not raise Rory "to be the kind of girl who sleeps with someone else's husband," and Rory argues Lorelai slept with an engaged Christopher (Episode 4.22, "Raincoats and Recipes"). The level of open communication about their respective sex lives speaks to the friend mentality (how did Rory know Lorelai slept with Christopher?), but it also blurs the mother/daughter boundaries. The writers highlight this in the next episode, when, the next day, Lorelai tells Rory, "I wasn't thinking we had to talk like mom and kid; I thought we could talk like friends, but hey, forget it" (Episode 5.1, "Say Goodbye to Daisy Miller"). Lorelai repeats the phrase "as your friend" throughout

Emily, Lorelai, and Rory. Emily and Rory are about to go to Europe. ***The WB / Photofest © The WB, Photographer: Patrick Ecclesine.***

this exchange, including, "I felt maybe I could help you figure out how to handle this, as your friend, who you usually turn to to help you figure out how to handle things." When Rory rebuffs her offer, Lorelai immaturely tells her she is too busy anyway. The boundaries get blurred and the two women eventually work out their issues, but the situation is not represented as perfect parenting by any means.

There is also a tension with Lorelai about wanting Rory to be like her but also *not* wanting Rory to be too much like her, and this is not just about getting pregnant as a teenager. The episode where Rory agrees to come out to society offers some insight into the complex dynamics between Lorelai/Rory, Lorelai/Emily, and Rory/Emily (Episode 2.6, "Presenting Lorelai Gilmore"). Lorelai delivers a poignant line when she tells Rory, "This is all the stuff I ran away from. I just assumed you'd be running with me," after Rory reveals that she is going to participate in the debutante ball "because it would mean a lot to Grandma." This scene is one of many where Rory differentiates herself from Lorelai, but there are also moments when she questions why she feels the way she does about certain things. After Rory gets hit by a deer and has a meltdown in class, Lorelai asks if the dream of Harvard was ever really Rory's or if it was something Lorelai put on her (Episode 1.4, "The Deer Hunters"). Rory insists it has always been her dream, but it does open up the theme of Rory trying to find a sense of autonomy from her mom. Dean argues Rory is just parroting what her mom says, first with her opinions on Donna Reed (Episode 1.14, "That Damn Donna Reed") and then when she does not return his "I love you" (Episode 1.16, "Star-Crossed Lovers and Other Strangers"). Lorelai then questions whether she has set a bad example where Rory is afraid to tell someone she loves him (Episode 1.20, "P.S. I Lo . . ."). The friend/mother/daughter boundaries are not clean and neat, and the writers do not necessarily take a stance on it being a "good" version of mothering. It is a version that is replete with issues but also benefits, similar to what we ultimately get from Emily's version of mothering.

SIMILARITIES ABOUND

A deeper dive into the series reveals that Emily and Lorelai Gilmore are sometimes as similar as they are different when it comes to mothering, a comment that would horrify Lorelai. Any suggestion to Lorelai that she is acting like her mother swiftly kicks her in the pants and causes her to change her behavior. During a rare Gilmore women sleepover, Rory watches Emily and Lorelai both apply their night cream in an identical fashion, commenting, "Behold, my future" (Episode 2.10, "The Bracebridge Dinner"). Lorelai is disturbed and promptly stops her routine. While in a fight with Rory after the sleeping-with-married-Dean fiasco, Lorelai storms around the Dragonfly, causing Sookie to ask, "Want to know the last time I saw staff and maids looking this scared of their boss? Your mother's house" (Episode 5.2, "A Messenger, Nothing More"). This stops Lorelai in her tracks.

And the similarities with Emily are not just on Lorelai's end. The relationship that Emily has with Gran (aka Lorelai the First, Trix) reveals a number of similarities in how she handles the overbearing expectations from the elder Gilmore to Lorelai's defense mechanisms. We find out Emily regifted a coat rack (a gift of substance to be sure) to Lorelai and Rory (Episode 1.18, "The Third Lorelai"), even though she was furious with Lorelai for returning the crystal candlesticks from Christmas (Episode 1.9, "Rory's Dance"). When Emily finds out Gran is coming for a visit, she runs to the basement and frantically starts digging through piles of antiques. She tells Lorelai,

> She doesn't just give you a present; she *gives* you a present. Then she tells you where to put it, how to use it, what it costs—for insurance purposes of course—and God forbid you should have a different opinion, or you don't think it works in the space, or you just get tired of waking up every morning with those horrifying animals staring at you. (Episode 1.18, "The Third Lorelai")

It is Lorelai who eventually gives Emily a suggestion on how to deal with Gran, and it is one that Lorelai uses to deal with Emily, thus reinforcing the similarities between the two dyads. Lorelai tells Emily, "Because one day I decided that instead of being hurt and upset by your disapproval, I'm going to be amused. I'm going to find it funny. I'm even going to take a little bit of pleasure in it" (Episode 3.10, "That'll Do, Pig"). At dinner that night, Emily gives it a try and manages to "make four green beans last an hour and a half."

The first visit from Gran in particular reveals similarities between the women, even though Lorelai positions it as Emily getting in her head

(Episode 1.18, "The Third Lorelai"). Gran, offended by the loan of money between family members, offers to give Rory access to her quarter-million-dollar trust fund now, so that she can pay for Chilton herself. Emily tells Lorelai that if Rory "has that money, she won't need you anymore. . . . It's terrible not to be needed, you'll see." This comment reinforces what we already know: Emily sees money as the power she has to maintain a relationship with her daughter (and granddaughter). And Emily believes that when Lorelai and Rory do not need her money anymore, they will not need her. Lorelai balks at the suggestion that the money will affect Rory and her relationship but then does not tell Rory about Gran's offer. When Emily thinks the money is still on the table, she reveals to Richard that the money from Gran means that "Lorelai will never come back here. She won't have to." At tea, Emily and Lorelai are chagrined when Gran takes back the offer, realizing that they both affected Rory's chance to get money. Ultimately, Lorelai and Emily accept the terms of their standing agreement, with Lorelai reassuring Emily they are "good," and Lorelai not telling Rory about the money until it is no longer available.

In one of the quotes that opens this chapter, Lili Loofbourow suggests that "the show explores heredity and habit—the faults and defaults of our programming—not just in the 'you have my eyes' jokes, but in the ways the Gilmores unconsciously echo each other, often in exactly the ways they detest."[12] Loofbourow argues that where Emily controls via money, Lorelai controls via food and ritual. Both women are passive aggressive, using their words as weapons and their language as walls. The moments of direct communication between the two are few and far between, but this only serves to reinforce the similarities.

MY MOTHER'S DAUGHTER

The series allows us to admire a close relationship between mother and daughter that slowly becomes something else as Rory is exposed to a bigger world beyond Stars Hollow. Amy Sherman-Palladino responded to criticism of the shift in season 4 when Rory goes to Yale and their relationship suddenly takes place primarily over the phone or e-mail.[13] She says season 4 was about transitions because "we also needed to transition [Lorelai] out of working at the Independence Inn to owning her dream place—otherwise it becomes a show about a mother putting her life on hold while her daughter has a life." The series repeatedly explores what it means to have a life both inside and outside of motherhood.

At the same time that we are introduced to the best friends mother/daughter duo, we also meet a fractured mother/daughter relationship with Lorelai and Emily. As Rory finds autonomy from Lorelai (and Lorelai from Rory), issues of past, present, and future reveal the layers of pain, hurt, and love that reside under every quip and slight. Writer Janine Hiddlestone suggests, "The key to the show is, as it has always been, its unorthodox—and through that, unexpectedly realistic—take on family dynamics; Richard, Emily, Lorelai, and Rory form one of the most interesting and intelligent families on television."[14] It is a show that complicates definitions of motherhood in a way that is refreshing and interesting. Emily/Lorelai, Lorelai/Rory: We are rooting for you.

2

FATHERHOOD

"People die, we pay..."

When Amy Sherman-Palladino wrote Gilmore Girls, . . . she "never set out to create an 'alternative' family"; she envisioned "a mother-daughter relationship where they were more pals than mother and daughter."

—James Poniewozik and Jeanne McDowell[1]

At first glance this family unit of two is a perfect little insulated world. But upon closer inspection, Rory actually has three major and influential father figures in her life, each one appealing to a different aspect of her character.

—Miellyn Fitzwater[2]

On paper, Rory Gilmore has all the makings of a made-for-TV movie: raised by a single working mother, has an absentee father, wears a plaid schoolgirl outfit. But *Gilmore Girls* sets a different tone, one where fatherhood is represented by all kinds of different men. "In the year 2000" (in our best Conan O'Brien voice), *American Demographics* writer John Fetto outlined several television shows attempting to respond to research that indicated "ninety percent of parents say there needs to be more family-friendly shows on during prime time."[3] Fetto explains that "a subset of FFPF's [Family Friendly Programming Forum] 41 members put up a million dollars to fund 'family-friendly' script development at the WB" and "six scripts and three pilots later, *Gilmore Girls* finally found its way onto the network's Thursday night schedule." It is noteworthy that a show about a single mom, raising a child she had when she was sixteen years old, was considered "family friendly" in an era when the "nuclear family" continued to be "promoted as the ideal, healthy family and the foundation of society."[4] In many ways, *Gilmore Girls* can be seen as part of a cultural moment in U.S. history where definitions of family were transitioning from the traditional nuclear family to alternative family structures. This is not just a show about a mother and daughter; it is a series that demonstrates a community approach to parenting Rory, especially from the men in Lorelai's life. *Gilmore Girls* portrays zany fathers (Jackson), deadbeat fathers (Jess's dad), and invisible fathers (Mr. Kim), but the focus of this chapter is the role of Rory's and Lorelai's father figures in *Gilmore Girls*: Max (kind of), Richard, Luke, and Christopher.

Although motherhood is a central theme throughout *Gilmore Girls*, themes of fatherhood help to carry the narrative throughout seven seasons. In fact, fans of the series have speculated on "father figures in Rory's life" asking the questions, "Who do you think is the ultimate father figure for Rory?" and "How do you see that playing a role in Lorelai's love life?"[5] The theme of fatherhood also has a special function in the narrative in that it helps the writers tell the story of Lorelai and her romantic entanglements. The representation of fatherhood offers a larger cultural significance beyond the series because the "writers take care to have characters that are realistic—in that special, hyper-realized kind of way that television demands"—giving us men "who do not fill any typical television or movie father roles."[6] Through the portrayals of fatherhood in *Gilmore Girls*, the series highlights consequences, both positive and negative, of an alternative family structure forged by Richard, Luke, Christopher, and even Max.

THE AUDITIONING OF MAX: NO CALL BACK

Throughout seven seasons, *Gilmore Girls* presents Lorelai's romantic suitors as potential fathers for Rory. This is a sentiment that Emily brings up time and again, noting that she does not feel Luke is a "suitable stepfather" for Rory (Episode 5.7, "You Jump, I Jump, Jack"; Episode 5.12, "Come Home") or a suitable mate for Lorelai (too many episodes to list). It makes sense that each of Lorelai's potential suitors "auditions" to be Rory's father. Lorelai is hypercognizant and protective of introducing potential fathers to Rory, especially in the first couple of seasons. On her first coffee "run-in" with Max Medina, as he tries to persuade her to date him, Lorelai explains, "Rory is my life. She's my pal, my everything, and I would never, ever do anything that would hurt her" (Episode 1.5, "Cinnamon's Wake"). Both Max and Sookie remind her that Rory is not a baby anymore, but old habits die hard and Lorelai is hesitant to invite Max into her home, let alone her life. Later, she sympathizes with April's mother, Anna, telling her, "I went through a Sister Wendy phase myself once" (Episode 6.20, "Super Cool Party People"). When Rory meets a potential suitor of Lorelai's, we know that he is typically supposed to be a more serious relationship than a fling, even if Max throws a wrench in the plan because Rory meets him first as her teacher.

Max continues to "audition" to be Rory's father figure even after his engagement to Lorelai. In episode 2.3 ("Red Light on the Wedding Night"), Max pushes Lorelai to explain the "rules" about Rory and Dean. Lorelai tells him she takes a hands-off approach—and expresses that she expects him to take a hands-, feet-, and body-off approach—but Max wants rules and guidelines and apparently desires to take on a fatherly role within their family. It is apparent in this episode that Lorelai is uncomfortable with Max's approach, and viewers see the first red flag for why Lorelai and Max might not be a perfect match. After the wedding is called off, Rory is assigned the task to interview him as the students' favorite teacher for the school newspaper (thanks, Paris) (Episode 2.5, "Nick & Nora/Sid & Nancy"). The interview is a little awkward at first, but then Rory stops the recorder and admits to Max, "I really wanted you to be my stepfather," to which he replies with a beautiful mix of wistfulness and relief that they can address it and not pretend it didn't happen: "I really wanted to be your stepfather." The communication between Max and Rory throughout his relationship with Lorelai gives a little hint of what Rory might be missing in terms of a father figure but also reveals how hard it would be for someone to come into the Gilmore girls' world.

RICHARD GILMORE: GRAND-FATHER

Richard Gilmore represents a father to Lorelai and a father figure to Rory throughout the series. Richard plays a consequential role in the narrative, providing a fuller picture of who Lorelai was as a teenager and who she is as a woman. In the first season, viewers encounter a distraught Lorelai confronting real fears of losing her father (Episode 1.10, "Forgiveness and Stuff"). Luke drives Lorelai to the hospital, and on the way, she tells him about Richard: "My dad is not a bad guy. . . . He lived his life the way he thought he was supposed to. He followed the rules taught to him by his non-fishing, non-Barbie-buying dad." In this scene, viewers see that Lorelai cares deeply for her father even though they are still somewhat estranged. Viewers are also encouraged to understand that Richard looks out for Lorelai in his own way. When Emily sets Lorelai up on a blindsiding blind date, and both Richard and Lorelai find the man repugnant and boring, he allows her to escape out her bedroom window; a favor that prompts a "Thank you, Daddy" from Lorelai (Episode 1.16, "Star-Crossed Lovers and Other Strangers"). In later seasons, Richard continues to provide financially for Lorelai, even in unconventional ways. For instance, Richard made a real estate investment in Lorelai's name when she was born, and he gives her the proceeds of the sale of that real estate with a fat check for $75,000 (Episode 3.18, "Happy Birthday, Baby"). Ironically, it is this money that allows Lorelai to pay her parents back for the Chilton loan but also sets the deal in motion for Rory to have her grandparents pay for Yale.

Lorelai struggles to connect with Richard throughout the series. For instance, Lorelai has a difficult time finding a gift for him for his sixtieth birthday. When Rory says she found Richard a *Chuck Berry Live at the Fillmore* album on vinyl for his gift (the perfect gift for him), Lorelai asks Rory to help her find another perfect gift (Episode 3.10, "That'll Do, Pig"). This is one of many instances that reinforces the special connection between Rory and Richard (Rory simply asked Richard what he wanted); one that leaves Lorelai repeatedly baffled and envious. Richard, like many men of his generation, is task-focused in his time with his daughter. Upon his first visit to Lorelai's home in Stars Hollow, he puts on his insurance-man hat and does a quick inspection of the house, citing the need for her chimney to be inspected (Episode 1.6, "Rory's Birthday Parties"). When Richard unexpectedly retires, he visits Lorelai at the Independence Inn and critiques her management style, providing some unwanted suggestions and feedback (2.12, "Richard in Stars Hollow").

When Richard does give her praise, Lorelai appreciates it, as when he says he is proud of her during a visit to the Dragonfly Inn (Episode 5.16, "So . . . Good Talk"). He tells her that she has done a wonderful job and that she should think about selling the inn to a major chain—a high compliment coming from Richard. Near the end of that same season, Richard calls Lorelai to tell her that someone wants to take a meeting with her about the Dragonfly. He closes the phone call by telling her, "I'm quite proud of you, Lorelai," and she beams (Episode 5.20, "How Many Kropogs to Cape Cod?"). After helping Rory with her class project, Richard decides to start his own business, and it is Lorelai who sets up his office and impresses him with her competence (Episode 2.20, "Help Wanted"). And when Rory tells Richard and Emily about Lorelai's graduation from community college, it is their proud faces Lorelai sees when she crosses the stage (Episode 2.21, "Lorelai's Graduation Day").

Richard also represents a unique father role to Rory throughout the series. Sometimes he is her financial provider as is the case when he and Emily willingly agree to fund her Yale education (Episode 3.22, "Those Are Strings, Pinocchio"). Sometimes Richard is Rory's conspirator, like the time Richard runs into Logan at Yale and says that he heard that Logan professed his feelings for Rory in the middle of class. Richard scares Logan by saying,

> I dropped by to tell you I've spoken to your father. We pounded out a few things—property agreements, prenups, that sort of thing. Oh, we came to a very fair agreement. I'm sure you'll be pleased. Now, we're setting up a dinner for next week to finalize the engagement. And start talking about the ceremony. Emily is handling all the newspaper announcements, so not to worry. That's all taken care of. . . . Welcome to the family, son. (Episode 5.10, "But Not as Cute as Pushkin")

Immediately after, viewers find out that Rory put him up to it to get back at Logan for embarrassing her in class. Although Richard has his flaws, this conspiratorial stunt gives him the title of best grandpa ever, in addition to showing he has a good sense of humor. Time and again, Richard expresses how much he loves Rory and appreciates her intelligence, hard work, and focus. He tells Gran (Trix) that Rory reminds him of her (Episode 1.18, "The Third Lorelai") and tells Straub she will give him a run for his money, even if she fumbles to help him prove that point (Episode 1.15, "Christopher Returns"). When Richard acts like a you-know-what when Rory brings Dean to Friday night dinner, Lorelai defends her father in a rare moment, telling Rory, "I don't think that my father has ever loved anything in this world as much as he loves you. . . .

You are the great white hope for the Gilmore clan" (Episode 2.1, "Sadie, Sadie"). Richard offers Rory the attention that she lacks from her own father, as well as being a fellow bookworm and intellectual. And Rory offers Richard a chance to see what it would have been like if Lorelai had been a better fit for the Gilmore world.

LUKE AS GUARDIAN? PROTECTOR? FATHER? YES, YES, AND YES!

Much academic scholarship exists on defining representations of the "good mother" in popular culture. "Good moms" are "fun . . . protective . . . selfless and loving . . . remain upbeat and supportive . . . [and] offer maternal insights."[7] In contrast, very little exists on fatherhood, and particularly absent is research on "good" fathering. Although fathers do not play a primary caregiver role as mothers do in the series (and in the majority of popular-culture narratives), *Gilmore Girls* advances a definition of "good fathering" through Luke's character.

In addition to being a go-to guy and protector for Lorelai, Kirk, and his sister, Liz, Luke has what appears to be an almost daily presence in Rory's life. When she lives at home with Lorelai, Rory is in the diner almost daily. Luke talks to her, cooks for her, and shows concern over her. He makes a birthday coffee cake for Rory's sixteenth birthday and places balloons at a table for breakfast before she goes to school (Episode 1.6, "Rory's Birthday Parties"). He tries to get her to move to a different table to protect her from falling debris when there is construction in the diner (Episode 2.16, "There's the Rub"), he worries about her nutrition (throughout the series), and he attends her Chilton graduation, even when her own biological father does not (Episode 3.22, "Those Are Strings, Pinocchio"). As Rory is leaving for Yale, Luke tells her that she is important (Episode 4.2, "The Lorelais' First Day at Yale"). He then spends the day moving her mattress back and forth from Yale. Good fathering happens in these small moments throughout the series through Luke's actions.

Beginning in season 2, after Jess arrives to Stars Hollow, Luke takes a fatherly approach to him as well, although sometimes the approach is misguided. Viewers see that Luke takes this role seriously. In fact, the first time Luke and Lorelai get into a serious argument, it is because

Luke Danes and Jess Mariano. ***The WB / Photofest © The WB.***

Lorelai attempts to give parenting advice to him (Episode 2.5, "Nick & Nora/Sid & Nancy"). He is insecure about his parenting abilities and takes it out on Lorelai. Shortly after their fight, out of frustration, Luke pushes Jess into the lake, demonstrating a slightly misguided though hilarious approach to child-rearing. Later in the same episode, Luke shows his version of fatherly guidance by buying Jess a bunch of items to help him quit smoking. Luke throws products at him while saying, "We got the patch, the gum, hypnosis tapes, Chinese herbs, self-help books, and several pictures of diseased lungs to hang on the fridge. Pretty, huh?" When Rory and Jess start dating, Luke explains what it means to be with a Gilmore girl, telling him, "When you date a girl like Rory, you are involved with her whole family. . . . These people come in a package with this girl" (3.14, "Swan Song"). He tells Jess that he has to communicate with Rory. Luke also supports Jess's achievements. For instance, Luke goes to the "ceremony" when Jess is chosen as Walmart's employee of the month (Episode 3.17, "A Tale of Poes and Fire"). There is ample evidence across several episodes that reveals Luke's attempts to be a good guardian to Jess, including when Luke gives Jess an ultimatum after he finds out Jess isn't going to graduate from high school (Episode 3.20, "Say Goodnight, Gracie"). Jess is told that he cannot stay at Luke's if he doesn't go back to school. When Jess leaves, Luke feels like he failed at being Jess's guardian (Episode 3.21, "Here Comes the Son"). But, as Jess matures, he develops some respect for Luke's advice, most notably when Luke shares some self-help rhetoric with Jess (Episode 4.20, "Luke Can See Her Face"), and Jess reads the books and tries to communicate openly with Rory (Episode 4.21, "Last Week Fights, This Week Tights"). Rory doesn't reciprocate his feelings (she's too busy trying to bag a married Dean), but Luke is the person who gets Jess to start thinking about being a different version of himself and helps make him the stellar novelist who convinces Rory to go back to Yale.

Luke takes on a complicated dual father/guardian role when Rory and Jess begin dating in season 3. So much so that, at one point, Jess says to Luke, "You know you're my guardian, not hers" (Episode 3.8, "Let the Games Begin"). When Lorelai and Luke argue over Jess and Rory getting in a car accident, Luke shouts at her, "You know I care more about her than I do myself, but at least you know where Rory is, and you know she is okay" as he runs off to find Jess (Episode 2.19, "Teach Me Tonight"). After Jess and Rory begin dating, Luke freaks out when Lorelai informs him that Jess and Rory planned a secret meet-up, telling Lorelai, "Wake up, the guy's trouble" as he races out to find Rory (Episode 3.8, "Let the Games Begin"). In these examples, it is clear that Luke takes his role as father figure (to both Jess and Rory) seriously.

Luke is consistently protective about Rory in terms of her boyfriends. For example, Lorelai tells Luke that Dean broke up with Rory and he gets pissed, showing his fatherly tendencies toward Rory (Episode 1.17, "The Breakup, Part 2"). In the same episode, Luke tells Dean to "turn around, bag boy," and then puts him in a headlock because he doesn't want him going into the diner where Rory is. It is clear that Luke is not happy when Dean and Rory get back together after Dean's marriage ends. In fact, Luke and Dean scuffle over "Bop It" after a double date with Rory and Lorelai (Episode 5.5, "We Got Us a Pippi Virgin"). Although he "feels awful" for ruining the double date, Luke reveals to Lorelai that Dean is

> not right for her. . . . He's a punk. . . . He broke her heart before. He got married and bailed out before the honeymoon was even over. He was pining for Rory and he got married. That's unstable. He doesn't know what he wants. He's proven that. How can Rory trust him now? He's not good enough for her.

The irony in this statement is that Luke got married to Nicole while pining for Lorelai.

Although Rory is upset with Luke about how he treats Dean on Bop It night, overall, she seems to respect Luke's fatherly concern over her. After Luke overhears Dean (under the influence of alcohol) at his bachelor party say he misses Rory, Luke insists that Rory not go to Dean's wedding and she abides (Episode 4.4, "Chicken or Beef?"). Luke offers Rory dating advice when she calls her mom (while Luke is over for a movie night). After revealing that her date chose to sit on the same side of the table as her, Luke suggests she say there is a draft and switch sides (Episode 4.5, "The Fundamental Things Apply"). Good idea but unfortunately it doesn't work—Drafty McDrafterson said he felt it too. At the twenty-first birthday party that Emily throws for Rory, Luke gives her a thoughtful gift: a necklace that belonged to his mother. When a passerby admires the necklace, Rory says, "It's from Luke, my stepfather to be" (Episode 6.7, "Twenty-One Is the Loneliest Number"). These examples indicate that Rory is supportive of Luke's efforts to be a father figure in her life (even if she does give him weird side-hugs a lot of the time—what's with those?).

Lorelai does not directly acknowledge Luke as a father figure to Rory until she writes a character reference for use in his custody battle with Anna (Episode 7.12, "To Whom It May Concern"), but she knows how important they are to each other. When Emily breaks Luke and Lorelai up the first time, Lorelai explains to Richard that Rory has every right to be rude to Emily because "Rory loves Luke, Dad. She did not want to see him hurt and humiliated like he was. She cares about him" (Episode 5.16, "So . . . Good Talk"). Sometimes Lorelai uses this information to her advantage. For example, Lorelai borrows Luke's truck to move Rory into Yale (Episode 4.2, "The Lorelais' First Day at Yale"). After Rory and Lorelai's first goodbye, Rory sends Lorelai a page (remember beepers!) that says, "Come back." Lorelai demands to borrow Luke's truck again because it will save time. He is resistant to her request but then Lorelai says, "Don't you care about Rory?" He replies, "Have it back by seven." Luke is the one who goes to Rory's high school graduation and birthday parties and provides most of her meals, which makes him the most present father figure for the longest portion of her life.

CHRISTOPHER—PROVIDER? FRIEND? FATHER? KIND OF?

Season 1 sets up an interesting contrast between Rory's biological father, Christopher, and Luke, Rory's surrogate father. Viewers do not meet Christopher until more than midway through season 1 (Episode 1.14, "That Damn Donna Reed"). Christopher is introduced to viewers when he rides into Stars Hollow on a motorcycle and tells Lorelai to take her shirt off. That viewers do not meet Christopher until late into season 1 establishes his lack of consistent presence in Rory's life.

Rory and Christopher's father/daughter relationship is supportive yet inconsistent. He seems to be there, sometimes, when requested. For instance, Lorelai calls Christopher to ask if he will escort Rory at the debutante ball, but neither Lorelai nor Rory thinks he will actually show (Episode 2.6, "Presenting Lorelai Gilmore"). When he shows up, Lorelai is impressed that he has a steady adult job and a grown-up car. Christopher also demonstrates fatherly tendencies toward Dean when he shows him how to tie a bow tie and dance. Later in season 2, Christopher appears to want to have a more consistent presence in Rory's life. This is especially emphasized after Christopher begins dating Sherry. In episode 2.10 ("The Bracebridge Dinner"), Christopher wants Rory to spend a couple of nights with him and Sherry over her break. Lorelai seems uncomfortable with this idea and she overreacts and is jealous and possessive of Rory. That she doesn't want Rory to go to her dad's indicates she is uncomfortable with the idea of someone else parenting Rory, and Rory suggests Lorelai's jealousy is as much about Sherry as it is Christopher.

In general, after the first season, Christopher appears when his presence is requested. In addition to the debutante ball, Lorelai invites Christopher to Rory's school debate on doctor-assisted suicide and he shows up with Sherry (Episode 2.14, "It Should've Been Lorelai"). Christopher comes over after Rory gets a hairline fracture in the car accident (Episode 2.19, "Teach Me Tonight"). Christopher shows up at the doctor when Rory gets her cast off (Episode 2.22, "I Can't Get Started"). It is this episode where Christopher indicates his desire to be a family with Rory and Lorelai, until he gets a call from Sherry letting him know she is pregnant. Then he splits again. In the aftermath of that decision, it is Rory who tells Christopher, "You promised me at Sookie's wedding that this was going to work . . . that you were going to be there. You promised me. . . . No, I always understand! . . . I've got Mom, that's all I need. Go be somebody else's dad" (Episode 3.2, "Haunted Leg"). His lack of communication, his flighty attention, and his abandonment tendencies have caught up to him, and Rory tells him it is his fault. It is the first time Rory distances herself from her father, at least until she is ready to forgive him.

Christopher is absent for much of Rory's first year at Yale and their relationship becomes strained after he calls Lorelai and asks for her help with Gigi (Episode 5.6, "Norman Mailer, I'm Pregnant!"). In this episode, viewers find out that Sherry has taken a job in Paris, leaving Christopher to raise Gigi alone. After Rory finds out Christopher has reached out to Lorelai for help, she sternly asks her dad not to call Lorelai anymore in fear that he will mess up her relationship with Luke. He complies, for the time being, until Lorelai reaches out, causing Rory to ice him out again. Then Christopher's father, Straub, dies, and Rory reaches out (Episode 5.11, "Women of Questionable Morals"). All is copacetic until, at the urging of Emily that "if you want a chance with Lorelai, you had better do something" (5.12, "Come Home"), Christopher attends and disrupts Emily and Richard's renewal nuptials (5.13, "Wedding Bell Blues"). In this episode, Lorelai, Christopher, and Luke catch Rory and Logan undressing each other in a back room. Christopher and Luke have similar reactions. Christopher says: "What the hell are you doing in here with my daughter? Get away from her. That is my daughter. I will kick your ass! I will kick your ass, you little weasel!" When Luke realizes "there is a guy in there with Rory?" he yells at Logan, "Hey, get your hands off her. I mean it. Right now. Hands in the air. I wanna see hands in the air." Although Christopher takes a ruffian approach and Luke takes a law enforcer approach, the sentiment behind their threats are the same: They are protectors over Rory. Afterward, Christopher and Luke argue over Rory in the hallway:

> Christopher: It's none of your business what's going on with Rory.
>
> Luke: It sure is my business.
>
> Christopher: Rory is my daughter.
>
> Luke: Oh, really? Then where the hell were you when she got the chicken pox and would only eat mashed potatoes for a week? Or where were you when she graduated high school or started college, huh? Who the hell moved her mattress into her dorm and out of her dorm and back into her dorm?

Yeah, Christopher—how convenient that you only show up for parties and to have sex with Lorelai. More importantly, this exchange provides insight into how the show is defining "good fatherhood." Good fathers are not just biological. Good fathers are present in Rory's life and know small details about Rory's childhood, as implied in Luke's statement about Rory eating mashed potatoes for a week. Even Emily questions Christopher's parental rights when Rory lets Christopher pay for Yale in an attempt to cut the strings from her grandparents (Episode 6.13, "Friday Night's Alright for Fighting"). Rory explains, "I let him pay for Yale. He's my father." Emily maniacally laughs and responds, "How convenient that he's her father now." The character of Christopher allows the writers to complicate definitions of fatherhood. Christopher is not a "bad" father, but he is an unreliable father, despite his good pedigree and love for both Lorelai and Rory.

CONSEQUENCES OF THE ALTERNATIVE FAMILY STRUCTURE

Parenting in *Gilmore Girls* is a community affair, and some father figures function as "othermothers" or "fictive kin," where "biological and non-biological people who are important sources of guidance and support participate in childrearing."[8] This alternative family structure stands in stark contrast to the idealized nuclear family that "presumes a self-supporting independent unit composed of two legally married heterosexual parents performing separate masculine and feminine family roles."[9] This alternative family structure has been critiqued for what messages it sends about fatherhood. Alysse Elhage, contributor to *Verily*, writes, "We get the message that because she [Lorelai] chose not to marry the father of her child, all of them, including Rory, are better off. Intentionally or not, *Gilmore Girls* communicates that fathers are nice to have around, but not necessary."[10]

Alternatively, we suggest that consequences of the alternative family structure advanced in *Gilmore Girls* are both positive and negative. On a positive note, Rory has multiple father figures who care about her well-being and are invested in her upbringing. Who wouldn't love to have not one, not two, but three people who will do whatever it takes to ensure your success? On the negative side, however, there is something to say about potential implications of the lack of a stable father figure. As some fans and critics have noted, especially after the Netflix revival ten years later, Logan (who has the smallest "team" for Rory's suitors) is the one who most embodies her biological father's qualities and it can be argued that Rory being drawn to Logan indicates that this relationship is motivated, in part, by Christopher's relative absence from her childhood.

Regardless of the implications, good fathering in *Gilmore Girls* is simply showing effort to be involved in Rory's life but not to control her life. Although Elhage criticizes the show in "its failure to reflect the real-life struggles that millions of women . . . actually experienced growing up in single-mother households,"[11] we argue that Lorelai does a great job of "auditioning" potential fathers who respect their mother/daughter bond and allow Rory to be herself.

3

ROMANCE

"I'm afraid once your heart is involved, it all comes out in moron."

Jason didn't meddle in [Lorelai's] business affairs. Face it, Christopher would have been making promises he didn't intend to keep, Max would have been moping in the unfinished corners, and Luke would have belittled her every decision. Those were a critical 5 months for the inn, and Jason was the perfect man for Lorelai for that season.

—Allison Pittman[1]

I would love to find out what happened to Marty (aka, Naked Guy), smart and interesting enough to be at Yale without the silver spoon and with good enough taste to like the Marx brothers.

—Mary Chase[2]

We start this chapter with quotes from writers referencing two men in the series (Jason and Marty) who do not make it far with Lorelai or Rory, but who both offer an intriguing opportunity to assess what their relationships say about the Gilmore women. We feel this is particularly fitting in regard to *Gilmore Girls*, where "many of the romantic relationships divide audience members in terms of support"[3] and when so much of the fan discussion occurs on blogs, Reddit, and fan sites devoted to the series.

For Lorelai, most fans have chosen Luke as the one she is meant to be with or, less often, Christopher as her soul mate. A few put their hat in the ring for Max and even fewer for Jason "Digger" Stiles. In fact, there seem to be more fans in favor of the three-episode coffee man, Alex Lesman (played by Billy Burke, who went on to be Bella's dad in the *Twilight* series), than Jason. For Rory, most fans are divided between Dean, Jess, and Logan (full disclosure: we don't get Team Logan fans, but we'll do our best to represent what you could possibly be thinking as we work through what he says about Rory . . . and you).[4] Tristan Dugray is an early version of Logan, so we do not need to scratch that surface, and Marty is in a category where the love is not reciprocated.

The romantic interests in the series represent choices and opportunities, both taken and lost, that tell us something about the way the Gilmore girls work. The variety of support for those romantic interests by fans reveals how we view compatibility, soul mates, and relationships in general. In this chapter, we detail the parallels within the series focusing on Logan and Christopher, Luke and Dean, and then the less obvious Lorelai and Jess. We also analyze how the ladies, with Lorelai in particular, use their verbal aptitude to test potential suitors but also to keep them at bay. This allows Lorelai and Rory to establish a terrible track record, turning down men who (in their own way) are perfect, or at least offer perfect moments. The lesson: Perfection is not always good enough, particularly when wonderful women like Lorelai and Rory have their own flaws and issues.

THE PARALLELS OF LOVE

One of the central themes in *Gilmore Girls* is the push and pull between Lorelai and Rory, both in their dependence on one another but more importantly in the continual assessment of how far the apple falls from the tree. They have the same eyes, and Lorelai tells her, "You are me!" in the premiere episode, with Rory pushing back, "I am not you" (Episode 1.1, "Pilot"). This discussion happens in a variety of iterations over seven seasons and is expressed in one way through the parallels between love interests and characters throughout.

Christopher and Logan: "Good man."

We certainly are not the first to point out how Christopher and Logan are paralleled throughout the series, and if there is any doubt, the Netflix revival, *Gilmore Girls: A Year in the Life*, presents a discussion between Rory and Christopher that makes it much more obvious and reopens it to fan fodder (Episode 1.4, "Fall"). It is worth exploring, however, what this parallel says about both Rory and Lorelai. Additionally, it accentuates a message that Sherman-Palladino delivers so well from the beginning of the series: Being a single mom, even one who manages to get her life together as well as Lorelai, is not a shiny fairy tale and has disadvantages for everyone involved. Lorelai cannot control how present Christopher is in their lives, although she leaves "the door open" for that relationship again and again (Episode 1.15, "Christopher Returns"). Christopher being mainly out of the picture—or flitting in as the wind brings him—for the majority of Rory's life has consequences. No matter how functional her mother can be and how close the two women are, Rory is going to have daddy issues, and that is manifested most clearly in her attraction to the (deplorable) character of Logan.

Logan's track record with stunts and his desire to avoid being what his father wants hearkens back to how we get to know Christopher in the beginning of the series. On his first visit to Stars Hollow, Lorelai tells Christopher, "I've known you since I was six, Chris. You're the guy who crashed his new Porsche two hours after his parents gave it to him for his sixteenth birthday" (Episode 1.15, "Christopher Returns"). Christopher has animosity with his parents, minimally with his mother, Francine, who harps on him to straighten his tie, and more extensively with his father, Straub, who is disappointed in Christopher's lack of ambition and blames it on Lorelai and, by extension, the existence of Rory. Similarly, Logan barely tolerates his family and only seems to relate to his sister, Honor, battling the weight of family expectations by rebelling with Life and Death Brigade stunts and occasionally writing a story for *The Yale Daily News*. Midway through the last season she wrote, Sherman-Palladino makes this parallel more obvious when Christopher and Logan meet for the second time (the first meeting involved a disrobed Logan and a drunk Christopher at Emily and Richard's vow renewal). Rory, reluctant to reveal her new roommate, brings her dad home, and Logan and Christopher immediately bond over big TVs, gaming systems, and getting kicked out of (all the) prestigious boarding schools on the eastern coast (Episode 6.14, "You've Been Gilmored").

Although we are not personally fans of Logan, other viewers are, and we do like Christopher, even if the way he treats Rory makes him a less-than-stellar father at times. Why are these characters likeable? Christopher is a kid of privilege who, in his mid-thirties, is just starting to get his life figured out, and Logan is kicking and screaming his way into a life of even greater privilege, but both offer charming complements to Lorelai and Rory. Christopher knows Lorelai better than anyone and refuses to let her wordsmith him out of a room, and Logan gets Rory to take more risks and appreciate the fun side to having a lot of money at your disposal. At the same time, both can be distant and offensive, with Christopher clearly leading Lorelai on when he already had a girlfriend (Episode 2.6, "Presenting Lorelai Gilmore"), and Logan running away when Rory calls him out on his bullshit (Episode 6.8, "Let Me Hear Your Balalaikas Ringing Out"). Writer Lili Loofbourow argues, "This is what *Gilmore Girls* has always done well: If it fully and even seductively portrays the rich boys as witty, debonair, and even thoughtful, they're also *total assholes*—and the show is unstinting in its portrayal of that too."[5]

The appeal of the two men for their respective love interests stems from the potential risk they pose for both Lorelai and Rory (particularly Rory, because with Logan's track record, she is exposed to a walking petri dish of unwanted STDs and venereal disease). When Lorelai reminds Christopher about crashing his Porsche, he in turn reminds her, "You were the girl in the Pinky Tuscadero T-shirt sitting right next to me" (Episode 1.15, "Christopher Returns"). He is also the one who continually gets her hopes up and then doesn't follow through. Dating him is risky, but he is also attractive to Lorelai, based on a shared history, a shared level of intelligence, and a shared loin fruit. In a similar appeal to risk, Logan gets Rory to jump from a seven-story scaffold (Episode 5.7, "You Jump, I Jump, Jack") and inspires her to be spontaneous and reckless, including when she decides to steal a yacht with his help (Episode 5.21, "Blame Booze and Melville"). Additionally, both Christopher and Logan offer a path of least resistance financially, eventually. For example, in (the frustrating and not quite right) season 7, Christopher has enough money to get a restaurant to open at the crack of dawn, and Logan has enough money to fly back and forth from Europe to keep Rory and his relationship alive.

Ultimately, the two men stand up as parallels to one another, offering Rory and Lorelai something they do not quite get from anybody else and suggesting that Rory's daddy issues run closer to the surface than the jokes and quips can conceal. And maybe Lorelai's do too. Richard was stable and consistently visible in Lorelai's early life, but characterizations of him as an all-work-little-play father hint at how attention from a young Christopher would have been exciting and fun for a young Lorelai.

Luke and Dean: "They want more than this."

After detailing the appeal of the risky boys, we now move onto the stable boys (maybe literally, as Dean had three jobs in season 5 and one of them could have been taking care of horses). Some people might argue that Luke should be paralleled to Jess because he is Luke's nephew and both Luke and Jess pine for Lorelai and Rory respectively around the same time. We argue that is where the similarities end, for the most part. Although Jess eventually reenters the scene just in time to get Rory back to Yale, he does so in a way that Luke never would. Jess yells at Rory and then leaves her to figure out the next steps on her own (Episode 6.8, "Let Me Hear Your Balalaikas Ringing Out"). In contrast, if Luke and Lorelai had been in the same position, Luke would have hung back, looking at her through eyes mixed with lust and frustration, swooping in when Lore-

Dean and Rory and Lorelai and Luke double date: a pre–Bop It movie. ***The WB / Photofest © The WB, Photographer: Patrick Ecclesine.***

lai was desperate for saving, and then holding her hand (and purse) through the process.

Throughout the series,[6] the parallel between Luke and Dean is apparent in small ways; particularly in how helpful and patient they are with the Gilmore girls. For example, Dean changes water bottles, builds cars, and picks up spiders, and Luke provides hamburgers, gives rides to the hospital when people get sick, and bakes special birthday coffee cake. The more consistent parallels start in season 4, when Luke and Dean offer the shoulders the Lorelais cry on when they can't find each other (Episode 4.14, "The Incredible Sinking Lorelais"). As Dean comforts a sobbing Rory, she remarks that he is amazing for being so "nice" to her even though she was "horrible" to him. When Luke comforts a crying Lorelai she tells him,

> There are very few times in my life when I find myself sitting around thinking, I wish I was married. . . . But, every now and then, just for a moment, I wish I had a partner. Someone to pick up the slack, someone to wait for the cable guy, make me coffee in the morning, meet the stupid sink before it gets sent back to Canada.

Luke is frequently that person for her though. When Stella the baby chick gets loose, it is Luke she calls (Episode 1.14, "That Damn Donna Reed"). When the stage for the fund-raising fashion show will not stand up, it is Luke who brings his toolbox to fix it (Episode 2.7, "Like Mother, Like Daughter"). Luke makes Lorelai coffee every morning that they are not fighting. And it is Luke who moves Rory's mattress in and out and back in again at Yale (Episode 4.2, "The Lorelais' First Day at Yale").

In season 5, when Luke and Lorelai start dating and Rory and Dean start dating again, the double-date Bop It incident allows Luke to reveal his issues with Dean (Episode 5.5, "We Got Us a Pippi Virgin"). Luke argues that Dean isn't good enough for Rory because "he was pining for Rory and he got married" anyway, he bailed on Lindsay "before the honeymoon was even over," and he's going to "drag her down to his level," keeping her from the adventures she could have in life (just like Pippi). Luke might as well be talking about himself here, when he spontaneously married Nicole while pining for Lorelai and has planted firm roots from birth in Stars Hollow. After Dean and Rory break up, Dean tells Luke, "Your situation's no different from mine. . . . They want more than this, don't you see that? And all you are is this. . . . This town is all you are and it's not enough. . . . You're here forever" (Episode 5.18, "To Live and Let Diorama"). Luke absorbs this assessment, at first dissuading Lorelai from considering a job that would allow her to travel and then, perhaps fearing Dean is right and he is holding her back, encouraging her to look into it (Episode 5.20, "How Many Kropogs to Cape Code?"). However, once it becomes a real(er) possibility, he blurts out, "What about the kids?!" to a baffled Lorelai (Episode 5.22, "A House Is Not a Home"). Luke wants to settle down into the Twickham house and have kids, and he wants Lorelai to have the same dream. Dean's comment dredges up the real possibility that Lorelai has greater aspirations than Stars Hollow offers, suggesting that deep down, on Bop It night, Luke was really talking about himself and Lorelai, not Dean and Rory.

The blue-collar, truck-driving similarities are more than skin deep with Luke and Dean. However, just because Luke and Dean offer a similar parallel does not mean that that they equate to similar fates for the Gilmore women. Dean is right; Rory did want to leave Stars Hollow, and their relationship was doomed from the start. But that apple may fall farther from the tree than everybody realizes, when the tree just wants to stay put.

Lorelai and Jess: "It's about time for a Jess."

This next parallel is specifically focused on Rory and might be a bit weird for some fans to swallow at first; however, besides the background (or lack thereof) of privilege and money, Lorelai and Jess have the most in common of all of Rory's suitors. This comes out in particularly subtle ways such as when Rory says the snowman buffer is sure to get first place. Lorelai says it is "over the top," and then later Jess calls it "overdone" (Episode 2.10, "The Bracebridge Dinner"). Or when Rory orders Indian food for her perfect night alone, and both Lorelai and Jess (on separate occasions) make a joke about burning the house down afterward (Episode 2.16, "There's the Rub").

In a broader vein, both Lorelai and Jess are similar in how they deal with problems. They run away from family, icing out certain members or ignoring their existence, lashing out at the people who go out of their way to help them (even if the help involves a weekly dinner). They both use jokes and jabs instead of openly communicating their feelings. On one hand, both eventually make a life for themselves that is enviable by pulling up their respective bootstraps, a positive attribute and part of the drive that comes when you constantly try to refuse help from others. On the other hand, they both have a tendency to sabotage relationships with good people. Max was wonderful on paper, as we can tell from the article Rory writes about him, and he would have made the perfect husband and a great stepfather to Rory, but Lorelai didn't love him. Jess did love Rory, or at least told her he did (Episode 4.13, "Nag Hammadi Is Where They Found the Gnostic Gospels"), but he struggled with communication and follow-through. Like Max, Rory is perfect on paper, but young Jess is not ready for a girl like her. Jess seems to set himself up for failure, in ways that a young Lorelai might relate to, like when he fails out of senior year and gives Luke no choice but to kick him out.

Jess grows up and ostensibly becomes the man Rory knew he could be, and he is the one who gets her back to Yale (Episode 6.8, "Let Me Hear Your Balalaikas Ringing Out"). Jess challenges Rory to think about what she is doing. It is the first time she gets this pushback from someone other than Lorelai (or Paris, who always seems a little too high-strung and intense to take advice from). Rory is not going to listen to her mom at this point, but Jess is somebody who can tell her a thing or two. His reappearance in season 6, when Rory is seemingly at her lowest point, is when Rory finds out Jess wrote a book—and didn't need Mitchum (or Logan) Huntzberger to tell him he was good enough first.

During the subsequent fight with Logan, Rory tells him he has oodles of doors open to him, but in contrast to Jess, she has (or had) far more open to her than he did and she gave it up to plan tea parties and luncheons. This realization is just happening now, and it is due to Jess's innate ability to challenge Rory's way of thinking. Jess fell in love with her for her mind (although not being an uggo probably helped too), and she's wasting it. He never asks her to stay back with him or makes her feel like they can't make it work when she goes off to college; instead, he consults a map to find out how far away Yale is from Stars Hollow (Episode 3.18, "Happy Birthday, Baby"). In contrast, Dean asks what is going to happen to their relationship when she goes away to college, causing Rory to panic a bit (Episode 3.3, "Application Anxiety"). In fairness, Jess does try to get Rory to leave school and hit the road with him, but when she turns him down, he leaves, accepting her decision (Episode 4.21, "Last Week Fights, This Week Tights"). Overall, Jess lets Rory be herself, and he challenges her good-girl perfect exterior that she frequently bends over backward to present to those around her. It is important for Emily and Richard that Rory live up to her potential, especially since they did not get to see that realized with Lorelai (at least in the traditional sense). On the flip side, it is important to Rory that they see her as a talented success, so she goes out of her way to be perfect. Luke puts Rory up on a pedestal, a princess destined to be a queen. Even Dean moons around putting up with far more from Rory than most boyfriends would (or should) be willing to. Jess challenges her and is frequently a jerk when he does it (which turns off the Team Dean, Team Logan, and Team Rory fans), but it is an attitude that Rory needs sometimes, coming from someone who she cannot write off as a privileged douche.

Similarly, Lorelai is not afraid to challenge Rory when she makes mistakes, like kissing Jess while still dating Dean (Episode 3.1, "Those Lazy-Hazy-Crazy Days") or sleeping with Dean while he's still married to Lindsay (Episode 4.22, "Raincoats and Recipes"). Or when Rory reconsiders attending Chilton after she meets a pretty boy (Episode 1.1, "Pilot"). Rory needs to be challenged, and it is both Lorelai and Jess who do this best.

WORDS AND ACTIONS

One of the most frequent comments about *Gilmore Girls* pertains to the unusually fast and witty dialogue, a quirk that caused the casting directors headaches when they had a particularly hard time finding actors who could "be *on top* of" their lines and come "right in as soon as the other person stops talking."[7] The rapid-fire pace and pop-culture-layered dialogue not only resonates with fans and critics but also within the narrative, where it seems intended to test other people. The dialogue from Lorelai keeps Emily on the outside of most of the references, and the wit and wordplay weed out all but the most worthy of suitors. It is what attracts Lorelai to Max and eventually how he convinces her to date him when he can keep up with her back-and-forth repartee (Episode 1.5, "Cinnamon's Wake"). With Jason Stiles, the scene in his office where Lorelai bursts in to defend Emily's identity (and her right to a catering job) provides the spark to the kindling of their relationship when he also keeps up with her, not just jab for jab but quip for quip, causing writer Allison Pittman to contend, "Of all the men in Lorelai's life (and I'm including everyone from Christopher Hayden to Luke Danes to Peyton Sanders), only Jason 'Digger' Stiles met her wit for wit"[8] (Episode 4.6, "An Affair to Remember"). Both Max and Jason are worthy opponents to attempt to tackle her verbal barrier, and, against her better judgment, Lorelai dates them based on this connection. Similarly, Rory's first run-in with Logan involves a wordy debate (Episode 5.3, "Written in the Stars"). In our opinion, Rory wins when she says he is acting like Judi Dench, but the debate ends with Logan giving her a patronizing smile and telling her she should think that was fun (ugh). As grossly egotistical as Logan acts and as creepy as it is for Logan and his friends to hunt down a woman Finn met the night before (run, little lamb), Logan's intelligence is what draws her in.

Additionally, both Gilmore girls sometimes use their language as armor to ward off having to directly confront emotions and feelings. *New York Times* writer Virginia Heffernan argues that "in their purest incarnations, Lorelai and Rory shared the witty woman's challenge: to architect a wall of words so high and so thick that no silence, no stares, no intimations of morality or even love could penetrate it."[9] Heffernan further laments the change of the characteristically witty, rapid dialogue in sea-

Max and Lorelai's first date. ***The WB / Photofest © The WB.***

son 7 under Rosenthal, arguing, "Indeed, that was the charm of the old show: women, fundamentally women without men, were compelled to talk as fast as they could to keep their loneliness at bay."[10] In fact, it is only when Lorelai is truly surprised by lovers that she is silenced. When Max proposes with one thousand yellow daisies, it leaves "Lorelai uncharacteristically speechless"[11] (Episode 1.21, "Love, Daisies and Troubadours"). When Luke reveals he carried the horoscope around in his wallet for eight years, Lorelai abruptly stops joking and is forced to confront what the act means (Episode 5.3, "Written in the Stars"). Later, when they break up the first time, she "re-watches" that scene in a dream and berates herself to "say something!" (Episode 5.14, "Say Something"). For Rory, Jess's challenges tend to leave her stumped and grumpy. For example, when Jess asks her what she and Dean talk about, she cleverly responds, "Everything . . . tons of stuff. Whatever" (Episode 2.10, "The Bracebridge Dinner"). She is not ready to deal with the fact that Dean, as perfect as he is in many ways, does not challenge her intellectually and is thus an ill-suited long-term beau.

One of the most interesting takeaways from *Gilmore Girls* is that sometimes perfect is not good enough. Dean could not have done more, planned more, built more to be thoughtful, kind, and true. He sat at book fairs and bookstores for hours, watched TV and ate pizza with Rory and her mom, and frequently was the one picking up the pizza for all of them. All of this is in addition to the acts we've already noted like changing water bottles and building Rory a car, which is destroyed while on a "date" with Jess. Outside of all the acts of love that he shows her, he also withstands her cold-shouldering distance and clear attraction to Jess for far longer than most people could. Rory is a jerk to him, and in the end, Dean is the one who breaks up with her (Episode 3.7, "They Shoot Gilmores, Don't They?"). If we were Jess, we would be concerned and miffed that Rory could not quite pull the trigger to make that happen herself. Rory's choices in men defy the theory of love languages: acts of service, gifts, affirmations, physical touch, and quality time spent together are not enough to keep her interested. We see this again with Marty, who she has far more in common with than Logan freakin' Huntzberger.

At the same time, Lorelai has issues in her romantic relationships that are consistent enough to suggest that maybe turning down Christopher at sixteen was less about being logical and more about having her own undefined love language that works like a moving target. Jason Stiles is weird about not wanting to sleep in bed with her, so he shows her to the Xanadu of bedrooms, makes her breakfast (Episode 4.10, "The Nanny and the Professor"), and eventually gives her a key (Episode 4.17, "Girls in Bikinis, Boys Doin' the Twist"). Even Alex Lesman the coffee man, who barely knows Lorelai, somehow knows to book a spa day after a ceremonial show of attempting to fish (Episode 3.12, "Lorelai out of Water"). Christopher's graduation gift to Lorelai is the exact right mix of funny, practical, and sentimental: a variety of gag gifts for young graduates; a disposable camera, which serves a lovely purpose with Emily and Richard later; and then a beautiful (real) pearl necklace (Episode 2.21, "Lorelai's Graduation Day"). We're even willing to give season 7 a bit of credit when they take the perfect dates over the top with the barn-side drive-in movie with fully stocked car (Episode 7.4, 'S Wonderful, 'S Marvelous") followed by Christopher whisking her away to Paris for French food at dawn (Episode 7.7, "French Twist"). These men offer moments of perfection rarely seen in real life, and yet, it is not always enough.

WHOM SHOULD THEY CHOOSE?

Although we have detailed many of the problems with Lorelai's and Rory's romantic relationships in this chapter, we would be remiss not to mention how *Gilmore Girls* offers quite a few relationships that are enviable. Sookie and Jackson are like peanut butter and homemade raspberry jam. Kirk and Lulu are made for each other, much to everyone's surprise, including Kirk's. And even Richard and Emily, with a minor separation as part of their story, show what it means to support a partner through crazy and crazier.

So, whom should the Gilmore girls choose as their mates? Throughout the series, Christopher offers Lorelai glimpses of who she thinks he could be and that is enough to keep him as a possibility for a while. However, it is Luke's devotion to Lorelai, his dependability, and above all his love for Rory that ultimately makes him the one for her. The scene with Jason even hints at this pairing when Lorelai accuses Jason of waltzing in and trivializing Emily's life (Episode 4.6, "An Affair to Remember"). Jason quips, "I don't waltz at all. It's embarrassing and a little gay." When Lorelai falls for Luke, it is partly because Luke waltzes with her at Liz's wedding, a moment she emphasizes for Rory when she says, "Luke can waltz [suggestive eyebrow wiggle]" (Episode 4.22, "Raincoats and Recipes"). As for Rory, we are still divided (as authors and within the broader fandom) about who she is destined to be with, but Wayne Wilcox, who plays Marty, argues he is clearly the most reasonable choice for a grown-up Rory.[12] Who are we to argue?

4

FRIENDSHIP

"Tangerinama"

In the world of Stars Hollow, the family you made was just as important as the family you were born into, and that led to some truly amazing friendships over the course of the series.

—Sabienna Bowman[1]

I love the female friendships in the show. The way Paris started out a villain and ended up a life-long friend without really budging an inch from being an intense pain-in-the-you-know-what. Because people can love you even though you are incredibly flawed.

—Mary Chase[2]

Lorelai and Sookie, Lane and Rory, Rory and Paris, Emily and Sweetie; most of these friend dyads are key to the charm of *Gilmore Girls*. When Rory isn't ready to return to Lorelai but refuses to go back to her grandparents' house, it is Lane's place that offers refuge (Episode 6.8, "Let Me Hear Your Balalaikas Ringing Out"). When Lorelai attempts to sort out her horrible reaction to Rory getting along with the grandparents, it is Sookie who pulls no punches: "You're jealous because they like Rory better than you" (Episode 1.3, "Kill Me Now"). Rory is Paris's pace car, and she "stays in the room until I'm completely done talking. I need that" (Episode 6.1, "New and Improved Lorelai"). And Emily apparently was close friends with a woman named Sweetie, who dies in season 4 (Episode 4.16, "The Reigning Lorelai"). Although not perfect—the friendships can seem a little one-sided at times—*Gilmore Girls*' depiction of female friendships contributes to the cultural significance of *Gilmore Girls* due to its emphasis on the value of lessons *in* friendship.

In many ways, *Gilmore Girls* is just as much about friendship as it is about family. As suggested in the motherhood chapter, the relationship between Lorelai and Rory blurs the lines between friendship and mother/daughter—at least that is what the show establishes in episode 1.1 ("Pilot") when the mother/daughter duo confuse others, primarily men, as to whether they are friends or mother and daughter. Yes, part of the confusion lies in Lorelai's youthfulness; however, the other part of the confusion is grounded in the friendly, though not perfect, dynamic between Lorelai and Rory. The motherhood chapter fully discusses the complex family-friendship dynamic between Lorelai and Rory. In contrast, this chapter sets out to explore the Gilmore lessons in friendship, as evidenced between Rory and Lane, Lorelai and Sookie, and Rory and Paris.

RORY AND LANE

The friendship of Rory and Lane teaches us the first lesson: *Friends buy you a lunch; best friends slather lunch on your head to keep the bleach from burning*. Rory and Lane were not the typical teenage friendship on television. Whereas most forms "of entertainment portray teenagers as emotional, overly dramatic and immature subjects who cannot make rational decisions,"[3] Rory and Lane's friendship reflects two positive functions of female friendship: emotional support and practical help. In interpersonal communication research, one of the most important aspects of friendship includes "companionship—chances to do fun things together and receive emotional support."[4] This aspect of friendship is also called the "communal function" and "describes friendships that focus primarily on sharing time and activities together."[5] The show highlights Rory and Lane's practice of sharing time and activities together through all seven seasons.

Much of the time shared between Rory and Lane focuses on when they are pursuing and/or maintaining romantic relationships. In this way, the friendships help to advance the narratives of Lane's and Rory's relationships . . . with boys. For instance, viewers learn about Rory's excitement over Dean after she tells Lane (before Lorelai) about their first kiss

Lane Kim and Rory Gilmore at Rory's second sweet-sixteen birthday party. *The WB / Photofest © The WB.*

(Episode 1.7, "Kiss and Tell"). When Rory and Jess get back together, Lane is skeptical and still mad about the car crash. Rory asks Lane to give Jess a second chance and Lane complies (Episode 3.12, "Lorelai out of Water"). When Rory has sex for the first and second time (with a married man), she seeks out Lane, who is more accepting of her relationship with Dean than Lorelai (Episode 5.1, "Say Goodbye to Daisy Miller"). Rory tells Lane she was uncomfortable with Jess's unpredictability and comfortable with Dean's predictability, a sentiment that Lorelai cautioned her against when Rory was upset that Jess "left his best girl home on a Saturday night" (Episode 3.15, "Face-Off"). Whereas Lorelai challenges Rory in these ways, Lane cheerleads her into the fire-rimmed end zone, allowing Rory to rationalize that sleeping with a married man was not the worst mistake she could have made because he loves her (technically, they don't get to finish the conversation, but Lane's first reaction was not horrified). In each of these scenes that emphasize the shared time between Rory and Lane, viewers also get insight into Rory's romantic relationships, thus explicitly advancing the narrative without showing the actual relationships. More importantly, Lane's character is positioned as necessary emotional support for the sometimes taciturn (to a fault) Rory in these times spent with each other.

And, in an effort to meet Bechdel's test, spending time together talking about relationships isn't the only aspect of Rory and Lane's relationship. The show emphasizes the importance of making time to spend with one another, especially when one friend gets a boyfriend. One episode in particular spells out this importance in female friendships. When Rory and Dean start dating, Lane feels like a third wheel and can't get her distracted best friend to carve out time to hear about her crush on Rich Blumenfeld (Episode 1.8, "Love & War & Snow"). The lack of a sounding board in Rory causes Lane to make a major teenage faux pas, running her hand through Rich Blumenfeld's luxurious, loin-tingling hair . . . without his permission. A mortified Lane seeks refuge at the Gilmore girls' house and Lorelai talks her down, but Rory ultimately realizes she owes Lane an apology for being a neglectful friend. Lane says that she was just jealous and she feels like she does not fit into Rory's life anymore. Rory says that Lane came first, and Lane agrees, "That's right. I've got dibs." They hug and the friendship is repaired. On its own, this moment represents a nice reverse bros-before-hoes moment, but what is even better is that the friends maintain an "I've got dibs" attitude throughout the series. When Rory needs her, Lane gives up her band practice time (annoying her bandmates) to let Rory vent about losing her virginity to Dean (Episode 5.1, "Say Goodbye to Daisy Miller"). Lane is shocked ("You what?!") when Rory reveals, "I slept with Dean in my room last night, in my bed." Rory, out of breath, recaps getting caught with Dean by her mom. Lane wants details of the experience, even though her band is in the other room yelling for her to join them for practice that started thirty minutes ago. Lane asks Rory, "How was it? Was he nice to you?" These questions and Lane's advice seem to serve a double function. In one way, Lane symbolizes the show's emphasis on the importance of the communal function of female friendships as she yells at her bandmates who are pressuring her to start with practice: "Hey, shut up, all of you. Now, that is my friend. And she is here in desperate need of some girl talk, and in case you haven't noticed, I am a girl. And this is what it's like to have a girl in the band, so all of you—deal!" As a second function, Lane's questions and morbid curiosity emphasize her (and Rory's, by default) immaturity and naïveté about sex. Lane is the person who Rory seeks out to discuss losing her virginity to a married man. After yelling at her bandmates, Lane goes back into the room and Rory asks her for some much-needed perspective on what she did. Lane's advice to Rory first includes seeking advice from Lorelai, but Rory says that is not an option. Here, the scene emphasizes that Lane is Rory's emotional sounding board when Lorelai is not. In this situation, the show emphasizes the important time they need to share with each other and Rory's need for emotional support, thus highlighting the communal aspects of their friendship.

Through sharing time together, sometimes the show emphasizes a much-needed perspective that female friends can provide. For instance, it is Rory who notices that Yiung Chui is in love with Lane (Episode 3.17, "A Tale of Poes and Fire"). Later, Lane needs Rory to help her sort out her feelings, asking, "Am I in love with Zack?" (Episode 5.2, "A Messenger, Nothing More"). A few episodes after that realization, Lane talks to Rory about liking Zack and her hesitations with "intra-band dating" (Episode 5.4, "Tippecanoe and Taylor, Too"). Lane cites the Cramps, Yo La Tengo, Kim and Thurston (a reference to Sonic Youth)—all intra-band dating success stories. After allowing her time to vent, Rory encourages Lane to tell Zack how she feels. In short, the emotion-sharing aspect of Rory and Lane's relationship allows the writers to carry the narrative forward for their respective romantic relationships. More importantly, however, the communal aspect of their friendship helps the series build a lesson in female friendship—that a non-negotiable part of female friendships is the act of sharing time and activities together, even if the primary emphasis of that time is spent on the stereotypical notion that all teenage girls talk to their BFF about is boys.

Sometimes Lane and Rory do not emotion-share or gossip about boys but instead help each other in practical ways. The agentic function in friendship refers to the practical aspects of friendships that "help us deal with problems or everyday tasks."[6] Although many of the communal aspects of their friendship revolve around discussion of boys, Rory and Lane also help each other with practical things, like covering for each other when Mrs. Kim or Lorelai might disapprove. This plays out in a variety of ways, from providing pizza and junk food (Episode 1.2, "The Lorelais' First Day at Chilton"), to lying to Lorelai so that Lane can go on a date with Dean's friend, Todd (Episode 1.12, "Double Date"), to hiding the New Pornographers CD in a book (Episode 4.11, "In the Clamor and the Clangor"), or offering a bed, like when Rory offers Lane a place in her small dorm room (Episode 4.12, "A Family Matter") after a fallout with Mrs. Kim.

Perhaps one of the most unforgettable episodes that demonstrates the agentic aspects of their friendship is when Lane decides to dye her hair in protest of her strict mother who is making her apply to conservative colleges, including all of the Seventh-day Adventist schools, Quaker schools, and an Amish school in Nicaragua (Episode 3.4, "One's Got Class and the Other One Dyes"). In this episode, Rory, albeit reluctantly, helps Lane choose a hair color and buy supplies for dyeing her hair. Rory suggests the color purple and then reminds Lane she needs bleach and gloves. In addition to helping buy the supplies, Rory also bleaches Lane's hair. A hilarious scene ensues:

> Lane: I have to do something [because her head is burning from the bleach].
>
> Rory: Run around the block!
>
> Lane: Why?
>
> Rory: I don't know.
>
> Lane: Good enough for me [runs frantically out of the bathroom].

After the bleaching (and the pain) is over, the two girls talk about Dave and Dean, as Rory is dyeing Lane's hair purple. When Lane hears the bells ring on the front door signaling Mrs. Kim is home, her face goes "white" and she tells Rory, "I can't do this. . . . We've got to put it back." She tells Rory to go get supplies to fix her hair . . . and she does. She climbs out Lane's window so as to not run into Mrs. Kim. This episode highlights a practical aspect of their friendship. Rory goes to great lengths, albeit hesitantly, to help Lane with her "hair emancipation." Additionally, this scene says something about Rory because she is trying to sort out her feelings for Jess and she does not communicate that to Lane. Rory doesn't always communicate everything to Lane and that is part of their friendship. In this scene, not saying anything is saying something and that is OK too.

Although Lane and Rory primarily talk about boys, it is significant that their ongoing and evolving relationship demonstrates a friendship that regularly epitomizes both emotional and practical aspects of female friendship. This emphasis creates a more complex depiction of a typical teenage female friendship. By highlighting a functional teenage friendship that has both emotional and practical aspects, the series' creators challenge a problematic one-dimensional female friendship stereotype. Instead of only centering Rory and Lane's relationship on emotional support about boys, the writers offer a teenage relationship that is at least two-dimensional. As writers Nathan Phan and Sania Syed conclude, "Just like any age group, teens are human beings learning to adjust to a new stage in their life. They should be depicted as individuals, not stereotypes."[7] Rory and Lane, though not a perfect representation of female friendship, model excellent communal and agentic strategies for friendships, thereby complicating the stereotypical one-dimensional teenage friendship archetype.

LORELAI AND SOOKIE

Similar to Lane and Rory, the friendship between Lorelai and Sookie depicts a positive portrayal of female friendship. Their relationship offers us lesson two: *True friends rely on and inspire you . . . and sleep with the zucchinis*. The story of their friendship is told through actively engaging in relational maintenance, which is defined as "using communication and supportive behaviors to sustain a desired relationship status and level of satisfaction."[8] *Everyday Feminism* contributor Suzannah Weiss asserts that "friendships can be a means for women to help one another thrive when the cards are stacked against them [and] inspire one another to succeed in their careers."[9] Lorelai and Sookie do both for each other in the ways that they maintain their friendship, highlighting an important lesson in female friendships: to actively engage in relational maintenance.

Early in the series, it is established that Sookie is Lorelai's go-to friend for all of her relationship issues. Viewers learn the nuances of Lorelai's romantic relationships through her self-disclosures to Sookie. For instance, when Lorelai is trying to decide if it is OK to date Max even though he is Rory's teacher, Sookie is the one she turns to (Episode 1.5, "Cinnamon's Wake"). Later, Lorelai finds herself conflicted when she invites Christopher and Gigi to lunch at the Dragonfly but does not tell Luke (Episode 5.9, "Emily Says Hello"). Lorelai's cognitive dissonance

Sookie St. James and Lorelai Gilmore. ***The WB / Photofest © The WB.***

is apparent when she later reveals to Sookie, "I should have told him, right? Yeah, I should have told him. Now he's going to think I'm hiding something from him, and I'm not. Damn it. He's going to beat up my car." In fairness, Luke would have beat up Christopher's car, but it is through this self-disclosure that viewers learn Lorelai regrets that she didn't tell Luke about Christopher. Similarly, through Sookie's self-disclosures to Lorelai, viewers get insight into Sookie's life choices with Jackson, such as her hesitations about being a mom (Episode 4.3, "The Hobbit, the Sofa and Digger Stiles"). Self-disclosure is a "strategy for friendship maintenance" because "all friendships are created and maintained through the discussion of thoughts, feelings, and daily life events."[10] The self-disclosures, then, not only advance a deeper narrative about the romantic relationships that Sookie and Lorelai experience but also model an effective relational maintenance strategy between them.

Sookie and Lorelai also maintain their friendship by helping each other thrive in difficult times. After the Independence Inn burns down, Sookie approaches Lorelai about starting a catering business together so that they can generate income until the Dragonfly opens (Episode 4.3, "The Hobbit, the Sofa and Digger Stiles"). Although this does not go as well as they planned (e.g., Sookie gets mad at a little girl who returns a used carrot to the tray, makes green mac and cheese and crudité platters for dinner, and then makes another little girl—played by Victoria Justice—cry after she asks for a juice box), Sookie's suggestion to go into business with Lorelai indicates to viewers that in addition to herself, Sookie is looking out for Lorelai. Looking out for each other is a common narrative arc in Lorelai and Sookie's friendship.

Sookie is always supportive of Lorelai regardless of the implications for her. For instance, Sookie does not get upset with Lorelai when she calls to let her know the wedding (with Max) is off, as she is literally putting the final touches on "Clyde," the name she gave to their five-tiered wedding cake (Episode 2.4, "The Road Trip to Harvard"). Sookie is always there when Rory and Lorelai are in need. When Lorelai can't sleep in her house because she "hears the termites," she and Rory go to Sookie's house. Sookie does not just open her house to them but also makes them Häagen-Dazs milkshakes at midnight and forces Jackson into the pantry (Episode 2.11, "Secrets and Loans"). When Lorelai insists on Sookie's famous zucchini soup for the opening of the Dragonfly Inn, Sookie gets Jackson to sleep with the zucchini in case the cold front comes in (Episode 4.20, "Luke Can See Her Face"). Sookie covers for Lorelai when she fails to show up to a birthday party she planned at the Dragonfly because Luke breaks up with her in Doose's Market (Episode 5.14, "Say Something"). When Sookie finds out, she immediately calls Rory to help her mom: "Look, uh, something happened with your mom and Luke and your mom's in bad shape, I mean, she's down, hon. And I–I'm here now, but I think you ought to come. She needs you." When Lorelai has to throw an impromptu bachelorette party, it is a half-asleep Sookie who shows up with a pan of pot stickers (Episode 5.13, "Wedding Bell Blues"). In the next episode, Sookie says she will hate Luke to support Lorelai (Episode 5.15, "Jews and Chinese Food"). Then Sookie worries that Lorelai is becoming a "couch potato girl" so she wants to take her for a girls' night out, even though she is pregnant and exhausted (Episode 5.16, "So . . . Good Talk"). In each of these examples, viewers witness Sookie's efforts to maintain her relationship with Lorelai by helping her during difficult times.

Lorelai and Sookie's friendship also demonstrates that female friends should inspire each other, sometimes in small ways. For instance, when Lorelai and Sookie attend a boring cram course on "starting an inn,"

Lorelai makes a "cootie catcher" and Sookie excitedly participates (Episode 3.11, "I Solemnly Swear"). In a much more important plot point, when Lorelai blurts out a rude comment about Sookie's lack of relationships, it seems to be the push she needs to ask Jackson out on a date (1.11, "Paris Is Burning"). And, later, after Sookie throws Lorelai under the bus to tell Jackson that four kids in four years is crazy, Lorelai convinces Sookie to have better communication in her relationship (ironically, since Luke and Lorelai seem to fall apart based on a lack of communication) (Episode 3.7, "They Shoot Gilmores, Don't They?"). When Lorelai tracks down the ghost stealing Toblerones, she again reinforces that Sookie needs to communicate what she needs to Jackson but then joins her for the episode of *Dark Shadows* (Episode 5.12, "Come Home").

Lorelai and Sookie consistently rely on and inspire one another to be the best versions of themselves. They both sort out relationship issues in conversation with one another and conduct acts of kindness from making wedding cakes (again and again and again) to keeping secrets. They do fight, but they also resolve those fights on-screen in a way that allows them to maintain their friendship and continue as business partners and best friends. And if the relationship ever feels one-sided, with Sookie providing a few too many trays of food, think of Lorelai as wingman on the date from hell with Rune. It goes both ways.

RORY AND PARIS

The unlikely friendship of Rory and Paris seems to embody the Oscar Wilde saying, "True friends stab you in the front." Lesson three from *Gilmore Girls* friendships: *Sometimes allies appear in the least likely of places*. Traditionally, "women's friendships in the media are often exclusive, appearance-based, unrealistically perfect, and based on stereotypes."[11] The relationship between Paris and Rory is unique in that they defy these stereotypes of female friendships. They are not exclusive friends, they generally are not concerned with their appearances, and their friendship is far from perfect. It seems that on paper, Rory and Paris should not be friends: "From their first meeting at Chilton to their rocky roommate relationship, they spend almost as much time fighting as they do friends. But in many ways, Rory and Paris are two sides of the same coin."[12]

Interpersonal communication scholars outline several "friendship rules" or "general principles that prescribe appropriate communication and behavior within friendship relations."[13] Those ten rules are showing support, seeking support, respecting privacy, keeping confidences, defending your friends, avoiding public criticism, making your friends happy, managing jealousy, sharing humor, and maintaining equity.[14] Paris and Rory violate many of these friendship rules, including keeping confidences, avoiding public criticism, and maintaining equity. It seems, then, that based on these rules we could conclude that Rory and Paris should not be friends. However, Paris and Rory overcome these deficiencies in friendship by providing support of each other's valued social identities. Because Rory and Paris actively engage in identity support, or "behaving in ways that convey understanding, acceptance, and support for a friend's valued social identities,"[15] Rory and Paris's relationship models a more complex picture of what "friendship" looks like than is typically seen on television.

Although Rory and Paris's relationship is centered on competition, the writers frequently indicate that Rory is the most consistent relationship in Paris's life, especially after they move to Yale. This relationship is less visible in the first few seasons as the show portrays their relationship in a competitive manner. Paris is threatened by Rory's arrival at Chilton, telling her, "You'll never catch up. You'll never beat me" (Episode 1.2, "The Lorelais' First Day at Chilton"). Paris is also jealous of the attention Tristan gives Rory. They seem to come to terms with one another, and then Tristan ruins that at the end of season 1 and they are enemies again. The waffling between friends and enemies continues in season 2 where Paris sees Rory more as competition than as a friend. For example, Paris wants to know what all of her friends scored on the PSAT, but Rory won't tell her (Episode 2.11, "Secrets and Loans"). Paris intentionally worries Rory about the importance of volunteer work to get into Harvard, which propels Rory to volunteer with Habitat for Humanity (Episode 2.2, "Hammers and Veils"). And when Paris finds out that Lorelai and Max broke up, she assigns Rory to interview Max for the school paper (Episode 2.5, "Nick & Nora/Sid & Nancy"). Rory seems to both cultivate this competition (refusing to reveal her PSAT scores just to keep Paris twisting) and understand there is more to Paris. When Rory has more social currency than Paris because she gets invited to the coveted secret society lunch table, she then convinces the Puffs to invite Paris to the table as well (Episode 2.7, "Like Mother, Like Daughter").

Their odd-pairing friendship continues throughout the series, with both friends violating important friendship rules. Paris wants to celebrate (go over their "words per minute") after their winning debate on doctor-assisted suicide, but Rory says she has plans and a rebuffed Paris runs off (Episode 2.14, "It Should've Been Lorelai"). At Yale, Rory violates Paris's trust when she tells Lane about Paris's relationship with Asher Fleming (Episode 4.14, "The Incredible Sinking Lorelais"). In season 5, Paris has a dream that Rory made veal parmesan, and she is convinced it means Rory is going to try to get the religion beat from her (Episode 5.6, "Norman Mailer, I'm Pregnant!"). In short, these multiple and frequent examples demonstrate the role of competition between Paris and Rory and highlight examples of the pair violating friendship rules.

Although friendship rules are often violated and they exhibit ongoing competitiveness with each other, Paris and Rory demonstrate a positive aspect of friendship in identity support. In some ways, the two are similar

Paris Geller and Rory Gilmore. *The WB / Photofest* © *The WB.*

in their comfort with being alone. Stephanie Whiteside reminds us that "Paris's caustic wit and competitive nature offend nearly everyone she comes in contact with and Rory prefers the company of her books to that of her classmates."[16] Rory frequently seems annoyed with Paris, but she also frequently helps her because in many ways, she gets her. For example, Paris comes over to Rory's house in a panic because she needs help studying. Rory reluctantly agrees to study with Paris for one hour (Episode 2.16, "There's the Rub"). In this example, Rory is sympathetic to Paris's academic goals because she shares them. In exchange for this identity support, when Dean catches Jess at her house after she said she wanted to be alone, Paris covers for Rory and says she is the one interested in Jess (Episode 2.16, "There's the Rub"). In these examples that emphasize identity support, Rory and Paris also demonstrate equity, in that "two people give and get in roughly equitable proportions."[17]

Sometimes identity support is evident in moments when they watch out for and support each other. When Paris doesn't get into Harvard, Rory is the one who comforts her by letting her cry on her shoulder (Episode 3.16, "The Big One"). When Paris starts her relationship with Asher Fleming, Rory covers for her at the newspaper and with Jamie (Episode 4.10, "The Nanny and the Professor"). Rory supports Paris's quirky requests like holding a wake at their dorm for Asher (Episode 5.3, "Written in the Stars"). And it isn't all one-sided. When Rory suffers a panic attack after she realizes Mitchum Huntzberger is at her DAR event, Paris offers a medicine cabinet of a purse (Episode 6.5, "We've Got Magic to Do"). When Rory needs a place to stay upon her return to Yale, Paris opens her door (Episode 6.11, "The Perfect Dress"). After Logan's cliff/parachuting accident, it is Paris who gets Rory answers from the hospital even though she is not family (Episode 6.20, "Super Cool Party People").

After being at odds over Paris's affair with Asher, and particularly how she treated Jamie, Rory and Paris experience a turning point on the spring break episode (Episode 4.17, "Girls in Bikinis, Boys Doin' the Twist"). This episode emphasizes their commonality. Instead of spring breaking, for example, they decide to watch *The Power of Myth* while consuming pizza, Coke, and chips in their hotel room. Later, they ask, "Are we doing this right?" They decide that they will commit to spring breaking. But then decide tomorrow's fine too.

Although Paris and Rory have a complex love/hate relationship, their friendship lesson is hopeful in that it says friendship rules can be violated as long as each other's valued social identity is affirmed by the other. Because "valued social identities are the aspects of your public self that you deem the most important in defining who you are,"[18] friendships that affirm this core aspect provide a way to understand how some friendships can overcome apparent incompatibilities. Over the seven seasons, Rory and Paris offer recurring representations of what identity support looks like, and, more importantly, give us what writer Mary Chase argues is important: a flawed person who can still be lovable.

TREATING EACH OTHER WITH LOVE

When "women are [still] underrepresented in U.S. media, regardless of the form, both in front of and behind the camera,"[19] *Gilmore Girls* is culturally significant in that it offers viewers a vision of female friendship created by a female writer/director. And the three lessons in female friendship offered in this chapter define different types of friendships that are all desirable and interesting.

Modern-day representations of friendship in media tend to portray a lack of friendship between female characters as well as a lack of female-to-female support. *Gilmore Girls*, in contrast, presents a plethora of female friendships that exhibit three lessons in female friendship. *The Guardian* writer Abigail Radnor suggests that "Sherman Palladino kept the schmaltz, or what she calls 'treacle matter,' to a minimum: 'We don't want a lot of "I love you" or hugging because I feel the love was shown through the way people treated each other.'"[20] The ways in which the female friends treat each other demonstrate that friendships aren't always perfect but can still be fulfilling and mutually beneficial when there is identity support, effort, and opportunities for emotional and practical fulfillment.

Part II

Culture: "She's Anthony Michael Hall in *Breakfast Club* smart."

Lunch with Norman Mailer. ***The WB / Photofest © The WB, Photographer: Danny Field.***

5

FEMINISM

"Does Susan Faludi know about this?"

> I think it's absurd to say that *Gilmore Girls* was anti-feminist. . . . I literally think it's the worst thing I've heard since Donald Trump was elected. Literally, Donald Trump is the new president might actually now be second to *Gilmore Girls* isn't feminist. I think that's ridiculous.
>
> —Amy Sherman-Palladino[1]

> The most central love story is neither the entanglements of single mom Lorelai (Lauren Graham) nor of her brainy offspring Rory (Alexis Bledel). It's the one between the two of them: sharp, witty and highly caffeinated, they're Tracy and Hepburn as mother and daughter.
>
> —James Poniewozik[2]

In today's society, "feminism" is a loaded word, with both women and men resisting the label, as well as the bra-burning (myth), man-hating (stereotype), hairy-legged (cold-climate necessity), Birkenstock-wearing (practical) image of the 1960s/1970s feminist woman. However, contemporary images of feminists reside as much in the images of female empowerment, from Gal Gadot's Wonder Woman and *Hunger Games'* Katniss Everdeen, as they do in political and social leaders who fight for equal pay and health-care bills that consider women's bodies. With that in mind, we suggest that *Gilmore Girls* is not a feminist manifesto as much as it is a narrative about how feminism exists in everyday lives. As Rory and Lorelai cry, "Solidarity, Sister!" (Episode 2.5, "Nick & Nora/Sid &

Nancy"; Episode 3.1, "Those Lazy-Hazy-Crazy Days") and Emily icily informs nurses that she is not a "Cosmo girl" (Episode 1.10, "Forgiveness and Stuff"), the series subtly articulates and occasionally overtly debates issues of feminism and gender expectations across generations. *Gilmore Girls* is known for its quick and witty dialogue, and we argue that it is in those conversations that a truly feminist story gets articulated.

"LOSE THE WORD 'MANIFESTO'"[3]

Responding to the criticism of *Gilmore Girls* as an anti-feminist series, Amy Sherman-Palladino balks at the idea, calling it "absurd" and "ridiculous."[4] And this makes sense when, in the premiere episode of the series, a flustered and babbling Rory explains to Dean that when Lorelai named Rory after herself, it was a moment when "her feminism just kind of took over" (Episode 1.1, "Pilot"). Overt references to and discussions about feminism pepper the first season in particular and continue throughout the entire series. Perhaps the cast is a little too white and the Gilmore girls' problems a little too champagne, but what makes a show feminist? Clearly, Sherman-Palladino's intention is that the show is feminist, but defining that is as difficult as defining pornography. We know it when we see it.

When *Gilmore Girls* aired in 2000, *Time* declared, "A charming story of a happily unwed mom and a brainy teen whose life isn't defined by boys, it shows that feminism and family values aren't mutually exclusive."[5] We'll put aside the fact that there was at least one episode of *Murphy Brown* that addressed this supposed tension ten years prior, but we agree that a narrative about the lives of women and their relationships with each other is an important and infrequent occurrence in television. Not only do we have Lorelai and Rory's relationship but also their relationships with best friends Sookie and Lane, respectively. Even sometimes-enemy Paris offers an important female friendship for Rory that stretches the entire series. Additionally, the character of Emily—"despite her autocratic approach to things—is a smart, fiercely loyal woman whose complicated emotional life receives a level of attention and care rare for a woman of her age on the big or small screen."[6] In the second quote that opens this chapter, James Poniewozik writes that "the central love story" is really between mother and daughter. This quality not only allows the show to pass the Bechdel test, in that the dialogue is focused on two women having conversations about something other than men a good portion of the time (or, as Bechdel requires, at least once), but it also suggests that female relationships are important on their own. Like on *Buffy the Vampire Slayer* and *Xena: Warrior Princess*[7] before it, the representation of and the relationships between the women of *Gilmore Girls* are relevant to a feminist focus on sisterhood and community.

At the same time, the showrunners cannot fully control how the show is perceived and viewed by all audience members. Male journalists were quick to point out the sex appeal of the women, in addition to the witty dialogue. *Rolling Stone*'s Joe Levy commented early in the airing of the series that "Lauren Graham has comic timings so deft that she can get a laugh out of a straight line. Plus, she wears jeans really well."[8] By season 5 of the series, *Esquire*'s A. J. Jacobs takes it a step further, initially calling Lorelai and Rory "quite hot" and then driving home the point: "And, men—in case I didn't make the hot-actress point sufficiently clear: This is a show worth watching even if the sound is muted, especially now that Rory—played by the stunning Alexis Bledel—is out of high school and you can leer at her without feeling like you should be chemically castrated."[9] (And this is why #MeToo is important.) In both articles, the male journalists admit that they feel a little embarrassed to be watching the show, and apparently witty dialogue and smart acting are not enough to fully justify their choice of viewing. This is kind of the equivalent to attaching those fake balls to the back of a pickup truck . . . because the truck isn't already masculine enough on its own?

One of the tenets of contemporary feminism, and something that stems from the third wave of feminism from the 1990s and early 2000s, is described as a type of "feminine feminism."[10] Feminine feminism says that women can be attractive and independent, and those ideas are not mutually exclusive or even deviant from feminism. In an article for *The Guardian*, writer Abigail Radnor argues:

> When it first aired, *Gilmore Girls* was refreshing television. While Sherman-Palladino didn't set out to break ground, exactly, she was aware of the climate in which she was writing. "Women at the time, in TV, were split into two groups: there was the popular pretty girl, or the angry girl who wore combat boots. As the cries of 'make women stronger' came out, all they did was take the same pretty woman and put a gun in her hand and have her run around in heels. The concept of

> strong women is still, and was especially then, a terrifying concept to a lot of networks, because they were afraid that that's not how people want to see women. But it is how women wanted to see women."[11]

Just because Lorelai and Rory are attractive or, more explicitly, "quite hot," does not mean they are not also feminist representations, and this is an important cultural representation for the time. Sherman-Palladino created strong women who rely on witty dialogue as much as their good looks.

One of the ways this feminine feminism plays out in *Gilmore Girls* is through the focus on Rory's love of reading. In a series devoted to popular-culture references, many of those stem from the literary world as much as the celebrity gossip rags. For example, early in their relationship, Rory convinces Dean to read Jane Austen (Episode 1.8, "Love & War & Snow") and tries to convince him to read *Anna Karenina* (Episode 1.16, "Star-Crossed Lovers and Other Strangers"). She nicknames Jess "Dodger," after the Artful Dodger in *Oliver Twist*, when he "borrows" her copy of Ginsberg's *Howl and Other Poems* (Episode 2.5, "Nick & Nora/Sid & Nancy) and calls him a Holden Caulfield wannabe when she is particular-

Jess (aka "Dodger") gives *Howl* back to Rory (with some additional notes). ***The WB / Photofest © The WB.***

ly annoyed with his antics (Episode 2.8, "The Ins and Outs of Inns"). When Rory falls asleep talking to Marty her first year at Yale, a poster for *A Confederacy of Dunces* adorns the wall (Episode 5.9, "Emily Says Hello"). There are articles, Reddit sites, and Goodreads lists devoted specifically to the book references in the series; it's a big deal, but not just for the literary love. Sherman-Palladino argues, "This is a series where we've said, implicitly, 'Read a book, read the classics; I know you're cute, but you can still wear lipstick and read Dickens.'"[12] Many contemporary definitions of feminism resist the man-hating stereotype and attempt to embrace (what might be seen by some as) contradictions. In Sherman-Palladino's image, this means you can be smart and girly at the same time. A show can depict empowered women who also wear short skirts and lip gloss, but does that make it feminist?

Writer Chimamanda Ngozi Adichie writes about feminism, "My own definition of a feminist is a man or a woman who says, 'Yes, here's a problem with gender as it is today and we must fix it, we must do better.'"[13] Even more succinctly, novelist and writer Roxane Gay offers one definition of feminists as "women who don't want to be treated like shit."[14] Amy Sherman-Palladino constructed Stars Hollow as a fictive place where audiences can witness, reflect, and admire the feminist possibilities of two women who actively resist being treated like shit and regularly talk to each other about things other than men. This seems to be making an effort to "do better."

RORY AND LORELAI: FEMININE FEMINISM IN ACTION

In a series created as part of the late 1990s family values framework, introducing Lorelai Gilmore as an unwed mother by choice takes some explaining, and done by the savvy Sherman-Palladino, the resulting narrative provides clues to feminist underpinnings. The first season is particularly heavy with references to feminist advocates and discussions of gender roles and expectations. Mentions of Susan Faludi (Episode 1.9, "Rory's Dance") and Emma Goldman (Episode 1.20, "P.S. I Lo . . .") are aimed at male characters who tell Rory and Lorelai what women are supposed to be doing. Mid-season, Rory dons a 1950s dress and pearls to help end a fight with Dean about women's roles at home (Episode 1.14, "That Damn Donna Reed").

However, some of these same moments also represent the contradictions that contemporary feminism embraces, which might muddy the waters for some viewers when defining the series as feminist. For example, when Tristan continues to harass ~~flirt~~ with Rory right before the dance and tells her "guys are supposed to buy the tickets," Rory retorts, "Does Susan Faludi know about this?" (Episode 1.9, "Rory's Dance"). It's a good line as Tristan is "slimy and weaselly, yes," and continues to pester Rory into dating him. She consistently rejects his advances and at one point astutely tells him, "You don't even like me. You just have this weird need to prove I'll go out with you" (Episode 1.6, "Rory's Birthday Parties"). By the time of the dance, and even later in season 1, it is clear that Tristan does like Rory a lot; however, he is still the guy who pulls a girl's pigtails to tell her he likes her. Except Tristan is the teenage version of a hair-puller who struggles with boundaries of consent, like when he offers to share his notes if Rory shares her body (Episode 1.2, "The Lorelais' First Day at Chilton"), who tells people Rory's going on a date with him when she is not and resorts to holding her books hostage until she agrees to go out with him (Episode 1.21, "Love, Daisies and Troubadours"), or goes out of his way to poke at Dean just to upset her (Episode 2.9, "Run Away, Little Boy"). In the end, he does not get the girl, which sends a great message about what women in general should demand from men's behavior toward them; however, he does get a kiss and kindness from Rory after consistently tormenting her.

In the final scene in the series for Tristan, he and Rory share a moment where he says, "I'd kiss you goodbye, but uh, your boyfriend's watching" (Episode 2.9, "Run Away, Little Boy"). Instead of rolling her eyes, snorting in disgust, or even mustering up a generationally appropriate "as if," Rory looks demurely away, giving him a slightly wistful smile. This is after Tristan has tortured her for a week threatening to tell Dean that they kissed at Madeline's party—and after Tristan reveals that he is not going to be able to complete the class project due in twenty minutes. He treats Rory badly throughout the season and a half that we know him, but this final scene is written in a way that hints we should lament the fact that there is no final physical contact between them. What is fascinating about *Gilmore Girls*, and part of what we argue does make it feminist, is that it embraces these types of contradictions as a way to represent contemporary issues with female empowerment and feminism. In the same way that Lorelai and Rory make picnic baskets for the annual town auction and yet recognize that the practice is "the world rotat[ing] backward on its axis" (Episode 2.13, "A-Tisket, A-Tasket"), it is the contradictions that make the conversation about the event explicitly feminist.

"Well said, sister suffragette"[15]

One of the most blatant conversations about feminism in the series takes place in episode 14 of season 1 ("That Damn Donna Reed"). The episode opens with Lorelai and Rory mocking the mundanity of women's lives depicted in *The Donna Reed Show* and Dean attempting to argue that the wife taking care of her family is "kind of nice." The conversation about Donna Reed in these first few minutes of the episode articulates a fascinating contemporary conversation about feminism that plays out through the remaining forty minutes of the show but also in households across America. In this prologue, Lorelai and Rory mock Donna Reed's window washing, perfect hair, and pearls, but Dean points out that families spending time together and "a wife cooking dinner for her husband" is not a bad idea. He argues, "She seems really happy." To which Lorelai and Rory retort that she is "medicated . . . and acting from a script . . . written by a man." But, Dean continues, "What if she likes making donuts and dinner for her family and keeping things nice for them and . . ." He trails off and eventually shuts up entirely.

In the context of the narrative, the way Dean indicates that he feels like he has to shut up when he is saying something unpopular mirrors what happens to a lot of men who try to have conversations about feminism. This episode aired on February 22, 2001, and since then we have had the "He for She" campaign (launched in 2013 with Hermione, er, Emma Watson as spokesperson) advocating for bringing men into the conversation. And more recently the MeToo movement, started by Tarana Burke as a way for young African American women to seek help and find a community, was reappropriated to represent not only sexual harassment and assault in Hollywood but for everyone, men and women included. What has occurred with MeToo is the shutting down of male celebrities who try to have public conversations about the degrees of incident between assault and harassment or the gray area of a bad first date versus issues of consent (in the case of Aziz Ansari). The prologue for this episode mirrors a common reaction of women who do not want to have a conversation about the privilege that maleness provides but also reflects some of the consequences of that silencing. The remainder of the episode lets this conversation happen between Dean and Rory, and he does have a voice, resulting in a representation of progression, compassion, and support that can happen between men and women regarding feminism.

This opening scene is important because it sets up two sides to an argument that started with the first wave of feminism in the early 1800s through the second-wave feminist movement and continues today. If a woman is happy taking care of her family and home, that does not necessarily make her less empowered than a woman who has a career outside of the home and does not even mean she is not a feminist. Dean and Rory further articulate this conversation the next day, which turns into a fight. Rory asks Dean to help her watch Babette's kitten, Apricot, and he agrees to come over after his shift at Doose's Market. He quips, "For some reason Thursdays are always really busy. Lots of repressed housewives shopping for their husband's dinner." Rory doesn't like that comment and argues that Donna Reed was repressed because she embodied "the whole concept that her one point in life is to serve someone else." Dean says that Rory only feels that way because of Lorelai, which offends her. Dean explains that his mom used to cook all the time for his family and wants to know what it says about her if Donna Reed was repressed. Rory argues, "It says that she has a choice and Donna Reed didn't. . . . Yes, I know she wasn't real, but she represented millions of women that were real and did have to dress like that and act like that." They part ways in a huff.

Ultimately, Rory does some research (because she is Rory) and finds out Donna Reed the individual was actually a bit of a Hollywood powerhouse for her time. When Dean shows up to Babette's, Rory answers the door in a 1950s dress and pearls, proclaiming, "Honey, you're home!" Rory makes him dinner, like the perfect housewife. It is a little unclear at the beginning of this scene if she is trying to appease Dean or teach him a lesson. However, when she realizes she forgot to make the rolls, she gets legitimately upset and declares, "Donna Reed would have never forgotten the rolls. They're going to make me turn in my pearls." Dean kisses her as he pulls her onto his lap. He says he loved everything, but he doesn't want her to be Donna Reed. It's a nice bow on the package of their tiff and a cute exchange between Rory and Dean, but the scene represents the best of both worlds. Rory has a choice to dress up and make a special dinner. Dean is a supportive partner who shows his appreciation for her efforts. The whole point of the original conversation was about women who didn't have a choice. What is important is that the dialogue between Rory and Dean sets up the conversation for the viewers and, in this way, demonstrates how popular culture narratives help to serve a communicative function.[16]

As a parallel story, just next door, another interesting situation sets up a conversation between characters about women, sex, and empowerment. Lorelai loses Rory's midterm baby chick (Stella!) and desperately calls Luke to come help her. He shows up looking a little bit like the Cheshire Cat with his goofy grin, when he hears a peep and exclaims, "You really do have a chick loose in here!" Sookie later explains to a baffled Lorelai that Luke must have thought the chick was code for a booty call. Underlying Sookie's explanation is the idea that women cannot ask directly for sex; they have to set up a damsel-in-distress scenario to open that door. The characters do not discuss this further, as Lorelai is preoccupied with Sookie's suggestion that she called Luke because a part of her does want to have sex with him (or at least date him). What this moment and the scene with Rory, Dean, and the uncooked dinner rolls also demonstrate is how easily these conversations get mitigated when the people involved move on to other ideas. It mirrors the way many conversations about gender expectations and roles play out in everyday life, but it still plants the seed for conversational possibility for the viewers. It is through examples like revealing Donna Reed's feminist story and subtly suggesting the absurdity of making up a fake chick in order to have sex that *Gilmore Girls* articulates its own feminist story.

A FEMINIST STORY

The series grapples with the tension between themes of feeling comfort in independence versus comfort in romantic relationships, making your own way versus accepting help, adhering to social expectations versus attaining personal goals. At the core of the story, Lorelai gets pregnant at sixteen and Christopher is willing to marry her as teenagers. They would have suffered through a brief scandal, but in doing "the right thing," they would have been set up financially, and eventually socially, for success. Lorelai refuses to marry him, then names her daughter after herself, and ultimately runs away from home to make her way in life freed from the emotional and financial constraints of her wealthy parents (at least until she can't afford Chilton by herself). Lorelai Gilmore gives the middle finger to social expectations about gender norms at the tender age of sixteen and charts her own path, working her way up from housekeeper to running the Independence Inn to owning the Dragonfly Inn. This is a feminist story.

At the heart of that narrative is the way the characters grapple with love and relationships. Lauren Graham contends, "The show is sneakily feminist in that it's always been great for [Lorelai and Rory] to have love, but they're also okay when they don't. That self-sufficiency is the first strength and that allows them to have these relationships."[17] While we could debate the definition of "okay" when the show depicts Lorelai passive-aggressively cold-shouldering Max Medina out of fear (Episode 1.11, "Paris Is Burning") and then manically planning a spur-of-the-moment road trip instead of telling Rory she canceled her wedding (Episode 2.3, "Red Light on the Wedding Night"), Rory deviled-egging Jess's car (Episode 3.6, "Take the Deviled Eggs…"), Lorelai breaking into Luke's apartment to steal a desperate answering machine message (Episode 5.14, "Say Something"), and Rory lying on the bathroom floor sobbing about why Logan won't call her (Episode 5.18, "To Live and Let Diorama"), we agree with the sentiment and take it a step further to argue that the fact that they are not always okay being independent is also feminist. Breaking up is hard and when love (or lust) is not reciprocated, sometimes bitches be crazy.

That being said, Lorelai goes out of her way to not be the woman who gets married just because she thinks she should. She cancels her wedding to Max Medina days before the big event because she "didn't want to try on my wedding dress every night" (Episode 2.3, "Red Light on the Wedding Night"). She is not going to walk down the aisle just to check a box on her list, and she is certainly not going to marry someone she likes a lot but does not love. When she does decide she is ready to get married, she is the one to propose (Episode 5.22, "A House is Not a Home"), much to the chagrin of Miss Patty, Babette, and Kirk. And later, when Luke strings her along, she calls off the engagement and sleeps with Christopher (Episode 6.22, "Partings"), and then when Luke shows up to tell her he is finally ready and they should elope, she does not back down (Episode 7.1, "The Long Morrow"). Even Rory eventually gives Logan an ultimatum and bags the "whale" (Episode 5.19, "But I'm a Gilmore!").

As these examples indicate, the space that exists between independence and comfort in romantic relationships, and between making one's own way versus accepting help, is what articulates this feminist story. Roxane Gay writes, "I embrace the label of bad feminist because I am human. I am messy. I'm not trying to be an example. I am not trying to be perfect. I am not trying to say I have all the answers. I am not trying to say I'm right. I am just trying."[18] Perhaps the bad feminist in *Gilmore Girls* is just trying; trying to highlight the in-between, trying to avoid the either/or. *Gilmore Girls* is not always the perfect feminist story, but it is trying to do better.

GENERATIONAL DIVIDE

One frequent discussion in the field of gender studies is about the tensions that are revealed when comparing feminism and gender expectations across generations. There is no better foil for Lorelai and Rory's contemporary feminism than Emily Gilmore's conservatism. She embodies the Phyllis Schlafly rhetoric for what it means to be "*Mrs. Mrs. Mrs.* Gilmore. I am not a Cosmo woman" (Episode 1.10, "Forgiveness and Stuff") and manages to articulate her place as *Mrs*. Gilmore in dialogue as witty and sharp as Lorelai's. Emily represents the resistance to second wave but voiced toward her daughter who grew up in the generation of third wave and granddaughter who is living something new altogether. At the same time, all three women exist in the same world as contemporary feminism, and their discourse and arguments about gender rules, expectations, and responsibilities reveal an interesting generational divide.

For example, during the school dance episode (Episode 1.9, "Rory's Dance"), Dean honks to let Rory know he is outside, and Emily refuses to let her go meet him. She insists, "It is not a drive-thru. She is not fried chicken." Emily says they will wait until he figures it out . . . which takes him a half dozen honks. The next episode, when Richard gets sick for the first time (Episode 1.10, "Forgiveness and Stuff"), emphasizes how much Emily's identity exists within being Mrs. Gilmore, but we also see that that role does not make her submissive or second to her husband. Richard tries to talk to Emily about practical matters and financial affairs in the event of his death, as she is fluffing his pillows to make him more comfortable. Emily refuses to listen and eventually blurts out, "No. I did not sign on to your dying and it's not going to happen. Not tonight. Not for a very long time. In fact, I demand to go first. Do I make myself clear?" Richard allows her to go first (although sadly, we know from the revival, and Edward Herrmann's real-life death, that he was not able to keep his promise). In this way, Emily gets what she wants that night without being submissive, but it all occurs within the boundaries of her role as his wife. This is the representation of the anti-ERA rhetoric from the 1960s and 1970s, which continues today. Just because a woman identifies primarily as her husband's wife and enjoys her traditional role does not necessarily make her repressed.

And yet, the character of Emily also reflects the contradictions of her own position. One of the consistent themes for Emily Gilmore is coming to terms with her identity in a changing world. The younger Jason Stiles, as business partner to her husband, consistently condescends to her, calling her desire for a photo of the signing of Richard and Jason's partnership "cute" (Episode 4.6, "An Affair to Remember"). Emily politely but dryly responds that when the financial papers ask for it, it will be "just darling." When she privately voices her annoyance to Richard, he reminds her that Jason is young, but she is not pleased. Later, she is thrown for a loop when the classic party she planned to announce the launch of the partnership is canceled to account for a trip to Atlantic City. Jason explains that he is sick of "floral arrangements and stuffy cocktail parties," remarking that his mother is busy planning them for his father's business, not realizing that planning and maintaining the social ties associated with Richard's business has always been Emily's job as his wife. When Richard agrees to try something new with the trip to Atlantic City, Jason informs Emily she can just "relax and hang out." Emily then apologizes to Lorelai, who she had hired as the party planner, and comments, "Times change, Lorelai. Things that were once considered proper and elegant are now considered out of date . . . like canapés and cocktail parties and the people who plan them." It is a rare moment of vulnerability from Emily and reflects how fragile the identity of wife sometimes is for her.

In a slightly different turn, when Emily and Richard are having problems after finding out he has been seeing Pennilyn Lott for lunch once a year behind her back, and when Richard double-crosses Jason without consulting her, she decides to take a trip to Europe. In a slapstick comedy scene set in the basement of the Gilmore mansion, Emily informs Richard she will go on the trip without him and have two glasses of wine at lunch every single day (Episode 5.1, "Say Goodbye to Daisy Miller"). An appalled Richard gasps, "Only prostitutes have two glasses of wine at lunch," to which Emily responds, "Well, then buy me a boa and drive me to Reno because I am open for business!" Moments later, she climbs out the window, snags her skirt, and gets caught in a state of undress by the neighborhood security, all in an effort to spite Richard and show him that she does not have to do what he wants anymore. Right before trekking to the basement, Emily supposedly "leapt out of a moving car" because "everything cannot be on your schedule, Richard." This hilarious scene highlights the (temporary) end of Emily's identity as "Richard's wife" when their separation becomes public but also reinforces how much her actions, behaviors, and plans were tied to her identity prior to the separation.

In fact, the episode where she finds out about Richard's secret meals with Pennilyn Lott (we must always use the full name—perhaps this would be a fun drinking game?) is rife with "wife moments" (Episode 4.9, "Ted Koppel's Big Night Out"). Richard announces to Lorelai that the day is not just about the football game but that "there are all kinds of rituals and traditions we Gilmores take part in." Emily is attending the Yale vs. Harvard football game, at Richard's alma mater, as a Gilmore. She pulls out the flask and cups to toast Handsome Dan the bulldog, as a Gilmore. She organizes a tailgating party so that Richard can show Rory off to his friends, sing school-spirited a cappella songs, and reminisce about the old days, as a Gilmore. At no point prior to the revelation that Richard has secretly been seeing Pennilyn Lott does Emily seem annoyed to be a part of this tradition. She embraces these moments as Richard's wife, and it is seeing Lorelai talk to Pennilyn Lott—and realizing Richard has been keeping a relationship with his ex-fiancée from her for years—that enrages her. She "won" Richard from Pennilyn Lott. He went against Lorelai the First's wishes in order to marry Emily, and her identity as Mrs. Gilmore is threatened in this moment and ultimately leads to fractures in the relationship.

In the end, she does not want to be the ex-Mrs. Gilmore, and this is evident after she goes out on what most people would consider a successful date (Episode 5.9, "Emily Says Hello"). She and Simon McLane have a nice rapport, she seems to enjoy herself at dinner, and when he says he will call her again, she expresses her pleasure with this. However, the moment she closes the door, the tone changes as she looks around her enormous silent foyer and starts sobbing. Later, when Richard expresses his regret at their separation, she tells him, "Come home" (Episode 5.12, "Come Home"). This simple request, where, in her traditional role as the center of the home, she calls him back to her, reinforces her identity as Mrs. Gilmore again.

The writers do a wonderful job of contrasting Emily's traditional values and identity in her role as a wife and mother against contemporary expectations, and particularly those of Lorelai and Rory. Sometimes it is Emily who seems to wish for more to her life, like when she tells Lorelai she admires her business savvy and life, commenting, "I've never done anything" (Episode 4.15, "Scene in a Mall"). Or when, in the same episode during her rant in the department store, she says, "Maybe I should get a job so I can have my own life!" Other times it is seen in the reflection of others' perceptions of her, particularly Lorelai's and Richard's. Lorelai's response to Emily's comment at the mall is to insist she has "friends and family who love being with you and you have a house that you love and a whole life." However, Lorelai's somewhat vague protest implies that she does not have many substantive examples to point out. In episode 3.13 ("Dear Emily and Richard"), Lorelai asks Emily what she does when Richard is out of town. Emily replies, "I keep this house running. . . . And I have my DAR meetings and there is always a thousand calls to make. I have functions and fund-raising events to organize. A million different things." Lorelai keeps pressing and Emily eventually tells her to stop because she thinks she is insinuating that she doesn't have anything to do when Richard is out of town. At Rory's twenty-first birthday party, a distraught Richard has just found out he paid for a $40,000 "sex house" (and sex mattress and sex box springs), knows Rory dropped out of Yale because her dreams were squashed, and realizes he should have listened to Lorelai (Episode 6.7, "Twenty-One Is the Loneliest Number"). Emily demands he come to the party, and he tells her they have failed because he wants Rory to do more than plan DAR "fund-raisers and tea parties: It's frivolous and meaningless. She has more to do; more to be. I don't want that life for her." Emily clarifies, "You mean my life. You don't want her to be me."

The collection of scenes with Emily contrasts with the "That Damn Donna Reed" episode (1.14) and offers an alternative view where Emily is not necessarily depicted as repressed by her role but does express feeling unfulfilled. In the Netflix revival, ten years after the series ended, this lack of fulfillment is something Emily labels as being over all the "bullshit,"[19] but in the cultural history of the original series, the conversation reflects the complex layers of gender and social expectations that an aging housewife encounters.

VALUE OF THE REFLECTION INSTEAD OF A MANIFESTO

Proclaiming *Gilmore Girls* "feminist" or "not" perhaps participates in a misguided debate.[20] *Gilmore Girls* successfully reflects the possibility of moving past an either/or proclamation by giving us a multitude of characters who all embody feminist ideals at times and eschew them at other times. Beyond strong female leads like Lorelai and Emily, even the supporting cast features a variety of women who are not afraid to demand what they want, including Paris Geller, Miss Patty, Gypsy, and Sookie St. James. What *Gilmore Girls* offers is not a feminist manifesto but rather a reflection of feminist possibilities, riddled with contradictions, which accurately embodies contemporary discussions about feminism. And, in our estimate, this is an effort to "do better" on television.

6

POPULAR CULTURE

"I mean, who doesn't love Muzak?"

If most American TV shows are performed in English, the language of *Gilmore Girls* is pop culture.

—Maura Quint[1]

An obsessive relationship with TV and film makes total sense for Sherman-Palladino—*Gilmore Girls* quickly became labelled a "pop culture show" for Lorelai and Rory Gilmore's referential dialogue. The pilot alone references Hans Christian Andersen, Nick at Nite, the Menendez brothers, 1981's *Mommie Dearest*, *Rosemary's Baby*, Zsa Zsa Gabor and more.

—Anna Leskiewicz[2]

From the Stars Hollow Troubadour to Sebastian Bach playing in Hep Alien to the innumerable references about indie rock bands and David Lynch films, both classic and indie literature, and celebrity gossip, *Gilmore Girls* asks viewers to reconsider the "low-brow" label commonly associated with popular culture. Just two years into the series, *Entertainment Weekly* writer Allison Weiner suggested that "what keeps the blooming fan base glued . . . is the deep, respectful connection between mother and daughter, and their breakneck, pop-cultured-crammed dialogue."[3] Much of the discussion about *Gilmore Girls* and pop culture has focused on the *quantity* of their pop-culture knowledge. In many ways, the quantity of popular culture references is central to the Gilmore girls' identities and helps viewers figure out who these characters are. The sheer volume of the Gilmore girls' knowledge of pop-culture trivia is part of what makes Lorelai and Rory so cool. In fact, Rose Maura Lorre of *Vulture* writes, "Much like Lorelai and Rory once opined about *The Donna Reed Show*, *Gilmore Girls* isn't just a show. It's a lifestyle, a religion for fans who worship Lauren Graham and Alexis Bledel's mother/daughter duo as both zeitgeisty deities in their own right and fast-talking filters sifting through the whole of popular culture."[4] The quantity of references is on the minds of many fans, including Lorre,[5] who quantifies the movies, TV shows, books, plays, musicals, songs, musicians, and celebrities watched, referenced, or mentioned. As evidenced by the many articles, websites, and lists that take on the task of cataloging references in the series, fans seem to take pride in the pop-culture knowledge acquired just by watching the show. Quantity, therefore, is important for understanding who Lorelai and Rory are. However, the content of those references is just as important in establishing identities for the women as well. Perhaps more accurately, through the smattering of pop-culture references, the show helps answer the question "Who are the Gilmore girls?" which invites a diverse *Gilmore Girls* fan community.

WHO ARE THE GILMORE GIRLS? (AS TOLD THROUGH MUSIC, MOVIES, BOOKS, AND MORE!)

The quirky pop song "There She Goes" that introduces viewers to *Gilmore Girls* in the pilot episode is the same song in the also quirky 1991 film *So I Married an Axe Murderer*, a comedy about a butcher (played by Nancy Travis) who Charlie Mackenzie (played by Mike Myers) believes is either "too good to be true" or an axe murderer, of course. It is no coincidence that this off-beat song introduces viewers to the equally eccentric Lorelai Gilmore, who similarly represents contradictory qualities. Is she the woman of Luke's dreams or will she (metaphorically) put an axe in his heart? By the end of the series, she kind of does both, but the show creates a unique identity for Lorelai to keep viewers guessing about who she is.

The popular culture references presented in the series help to establish Lorelai and Rory as complex, multidimensional characters who transcend the one-dimensional, mother/daughter archetypes common in television

Hep Alien. ***The WB / Photofest © The WB.***

and film. Lauren Graham references this Hollywood tendency to reduce women to certain limiting stereotypes in her 2016 autobiography, *Talking as Fast as I Can*. She explains:

> In *The First Wives Club*, Goldie Hawn's actress character says there are only three ages for women in Hollywood: "babe, district attorney, and Driving Miss Daisy." This suggests that acting careers follow a three-act structure, which makes sense. For the people who are willing to do the ear-staple-neck-flap surgery, perhaps the second act lasts longer. I haven't gotten to my last act yet (Ole Granny Sack Pants? Cranky Irish Potato Maven?), but so far for me career-wise, I'd call my first two acts Gal About Town and The Mom.[6]

Graham then goes through the stereotypical qualities that describe each archetype. "Gal About Town," according to Graham, "is a career girl on the go. She's looking for love but can't be tied down yet because she's trying to get ahead at the office."[7] In contrast, The Mom "wears plaid shirts and sneakers, and is usually described as 'tired,' 'beleaguered,' or possessing a 'faded beauty.'"[8] But Graham understood Lorelai as "equal parts Gal About Town and The Mom, plus a magical mix of smarts and humor that made her totally unique,"[9] and thus demonstrates the complexity of her character.

Many writers and fans of *Gilmore Girls* similarly discuss the appeal of Rory Gilmore's character as an atypical teenage girl. Representations of teenage girls on network television are "motivated by love and romance [and] appear less independent than boys."[10] Rory, in contrast, has boyfriends but is a character portrayed as independent and more motivated by her educational and professional aspirations. Brenna Ehrlich, *MTV.com* writer, states, "Before 'Garden State' and Zach Braff made the Shins a totally mainstream thing . . . Rory asserted her loner status by listening to 'Know Your Onion!' alone at her prep school lunch table."[11]

The following pages explore the Gilmore girls' identities and their pop-culture-laden dialogue that suggest this aspect of the show is one part that invites a unique audience that transcends generations and gender. This aspect of the show reveals intentionality in building multifaceted and complex characters that appeal to "different generations, transcending age, gender, and class."[12]

Gilmore Music

As *Rolling Stone* contributor Melissa Locker writes, "Don't look for too much hidden meaning in the expression, 'Monkey Gone to Heaven,' because according to the song's scribe, Black Francis (a.k.a. Frank Black), 'The phrase "monkey gone to heaven" just sounds neat.'"[13] Unlike the Pixies' lack of hidden meaning, the *Gilmore Girls*' creators' sprinkling of music references throughout the series highlights intentionality. The purposeful pop-culture references sometimes help characters diffuse awkward situations. To diffuse Dean's anger about Tristan, Rory says, "And No Doubt is touring with U2. I know you're extremely disappointed in Bono" (Episode 2.9, "Run Away, Little Boy"). In most television programming, music is backgrounded and supplements the narrative. For instance, the musical score can guide viewers to feel a certain way about the characters, to establish when viewers are supposed to feel sorry for a character, for example, or be wary about the motives of an antagonist. In many ways, music in *Gilmore Girls* is an active part of what advances the narrative and not always to encourage the audience to feel emotion. Instead, the music creates a specific identity for the Gilmore girls and their relationship with each other, as well as those around them.

Sometimes, music centers the relationship between Rory and Lorelai, demonstrating their connection with each other. In one episode Rory and Lorelai tease each other about their guilty music pleasures. Lorelai's guilty pleasures include Barry Manilow, Duran Duran, and Olivia Newton-John; Rory's include Bryan Adams, Dido, Spice Girls, and "The Macarena" (Episode 2.7, "Like Mother, Like Daughter"). In this instance, the music knowledge of Lorelai and Rory is highlighted as well as their ability to use these references to make witty observations about each other. When they don't share the same taste in music, Rory and Lorelai make recommendations to each other. "It's Rory who asks her mom if she wants her to burn a copy of their [Arcade Fire] CD. 'I don't know, do I?' Lorelai asks. 'Yes,' Rory says, because 'Funeral' is a classic"[14] (Episode 5.13, "Wedding Bell Blues"). On a visit home from Yale, Rory burns a copy of the New Pornographers' (a band named after Jimmy Swaggart's suggestion that rock 'n' roll was the new pornography[15]) CD for her mom (Episode 4.11, "In the Clamor and the Clangor").

The music choices are noteworthy, in part, because they are distinctive, peculiar, and diverse. One does not typically turn on the radio and hear Kraftwerk or Neko. That peculiar distinction helps portray the identities of Lorelai and Rory. They are a unique mother/daughter pair. Their characters challenge the mother/[teenage] daughter stereotype of not relating to each other, particularly when it comes to music. One might expect a mother/teenage daughter relationship portrayed on a TV drama as filled with the teenage daughter's "need for separation and differentiation as an independent woman."[16] Instead, the quantity and quality of the Gilmore girls' pop-culture knowledge allows the show to portray an atypical relationship as one where they have an "unusually close familial bonding (Rory and Lorelai share the same taste in lip gloss and Macy Gray CDs)"[17] (Episode 1.1, "Pilot") and can create that distance between them and Emily (or at least Lorelai and Emily). In contrast, when Emily creates a room for Rory at the Gilmores' house, she gives Rory two options: N'SYNC or Backstreet Boys, neither of which mesh with Rory's musical sensibilities (Episode 1.19, "Emily in Wonderland").

In the episode that perhaps most clearly defines their atypical and close relationship through music, Sookie scores four tickets to see the Bangles in concert (Episode 1.13, "Concert Interruptus"). Rory shares with Madeline, Louise, and Paris that she is excited about going to the concert with Sookie and her mom. Madeline says, "You're kidding.

You're going to a concert with your mom?" They are amazed at this revelation and Rory later tells them that her mom is her best friend. In this scene, the creators use the Bangles reference as a way to establish Rory and Lorelai's close, atypical mother/daughter relationship. They not only appreciate the same cool, off-beat music, they want to spend time together listening to it.

In addition to portraying a distinctive and atypical mother/daughter relationship, the show also establishes Lorelai as a "hip" mom through the show's music choices that are associated with her character. Even sixteen-year-old Lorelai was cool as demonstrated when she takes herself to the hospital while in labor with Rory (Episode 3.13, "Dear Emily and Richard"). While she is waiting for a hospital room, sixteen-year-old Lorelai listens to Nena's "99 Luftballons" on her Walkman. In this episode, the show uses the Cold War song reference to mirror Lorelai's insistent independence from her parents and the upcoming future freeze-out she instills when she runs away from home with Rory.

The La's, B-52s, Grant Lee Buffalo, the Cure, Mazzy Star, Blondie, Yoko Ono, Velvet Underground, Neko, PJ Harvey, Siouxsie and the Banshees: This brief, not-exhaustive list of some of the non-mainstream music references are cited from only the first two seasons of the show. It is noteworthy that the series associates these non-mainstream and edgy bands with teenagers like Rory and Lane. One might expect representations of teenagers in popular culture, in the early 2000s, to be associated with mainstream pop icons of the time, like Britney Spears, Christina Aguilera, and N'SYNC. But, in Stars Hollow, the cool teens go to see PJ Harvey (except for Tristan, who thinks PJ Harvey is a man) (Episode 1.21, "Love, Daisies and Troubadours"), and school dances play XTC and Mazzy Star (Episode 1.9, "Rory's Dance").

Perhaps the character most clearly intersecting with music is Lane. In the beginning of the series, Lane's character is portrayed as "in the know" for particularly obscure classic and contemporary music. For example, when Lane catches Max and Lorelai kissing, she gets embarrassed and runs into Rory's room, turning on "Pictures of You" by the Cure, an English band formed in the late 1970s who were pioneers in the goth rock style (Episode 1.8, "Love & War & Snow"). In season 2 when Lane comes back from Korea, she brings Elvis Costello, Neko, and Iggy Pop "bootlegs from Seoul"—not the most obvious musical choices for teenage girls (2.4, "The Road Trip to Harvard"). When Lane decides to try cheerleading, she chooses the music selection for the dance and it is the 1980s ska band Madness (Episode 2.11, "Secrets and Loans"). In an attempt to keep her true musical identity away from her mother, Lane changes from a Dead Kennedys T-shirt to a "Trust God" T-shirt (Episode 3.3, "Application Anxiety"). She secretly listens to Coltrane in her closet and gives Rory CD copies of obscure bands like the New Pornographers and the new Sparks (Episode 3.4, "One's Got Class and the Other One Dyes"). As these examples illustrate, Lane's musical choices are atypical teenage picks and diverse in genre, complementing the complex and atypical identities of Lorelai and Rory.

The music choices also help advance the narrative of Rory and Jess's budding romance. Viewers see Rory and Jess bond over the popular culture knowledge of Björk (Episode 2.10, "The Bracebridge Dinner"). On a sleigh ride through town, Jess asks Rory about Dean, "Does he know Björk?" Here, Jess is implying that if Dean doesn't know Björk's music, then he is unsuitable for Rory (and Jess is available!). It makes the viewers (or at least all those who are not Team Dean) question how important it is that Rory have a partner who she can relate to about music and, by extension, books and films. *Gilmore Girls* successfully inter-

Lorelai and Rory with Björk the snowwoman. ***The WB / Photofest © The WB.***

twines sweet, relatable moments with drops of obscure references that may go over the heads of many viewers. For example, when Rory uncharacteristically skips school and hops on a bus to New York City to find Jess, he takes Rory to a record store that he says is just like the film *High Fidelity* (Episode 2.21, "Lorelai's Graduation Day"). In the background, the Pixies song "Monkey Gone to Heaven" is playing while Rory discovers the "perfect Lorelai present—the Go-Go's on Vinyl"[18] signed by Belinda Carlisle herself. In this scene, viewers encounter obscure music, closely associated with *High Fidelity*, while simultaneously appreciating the sweet bonding moment between Rory and Jess. Layer upon layer of pop-culture references set a tone that suggests Jess and Rory have a lot in common, and maybe they should explore that further. In a later episode, XTC plays in the background as Jess and Rory kiss as a couple for the first time, creating a very John Hughes moment (Episode 3.8, "Let the Games Begin"). Such examples demonstrate the show's intention in pairing obscure music references with a relatable narrative arc about young love and compatibility.

In addition to advancing the *Gilmore Girls* narrative in intentional ways, it is clear that the musical references help to bring a fan community together. There are message boards where fans can note the musicians mentioned on the show[19] as well as boards like "Music you like that the Gilmores hate/Music the Gilmores like that you hate."[20] Jeff Finkle, contributor to *The Good Men Project*, details "5 Reasons 'Gilmore Girls' Isn't Just for Girls" including "These Girls have excellent taste in music" and "These Girls know pop culture."[21] The music references bring together a diverse community that crosses gender, which is particularly important for a show that is predominantly focused on relationships between women.

So, who are the Gilmore girls as told through music? They are complex in quantity and are quirky in quality, just as their music preferences. To be "in the know" with pop culture is not only hip but smart. *MTV.com* contributor Brenna Ehrlich labels the Gilmore girls as "hipster" "before the word [had] gotten dragged into the mainstream and slapped on everyone wearing a plaid shirt with a predilection for synth-pop."[22] The musical choices help to establish the "coolness" of the Gilmore girls, which involves depth and breadth of music knowledge. In doing so, Lorelai and Rory transcend typical mother/daughter archetypes, both individually and together.

Gilmores on Film, Literature, and Celebrities

In addition to the central role that music plays in *Gilmore Girls*, the show is replete with film, literature, and even celebrity gossip. Such popular culture references reveal complexities and uniqueness in dialogue and continue to establish Lorelai and Rory as the coolest mother/daughter duo. Movie references are just as diverse as the music references. Some film references are mainstream, like *Cocktail* (1988) and *Fletch* (1985), while others are obscure and offbeat, like *Moment by Moment*—a terrible 1978 John Travolta/Lily Tomlin film rated "a Grade-A stinker"[23] by Rotten Tomatoes. Sometimes movies nod to the theme of the episode, like when Sookie and Lorelai go on a double date with Jackson and his cousin Rune (Episode 1.12, "Double Date"). Rune is disgusted by Lorelai, particularly by her height and general appearance, causing Lorelai to tell a nervous Sookie, "You're nervous? You don't have some guy staring at you like he's Cher and you're that kid from *Mask*!" When Lane and Rory also double date that night, they go to the Black & White & Read Bookstore/movie theater to watch the 1958 cult film *Attack of the 50 Foot Woman*. The series is immensely clever with the layers of references that build upon one another, and this is part of what makes it easy to watch again and again.

Amy Sherman-Palladino and Daniel Palladino create a colorful mother role for Lorelai through some of her film references and other popular culture knowledge. For example, Lorelai quips to Sherry's baby shower guests that she learned about parenting through *For Keeps*, a 1980s film about teenage pregnancy starring Molly Ringwald and Randall Batinkoff (Episode 3.6, "Take the Deviled Eggs . . ."). And in a later episode, Lorelai reveals to Sookie that she made a Bananarama onesie for baby Rory (Episode 4.7, "The Festival of Living Art"). Her nontraditional approach to parenting, learned partially through a popular 1980s movie instead of a more traditional approach, like Dr. Spock, tells viewers that Lorelai is not just a stereotypical "Mom" who reads parenting magazines and buys (not makes!) clothes for her child. It also allows Lorelai to joke about how unprepared she was as a new mother at the age of sixteen. Intentional choices like these create a consistent persona for Lorelai Gilmore as unique, peculiar, and multidimensional.

Part of her peculiar identity is her knowledge of television and film, and her ability to apply that knowledge in unexpected situations. When

Rory's midterm, a baby chick named Stella, gets out of her cage, Lorelai sees the open door, throws her head back, and does her best Stanley impersonation from *A Streetcar Named Desire* (1951) (Episode 1.14, "That Damn Donna Reed"). When Lorelai and Luke break into the church in order to dismantle the church bells, Lorelai opens the door with her gym card noting, "All of those years watching *Hart to Hart* is going to pay off" (Episode 4.11, "In the Clamor and the Clangor"). The writers were smart to make pop-culture references consistent throughout the series, and critics and viewers noticed. For example, Rory "turns down Dean's proposal to bring over *Boogie Nights* for a movie night," telling him, "You'll never get it past Lorelai. . . . She had a bad reaction to *Magnolia.* She sat there for three hours screaming, 'I want my life back!'" (Episode 1.7, "Kiss and Tell").[24] *Bustle.com* writer Shannon Carlin also notes that Lorelai brings this up again at Spiffy's Tavern on her first date with Luke; annoyed that the menu is too long, she cries, "Oh my god, did Paul Thomas Anderson write this? Edit, people"[25] (Episode 5.3, "Written in the Stars"). In these episodes, we see consistency in Lorelai's character in terms of not being a fan of Paul Thomas Anderson's long movies but, more importantly, for her character development. It is her knowledge of this filmmaker and his style as well as her ability to deliver a witticism about the filmmaker that makes both of these references humorous. Moments like this are rampant throughout the series.

The mother/daughter relationship between Rory and Lorelai is also told through their shared movie knowledge. In some ways, the movie references help them communicate with each other and show viewers that they are more than a mother and daughter; they are also friends. When Lorelai thinks she may have had a moment with Luke, she pulls Rory roughly outside, leaving Rory to ask, "What's your damage, Heather?" (Episode 4.22, "Raincoats and Recipes"). The fact that the two share this common knowledge of *Heathers* (1988) makes this both funny and telling about their breadth of film knowledge. Sometimes the movie references reveal possible pitfalls in the relationship. For instance, when they are watching *Grey Gardens*, the 1975 documentary about "Big Edie" and "Little Edie"—an eccentric mother/daughter pair from the Kennedy clan who became reclusive in their old age—the two both imagine that as their future at the same time, becoming increasingly horrified (Episode 3.9, "A Deep-Fried Korean Thanksgiving"). Rory and Lorelai's movie nights help to establish their mother/daughter dynamic. Their choices in film are rarely common mainstream Hollywood blockbusters of the early 2000s, instead ranging from classics like *Willy Wonka and the Chocolate Factory* (1971) (Episode 1.7, "Kiss and Tell") to obscure, like the made-for-TV movie *Tears and Laughter: The Joan and Melissa Rivers Story* (1994) (Episode 2.1, "Sadie, Sadie") or Rosie O'Donnell in *Riding the Bus with My Sister* (2005) (Episode 6.4, "Always a Godmother, Never a God"), which enhances the peculiarities of their mother/daughter dynamic.

Not only do they watch movies together but they discuss the reasons behind their movie choices. Rory says that she wants to rent *Godfather III* (1990) because Francis Ford Coppola defends hiring Sofia in the director's cut. On one hand, she is a teenager who is interested in a classic film, but on a deeper level, her line indicates that she understands trivia behind the making of the film. Diversity in their film references is significant to show the breadth of their film knowledge, but there is also a more unique element revealed when the show pairs a common mother/daughter celebration night with a viewing of *The Rocky Horror Picture Show* where Lorelai stars as Magenta and attempts to persuade Luke to go as Dr. Frank-N-Furter (Episode 2.11, "Secrets and Loans"). These small, intentional choices establish Lorelai and Rory as peculiar and unique.

Movies are not the only major pop-culture references, with Rory's identity in particular defined by her love of books. Rory notes in her graduation speech (can anybody get through this without crying?), "I live in two worlds. One is a world of books" (Episode 3.22, "Those Are Strings, Pinocchio"). Over seven seasons, Rory's character is shown reading 339 books.[26] The books, especially intellectually classic book references, help shape the narrative about Rory, where her "bookish character has helped make smart girls hip."[27]

The purposeful integration of book references not only builds a unique identity for Rory but also helps establish the appeal between Rory and Jess. In fact, Emma Dibdin notes in an article for *Elle* that "books were the defining thing that brought Rory and Jess together—so much so that their ship name is 'Literati' in some circles—and Jess's bookishness was endearing enough to offset his major attitude problem."[28] In his first appearance in the show, viewers see a disrespectful, angst-filled young man have an endearing moment when "Rory says 'Goodnight Dodger' to which Jess replies '*Oliver Twist*,' cementing a place in Rory's heart, and most viewers' through his literary prowess"[29] (Episode 2.5, "Nick & Nora/Sid & Nancy"). Jess is never without a book in hand, a trait that is well established with Rory starting in the first season. Later, when Jess outbids Dean for Rory's basket, they discuss Hemingway and Ayn Rand (Episode 2.13, "A-Tisket, A-Tasket"). This discussion is put in contrast to Dean's lack of book-love, when he waits patiently while Rory combs through the book sale for hours but does not buy anything himself (Episode 2.15, "Lost and Found"). Books continue to be central to Rory and Jess's relationship in season 3, when Jess calls Rory a "book tease" after she tells him about *The Holy Barbarians* but won't let him borrow it until she is done reading it (Episode 3.14, "Swan Song"). As these examples illustrate, the show creates an intentionally romantic narrative between Rory and Jess through their common love of books. This serves the purpose of foreshadowing for the viewers that Dean is not going to be a long-term romantic partner for Rory because, for all his good looks and chivalrous attitude, he is not intellectually on par with her, just as Richard tries to drive home in both seasons 1 and 2.

Jess, for all his faults, is Rory's intellectual equal, or at least close. Jess and Rory's relationship is not only pushed forward through their literature similarities but also in movie references. For example, *Bustle.com* contributor Carlin writes, "'As you wish.' Those three words work for Westley when he was trying to win over Princess Buttercup [in *The Princess Bride*], and they certainly help fuel the romance between Jess and Rory. It's those three words that lead Jess to keep driving Rory's car. And despite the scene ending in a car accident and a broken arm, it also results in their first kiss."[30] In short, viewers learn about Jess through his book knowledge and also accept Jess, with all of his faults, as a suitable boyfriend for Rory because of the deeper side of his character, which is told through film and book references.

The popular culture references not only help to define characters and relationships but also tell viewers when we should not identify with a character. Such was the case when Luke hired Brennon Lewis at the diner, and Rory refers to him as "the lost Farrelly Brother" (Episode 4.9, "Ted Koppel's Big Night Out"). In this episode, it is clear that Brennon Lewis is at best dumb and dumber or at worst Satan, at least according to Kirk. And the creators must agree because that is Brennon's only appearance over the seven seasons. In a separate episode, when Lindsay reveals that she likes Michelle Branch and Matchbox 20, Jess scoffs, suggesting to viewers that Jess views Lindsay as immature and superficial, or at least predictable and mainstream (Episode 3.19, "Keg! Max!"). Such pop-culture references help the creators of the show instruct viewers to not identify with Brennon and Lindsay, without explicitly saying you should not like these characters.

Andrew Husband of *UPROXX* writes, "Judging by the prevalence of cameos made by diplomats (Albright), journalists (Amanpour), and other celebrities whose renown originated outside the entertainment industry, Sherman-Palladino preferred a healthy dose of intelligence with her pop culture."[31] Furthermore, he writes, "More than any other show before, during and after its time, *Gilmore Girls* celebrated the modern intelligentsia—politicians, writers, scientists—the same way sitcoms prized pop culture's darlings. In doing so, Sherman-Palladino's creation became television's representative for the smartest people in the room, but never at the viewer's expense."[32] Now, the show is not without its celebrity gossip, commenting on J-Lo's marriages, Angelina Jolie's relationship with Billy Bob Thornton, and Leo DiCaprio's obsession with model-girlfriends, but "Sherman-Palladino featured the likes of Albright, Amanpour and Mailer in the hopes of elevating them to the level of pop culture icon without negating the series' intelligent character or audience."[33]

As we argue, *Gilmore Girls*, and specifically the popular culture references in the series, creates unique identities for Lorelai and Rory. Their uniqueness complicates the typical representations of the "mom" and the "teenage daughter" on TV. Instead of only seeing a mom on TV as "'tired,' 'beleaguered,' or possessing a 'faded beauty,'"[34] viewers see a more complex depiction of a mother. Instead of only seeing a teenage girl as boy-crazy and obsessed about her looks, viewers see an alternative teenage girl archetype, who, arguably, is still boy-crazy but who is simultaneously driven to succeed academically and professionally and has a wealth of knowledge about culture—both low and high brow.

We suggest that *Gilmore Girls*' use of popular culture is intentional in how it advances the narrative about Lorelai, Rory, and their relationships. But the show is also intentional in that it introduces viewers to must-see films and reminds other viewers about the expansive universe of popular culture. In a way, it seems that the intention behind the depth and breadth of the integration of pop-culture references is the creators' way of expanding and complicating the limiting universe of "Hollywood mainstream."

CREATING A UNIQUE CROSS-CATEGORY *GILMORE GIRLS* FAN COMMUNITY

It has been well documented that *Gilmore Girls* has appealed to diverse audiences, sometimes unexpectedly, "but in the time between its original series run and its Netflix revival on Friday," asserts *National Post* writer Sadaf Ahsan, "other viewers, outside of its intended demographic, have embraced the show."[35] When she originally created the show, Amy Sherman-Palladino was charged with creating a family-friendly show for the twenty-first century. Pamela Hill Nettleton writes that *Gilmore Girls* "proves that 'family friendly' need not mean prudish, out-of-touch, dull as tombs, or sugary sweet. The show is sassy, smart as a whip, and peppered with pop culture references and witty zingers. It is fun to watch."[36] The show hit a level of mainstream appeal as it was read as "family-friendly" by atypical audiences including "right-skewing media watchdogs"[37] and men.[38] In fact, *Esquire* writer A. J. Jacobs reveals, "I know that professing my love for *Gilmore Girls* is a bit like saying that I just went to a really super scrapbooking workshop. It's just not something straight adult males are supposed to say. I mean, the show has a Carole King theme song, for God's sake. Sally Struthers plays a recurring character. Doesn't matter. I love it, and you should, too."[39] This far-reaching allure that appeals to diverse audiences is due, in part, to the diverse and far-reaching pop-culture references that many times transcends Hollywood mainstream. The dialogue includes "tough stuff for older folks to identify with, to be sure, but we've all had a generation or more to grow accustomed to the fact that, while we ourselves may age, popular culture remains a kind of garden of attenuated youth."[40]

The popular culture appeal of the show has invited fan communities to develop message boards like "Movies Mentioned in the Gilmore Girls"[41] and "Every movie referenced/watched in Gilmore Girls (including quotes)!"[42] and a full film list of Gilmore Girls Film References compiled by Gilmoregirlsmovies.wordpress.com. *BuzzFeed* has compiled "All 339 Books Referenced in 'Gilmore Girls.'" A website titled "Black, White & Read Books: Reading all books referenced on Gilmore Girls" is organized by season and created by Wix.com. As evidenced by these examples, fans of the show are drawn to the series, in part, because of the pop-culture references.

THE VALUE OF POPULAR CULTURE

As we have demonstrated, the show walks a thin line between mainstream and non-mainstream references. Viewers encounter familiar 1990s celebrity references like when Lorelai tells Jason Stiles that the flowers she's been receiving signed from "Jason" she assumed to be from Jason Priestley (Episode 4.8, "Die, Jerk"). Then the show presents viewers with more obscure references like when Lorelai warns Emily about firing a maid for putting "walnuts in the salad" and says that this might lead to a "Frank Lloyd Wright situation" (Episode 3.8, "Let the Games Begin"). The continuous juxtaposition between well-known and deep cuts intentionally brings together diverse audiences and explains why some critics, like Andrew Husband, highlight that "the result was a smart show with smart people that didn't talk down to its audience, and that's a key, and sometimes overlooked, element of its enduring appeal."[43]

The Guardian contributor Abigail Radnor speculates why audiences continue to watch *Gilmore Girls*.[44] She writes that some might watch because they relate to the mother/daughter portrayal, and others might watch the show as an escape. We suggest that a third option is that the show appeals to diverse audiences who appreciate the cultural history of popular culture. Popular culture is often considered "common" and "low brow" and typically positioned opposite of other, more intellectual forms of discourse. But "popular culture tells us something about society."[45] It is part of the "rhetoric of everyday life"[46] that teaches us about societal attitudes, values, and belief systems. In the same way that Lorelai uses popular culture references to verbally keep her mother at a distance, she also uses them to cultivate a tighter bond with Rory.

As Ahsan suggests, "As a reference-laden series that pays respect to television and film throughout every single episode, *Gilmore Girls* itself has become that very paragon of pop culture it long prided itself on representing."[47] The show's use of popular culture builds unique characters who viewers are asked to identify with. The complexity and sometimes counterculture aspects of the characters and their relationships invite a diverse cross-category audience who may simultaneously understand cross-genre knowledge of musical artists like Dolly Parton and Bananarama and non-mainstream references like XTC and Kraftwerk. The series is "a brand of drama and comedy even with an encyclopedia of pop culture references"[48] that represents an expansive universe of popular culture. Viewers, then, can either take delight in the references they understand or can use the show to learn about references that are unfamiliar.

The result is a show that redefines smart as both "low and high brow," which appeals to diverse audiences that transcend "age, gender and class."[49] We've noted that being in the know on music and books is what brings Jess and Rory together, but being in the know as a viewer is what has created a fan following that, due to the release of *Gilmore Girls* streaming on Netflix and the desire for the ten-years-later revival (also on Netflix), has gone beyond a cult-following to a mainstream love of the girls. When Target carries a *Gilmore Girls* T-shirt, you know you've reached a broad group of viewers. The appeal of *Gilmore Girls* is centered in "Sherman-Palladino's protean gift for cultural references in some cross between Mystery Science Theater 3000 and Ulysses, [where] you lived each week, to borrow from critic Wilfrid Sheed, in 'an old world with a fresh coat of words'"[50] and boy, do we love that language.

7

ISSUES OF CLASS

"Money makes people shallow."

> *Gilmore Girls* is incredibly smart about all of the ways that the life Lorelai left behind, and all the easy cash that would've come with it, act as siren songs for Rory.
>
> —Todd VanDerWerff[1]

> For all their differences, the Gilmore women all understand money as a way of securing the dynamic they want, whether that means refusal and distance or obligation and acceptance.
>
> —Lili Loofbourow[2]

When it comes to issues of money and status, *Gilmore Girls* creates endless opportunities to see characters at odds with one another. It is difficult to miss how the series negotiates themes regarding social status and money when the opening story centers on a woman who purposely left her parents' world of fund-raisers, galas, and social expectations to first live in a shed and then a two-bedroom, termite-feast of a house in tiny Stars Hollow. The plot is driven entirely by the fact that Lorelai needs her parents' money to help Rory get into Chilton prep school. Cultural critic Lili Loofbourow reminds us, "Money matters in *Gilmore Girls*. It matters deeply. In a show with spirited characters who don't take direction well, it often functions as both a means of controlling others—emotionally as well as financially—*and* as an excuse to submit to that control."[3] If Richard had simply found his checkbook and Emily not tacked on the stipulation for a weekly dinner (Episode 1.1, "Pilot"), the show is over and Lorelai's bruised ego begins to heal on the ride home with the salve of a fat check in her wallet and no strings attached. But you've got to love Emily (and Amy Sherman-Palladino) when she seizes the opportunity, setting the plot in motion and creating situations that allow us to question how wealth and money function in the narrative as a means of getting what the characters want materialistically and emotionally.

Richard and Emily represent the upper echelon of society, whereas Lorelai represents the opposite—not just as someone who is poorer than they are but someone who actively resists what their world represents. When Emily and Richard are reintroduced to the lives of Rory and Lorelai, Rory relates to her grandparents and to their high-class world in ways that Lorelai was never able to. As such, Rory's struggle with her identity and her increasing autonomy from her mom can be explained, in part, by looking at how socioeconomic status is represented in *Gilmore Girls*. It is the idea that money plays two roles in control (giving and taking; accepting and resisting) that allows the series to battle tensions with wealth to create definitions of class. These tensions create opportunities for resistance and differentiation between Lorelai and Emily but also Rory and Lorelai. *Gilmore Girls* is particularly interesting in how money comes into play in romantic relationships in the series, frequently from outside sources, and what that ultimately says about American dreams and aspirations.

DEFINITIONS OF SOCIAL STATUS IN *GILMORE GIRLS*

Fans have noted that perhaps the ladies live a little too cushy a life to be in a single-parent household on the outskirts of Hartford, Connecticut. For example, Lorelai and Rory rarely repeat outfits and consume massive quantities of takeout on a supposedly limited budget. However, we note that the television show is not intended to be a gritty narrative of what it means to be a single mother in America, and watching Lorelai have to work three jobs to buy milk is not what Amy Sherman-Palladino was going for. So we ignore the financial depictions that do not quite ring true in an effort to understand the deeper themes of social status and class conflicts that course through the veins of each season. Writer Todd Van-

DerWerff notes, "That's how *Gilmore Girls* casts the classic screwball comedy story arc into a different light. The show is still a mostly silly, happy one, but it has an undercurrent of financial tension that divides generations of Gilmores."[4] And that tension, while not gritty, is pervasive and interesting.

The entire series is loaded with examples of what it means to be part of the upper class of society. The tensions between the haves and the have-nots come into play when Emily and Richard's opportunities and expectations are compared to Lorelai and Rory's, as well as when Rory gets thrown into the complicated social world of Chilton and becomes interested in an eligible Yale bachelor. Frequently, references to wealth and social status are layered into the witty dialogue in seemingly minor moments. For example, when Rory gets stuck at Emily and Richard's house during a snowstorm, Lorelai warns, "Tell Grandma you arrived there not a member of the Junior League; I'd like you to leave the same way" (Episode 1.8, "Love & War & Snow"). In the same episode, Emily and Richard express shock and disdain when Rory proposes they heat up a frozen pizza. Later in the first season, Richard and Emily find out that their regular rental in Martha's Vineyard is not available, so Lorelai suggests they go to Paris instead (Episode 1.14, "That Damn Donna Reed"). They refuse to travel to Europe in the spring because it is too expensive to fly first class. Lorelai's suggestion that they fly coach is met with stares of disbelief. In season 4, when Lorelai and Rory go to the Yale vs. Harvard football game, we find out that Emily and Richard's definition of tailgating is hiring a chef to cook steaks (Episode 4.9, "Ted Koppel's Big Night Out"). Upon seeing Richard and Emily's house for the first time, Luke remarks, "This is a house? . . . What a waste. See this is what causes peasants to revolt. This is how heads end up on pikes" (Episode 5.7, "You Jump, I Jump, Jack"). When Paris's parents run out of money and she finds herself unexpectedly poor, it only takes days for her to proclaim, "Karl Marx has come alive for me today. I never understood what he was yammering about before and now it just seems so obviously wrong that those who control capital should make fortunes off the labor of the working class" (Episode 6.5, "We've Got Magic to Do"). And Luke repeatedly receives a peal of laughter when he asks what the DAR is at Rory's twenty-first birthday party (Episode 6.7, "Twenty-One Is the Loneliest Number"). These seemingly small moments are but a few examples of the way social status is defined in the series, both upper and not.

And sometimes the conversations are more deliberate, and it is the contrast between those who have money and those who do not that produces the most blatant examples. Rory's first and second meetings with Logan Huntzberger highlight these issues of class but also foreshadow what VanDerWerff calls the "siren songs" for Rory. The first time is when Logan's friend Colin bumps into Marty and then blames him for the physical contact (Episode 5.3, "Written in the Stars"). Logan (eventually) remembers Marty as a bartender for his parties and asks if his "financial situation hasn't changed" because he wants to hire him again. As they walk away, Colin belittles Marty, criticizing his clothing and then, when Logan tells him to stop, comments, "I'm a friend of all people, large, and . . . very very small." Although Logan was not particularly rude to Marty in this meeting—"show me your friends, and I'll tell you who you are"—Rory and Marty agree that Logan and his friends are jerks.

Later, while Rory hangs posters for Asher Fleming's wake, she runs into Colin, Finn, and Logan searching for a blonde/redhead with a "short" name whom Finn met the night before. Logan and Rory get into a debate about social status with Rory telling him, "Just because somebody doesn't have money or a fancy family doesn't mean they are inferior to

Rory and Logan's second meeting, first debate. ***The WB / Photofest © The WB.***

you. . . . And just because somebody is a bartender at a party for you and your friends, it doesn't mean you can talk to them like a servant." Logan acknowledges the former is true but disagrees with the latter to a shocked and appalled Rory. He argues, "I hired him, I paid him, he served. That's what a servant does." They go back and forth, with Logan smugly guiding Rory through a debate until she tells him he embarrassed her friend and she doesn't like that. As he walks away, Logan tells Rory to call him Master and Commander from now on. FYI, Matt Czuchry, this is but one reason why most fans hate Logan.[5]

One of the most cringe-worthy scenes to watch in the entire series is in season 5 when Rory and Marty end up at a dinner with Logan and his privileged friends (Episode 5.15, "Jews and Chinese Food"). Logan and his friends swap boarding-school tales, and then Colin mocks Marty's question about whether he missed his family. At the end of the meal, they decide to split the bill evenly, and Marty cannot pay his $75 portion. Logan offers to pay for him, but Marty refuses and then runs out to find an ATM. When Rory follows him out, Marty reveals he only has $18 in his account and he does not know what to do. He is mortified to leave but also embarrassed to go back into the restaurant. Rory begs him to take money from her and Marty reluctantly does so, saying, "And I thought getting pantsed at the prom was going to be the low point of my life." This episode not only cements Rory's choice of Logan (although Marty's romantic interest was always one-sided, even if Rory gives him hope by draping her legs over his on the couch and insisting she wants to spend time with him—damn, girl—pay attention to what you are doing to men's hearts!), but it also marks a full turn toward the life that Lorelai refused. Logan is the rich, privileged douche of a man that Lorelai wouldn't be caught dead with.[6]

We saw the start of this difference between mother and daughter when a tipsy and bedazzled-with-diamonds Rory stumbles from a limo filled with eligible Yale-enrolled bachelors laughing and, to Lorelai's dismay, looking at home and happy (Episode 5.8, "The Party's Over"). And then witnessed the discomfort between the two women in the kitchen the night before Emily and Richard's vow renewal, when a slightly drunken Lorelai rants about the upper class (Episode 5.13, "Wedding Bell Blues"). She tells Rory,

> This is how it works in my parents' world. . . . These people live in a universe where they feel entitled to get what they want when they want it and they don't care who is in their way. I hate that world. It's vapid and selfish. It's like that Life and Death Brigade you wrote about. . . . A bunch of selfish rich kids, the children of entitlement, blowing off school, drinking for days, spending thousands on a stupid and potentially dangerous stunt, knowing full well that they're not going to get into trouble cause Daddy is important. They're all the same.

Thinking of her growing interest in Logan, Rory protests, "They're not all the same! You don't even know them." Lorelai looks shocked and backs off a bit, acknowledging that having money does not necessarily make a person terrible. The two handle the disagreement the way they do most issues in the later seasons, by nonverbally conveying that they feel weird but then changing the subject. Under the surface, this moment foreshadows how Lorelai will feel when she finds out Rory is interested in Logan, but it also articulates the difference in how the two women view the world of the upper class now. Back in season 2, when Richard attacks Dean for not having ambition or plans for his future, Rory is furious and calls him a snob (Episode 2.1, "Sadie, Sadie"). By season 5, however, she has now spent multiple years in private education surrounded by people who can not only afford private education but think it is necessary to get ahead in life, and she has gotten to know her grandparents and their world; an acceptance of what that world entails has seeped in. In this way, the depictions of social status make *Gilmore Girls* particularly interesting and complex in how these moments steer the Gilmore women in particular, both toward and away from one another.

LIKE MOTHER, (NOT) LIKE DAUGHTER

Lorelai resists the high-culture trappings of crinoline, crystal, and cotillions as a way to differentiate herself from her family, and more specifically, Emily. Whether that happens by simply staying away from them, as indicated in the first episode (Episode 1.1, "Pilot") when, upon finding Lorelai suddenly at their door, both Richard and Emily make a quip about it not being a holiday, or by actively seeking out items that would be considered gauche by her mother's standards, these moves exist within a deeply threaded theme of social status. For example, when Emily visits

Stars Hollow to see Rory go to her first dance, she stays to take care of an injured Lorelai and tries to hunt down the Baccarat crystal candlesticks she gifted Lorelai last Christmas (Episode 1.9, "Rory's Dance"). Lorelai begrudgingly reveals she exchanged them for the monkey lamp on the side table. An appalled Emily harangues Lorelai: "You traded my lovely gift for a semi-pornographic leering monkey lamp? How could you? This is not just about the bad breeding of returning a gift. This goes to the very heart of the question of taste. You were given something of substance and you cast it off for a ridiculous, slightly sinister barroom decoration?" Lorelai relies on fuzzy clocks to purr her awake, rhinestone sweatshirts to keep her sparkly and warm, and a Betty Boop vase to hold her flowers. According to Lili Loofbourow, "Camp and kitsch were her weapons. Excess, impracticality, and questionable taste became, for Lorelai, a kind of politics of resistance against the Gilmores as an institution."[7] At the same time, Emily's gift of crystal candlesticks is so impractical for Lorelai's life that she is also involved in a political game of trying to drill in good breeding and taste as defined by the upper class in which she exists. The rare moments when Emily considers what Rory and Lorelai might want and need are exceptional in the series and are singled out by Lorelai as possible turning points; for example, when Emily serves pudding at dinner because Lorelai and Rory like it and picks out an affordable light-up bracelet for Rory's birthday instead of buying her pearls or a pashmina (Episode 1.6, "Rory's Birthday Parties"). Or when she attempts to buy Lorelai and Luke a house for a wedding gift and it is exactly what Lorelai wants (Episode 6.21, "Driving Miss Gilmore").

The first season of the series in particular initially establishes an "us" versus "them" dynamic regarding wealth that slowly begins to erode as Rory gets to know her grandparents and also as she starts to call Chilton her second home. Although Lorelai attended a private school until the age of sixteen, Rory only just starts her private school existence at the same age. While Rory does not exactly embrace the wealth suddenly around her, it is the first time in her life that she experiences it outside of her mother's narrative about it. If we know anything about Lorelai, it is that sometimes she is an unreliable narrator, but a young Rory did not necessarily pick up on that. Early on, Rory does not crave wealth, but she is not unimpressed by it. After her first breakup with Dean, she takes Lane to a Chilton party thrown by not-really-enemy-but-not-really-friend Madeline (Episode 1.17, "The Breakup, Part 2"). An awed Lane asks if Rory's grandparents' house is as big as Madeline's and Rory responds, "No, I mean it's big, but it's not this Hearst-castle-y." Lane quips, "I mean there should be a map or a tour guide or Robin Leach or something." In contrast, Lorelai would have immediately found her way to the master bedroom to mock the owners because "rich people have hilarious sock drawers."

One of the first moments to reveal the new tension between how Rory and Lorelai view the wealthy comes in the third episode of the series (Episode 1.3, "Kill Me Now"). Emily talks Richard and Rory into spending the day together at the club, and when Lorelai tries to stop the setup, Emily remarks, "Well, isn't this interesting. You're afraid . . . that Rory will enjoy the club and have a good time without you." Rory and Richard both begrudgingly agree to go, and they end up bonding over a love of travel and books. When Lorelai finds out Rory had a good time, she unconvincingly remarks, "So, you had fun. That is great. That is really, really great." But Lorelai is clearly disappointed and feels disconnected from Rory for what is probably the first time ever. Later, she gets jealous when Richard calls to talk about books with Rory, and she resorts to passive-aggressively yelling at Rory for stretching out her sweater with her "totally" bigger boobs. Lorelai later laments her behavior in a conversation with Sookie, realizing, "It's not about the sweater. It's about the golfing thing. And the liking it thing. She had fun, Sookie. Just like my mother said she would." This episode sets up a consistent theme of Lorelai trying to sort out her feelings about Rory's relationship to Emily and Richard and to come to terms with the fact that Rory may want the wealthy world that Lorelai actively despised.

However, mo' money, mo' problems. When Lorelai and Rory go window-shopping because they are skint, they run into a whirling-dervish shopping tornado called Emily (Episode 4.15, "Scene in a Mall"). Emily is making the major mistake of shopping while angry (second only to the mistake of shopping online while drunk), after Richard makes fun of her spending habits by commenting, "You've done enough shopping for a lifetime. For Methuselah's lifetime." Emily barely pauses on her marathon through the store as she purchases fancy glass apples, Brioni suits (which Lorelai informs Rory cost "six months of my car payments, plus a car"), diamond watches, Manolo Blahnik shoes, and, according to Rory, a Vera Wang wedding dress for Lorelai, all without asking the cost of anything. When Lorelai questions the impetus for her shopping rampage,

Emily throws a temper tantrum, revealing that she is furious with Richard and feels left out of the new life he seems to be cultivating. To calm her down, Lorelai and Rory take Emily to a brand-new place: the mall's food court. Emily is disdainful of the plastic chairs, comments about all the food on sticks, and eventually tries an Orange Julius, remarking, "Your father and I know a man who owns a couple dozen of these stands as part of his holdings. Now I can sincerely tell him I like his product."

The entire scene is rife with haves versus have-nots tension, but it is the conversation between Emily and Lorelai that pulls back the curtain a bit on the upper-class world that Emily lives in. Emily tells Lorelai she admires her life because "I've never done anything. . . . Richard is right. I buy things, things I don't even want. It's all I have." This comment speaks to "the show's project of exploring what money means for women—particularly women seeking some form of emotional independence."[8] In Emily's world, spending money serves a variety of purposes, but Emily doesn't have her own money and she is criticized for shopping, an activity that helps her fulfill her role and is deeply tied to her identity in intricate ways. What she owns conveys something to those in her social circle, and how she outfits her life and husband is a reflection of how well she does her job as Mrs. Gilmore. The end of this episode depicts a particularly heartbreaking moment for Emily when Richard does not realize the glass apples now adorning his dinner table are a new purchase, thus trivializing the artifacts she uses to mark purpose in her life.

In one of the opening quotes for this chapter, Loofbourow articulates the importance of money for all of the Gilmore women when it comes to establishing a sense of power, either in being able to resist or refuse money and create distance or in establishing a sense of obligation and securing face time with each other. Emily frequently attaches strings to the money she loans both Rory and Lorelai, and Lorelai breaks her neck to avoid getting attached to more strings than she needs. When Lorelai pays back the money that she borrowed for Chilton, Emily is furious, remarking, "You must be very relieved. . . . Your debt is paid. You owe us nothing. . . . You don't need us anymore. . . . You don't have to deal with us. . . . You don't have to come over for Friday night dinners. . . . It all works out beautifully, doesn't it?" (Episode 3.18, "Happy Birthday, Baby"). Lorelai asks her, "Wouldn't you rather we came over here because we wanted to, not because of some threat you're holding over our heads?" Even Rory uses Christopher's offer of money to establish some independence after the stay with her grandparents ends on bad terms (Episode 6.10, "He's Slippin' 'Em Bread . . . Dig?"). *Gilmore Girls* deals with money in ways that depict the complexity of the power that it brings and takes away. When Emily is lonely in her marriage, no amount of shopping can fill that void (Episode 4.15, "Scene in a Mall"). When Lorelai's house is being eaten by termites, no amount of talking can convince a bank to loan her money without Emily as a cosigner (Episode 2.11, "Secrets and Loans"). Money matters in the Gilmore girls' worlds, and how that money negotiates relationships is a central theme of the series.

SUITABLE SUITORS: SUITING THE FAMILY

If *Gilmore Girls* has taught us anything, it is that the upper class is maintained by a willing agreement among the rich to only marry other rich people, with the exception of Logan's friend Juliet (played by Riki Lindhome), who won't eat anything until she marries a poor man and locks him into an iron-tight pre-nup, so that she can balloon up on fried shrimp and peanuts (Episode 5.15, "Jews and Chinese Food"), or maybe Robert "Grimaldi" who has grand plans for wasting away his family fortune, via multiple divorces and debauchery, and leaving whatever is left to a parrot (Episode 5.17, "Pulp Friction"). Luke is not good enough for Lorelai because he is a "filthy diner owner," according to Emily (Episode 5.17, "Pulp Friction"), who has long dreaded the outcome of Lorelai's attraction to him. Even Dean agrees that Luke is not enough for Lorelai, although whether that is based on intelligence, finances, aspirations, or all of the above, it is not entirely clear (Episode 5.18, "To Live and Let Diorama"). Dean is not good enough for Rory because he will not be able to give Rory the life she deserves, according to Richard (Episode 2.1, "Sadie, Sadie"). Rory is not good enough for Logan, according to Shira Huntzberger, which "has nothing to do with her mother" (yeah right, Shira), but everything to do with the fact that "a girl like Rory has no idea what it takes to be in this family, Logan. She wasn't raised that way; she wasn't bred for it" (Episode 5.19, "But I'm a Gilmore!"). Rich people marry other rich people, and the richer people marry the richiest rich of them all.

In the episode that best articulates the Gilmores' issues with Luke and Lorelai, Emily finds out they are dating (via Kirk), and she invites him to dinner (5.7, "You Jump, I Jump, Jack"). Emily offers Luke a beer and comments on the rustic charm of his diner, and Luke initially thinks that Emily is being "great." He gets mad at Lorelai for suggesting that Emily is actually insulting him, but then it turns out Lorelai knows Emily better than Luke does. Emily spends the rest of the evening talking about how she has heard of diners serving road kill ("probably not yours," Luke), offering him *beer* ("nitwit juice"), and calling his truck rustic ("crap pile"). At the end of the evening, a battered Luke asks Lorelai, "Do you know what's amazing? I mean truly amazing? . . . She never said anything directly bad about me or the diner or anything else concerning me. . . . 'Rustic' really did sound like 'crap pile' that time." But it's not over for Luke. When Richard finds out Luke came to dinner (this happens during Emily and Richard's estrangement), he wants a reciprocal moment with Lorelai's new boyfriend and takes him golfing. After a day at the club, a tipsy Luke calls Lorelai from the driving range, where Richard has insisted he practice, to tell her, "I franchised my place . . . the diner. There's going to be seven of them and that's just on the eastern seaboard. Then I'm going national." He reveals that he needs to get shaved, now has an art dealer, had to buy a set of golf clubs, and has been given a reading list. Emily is livid when she finds out Richard took Luke to the club. Richard calls Emily a snob but then reveals that he is "thinking ahead" and trying to "legitimize" Luke and "bestow some credibility on him" in case "this insane relationship between him and Lorelai continues"; then the Gilmores "can legitimately take him to places like the club . . . at least on holidays." At the crux of it, Lorelai, as a Gilmore, is intended to marry someone from the Gilmores' class status and Luke does not fit the bill, based on intelligence, occupation, or upbringing. Richard attempts to make Luke a more acceptable option, while Emily chooses sabotage.

Except *Gilmore Girls* also negotiates the hypocrisy of this plan. Emily was not good enough for Richard, after all, when Lorelai the First begged him to leave Emily at the altar (Episode 4.16, "The Reigning Lorelai"). And Emily reveals that Shira Huntzberger was not "bred" for the lifestyle that she claims to protect and uphold when she reminds her, "You were a two-bit gold-digger fresh off the bus from Hicksville when you met Mitchum in whatever bar you happened to stumble into" (Episode 6.5,

"We've Got Magic to Do"). It is in these contradictions that a larger conversation about wealth comes into play. Emily wants to see Christopher and Lorelai together and is self-righteous in her determination that they belong together, even though she "never thought much of" him and finds him to be a "weak but charming" boy/man (Episode 5.12, "Come Home"). After that glowing assessment, she informs Christopher that he is a match for Lorelai because "you have good breeding, you come from an impeccable family, and you love Lorelai. You have always loved Lorelai." It is nice to know that love matters to Emily, but Luke loves Lorelai too. Granted, Emily does not know Luke kept the horoscope in his wallet for eight years, but something tells us she would not find that as rip-my-pants-off-sexy as Lorelai did. She tells Christopher that Luke is an unsuitable match because "he owns a diner, he's a divorcé, he's uneducated, and he's not a proper stepfather for Rory." The irony is that Luke is more of a father to Rory than Christopher ever was, and Rory is twenty years old at this point, beyond the significant period for paternal guidance. Additionally, well-bred Christopher has two illegitimate children with two different women (April hasn't appeared to rip a piece of hair from Luke at this point, so he still wins on that count). Ultimately, Emily argues that Lorelai is "capable of greatness" and Luke will hold her back. She is not aware that when Lorelai is in dire straits for money while working to open the Dragonfly, it is Luke who invests the $30,000 she needs to power through (Episode 4.14, "The Incredible Sinking Lorelais"; Episode 4.15, "Scene in a Mall"). And they were not even in a relationship at that point; both were with other people. Emily and Richard are quick to pull out their checkbook, but clearly Luke is able to save money too, and the filthy diner owner has at least $30,000 to loan Lorelai by the next day.

Perhaps the biggest irony regarding wealth in the entire series is that it takes high school dropout Jess to wake up Rory and get her back to Yale. After a horrible (and accurate) introduction to Logan, Jess storms out of the pub and demands to know what Rory is doing with a guy like that. Baffled, he asks,

> What the hell is going on? . . . I mean with you, what is going on with you? . . . I know you. I know you better than anyone. This isn't you. . . . What are you doing? Living at your grandparents place? Being in the DAR? No Yale. Why did you drop of out Yale?! . . . This isn't you! Going out with this jerk? . . . We made fun of guys like

> this. . . . What's going on with you? This isn't you, Rory. You know it isn't. What's going on?

Rory doesn't have an answer for him. Jess has written a novel and Rory is floundering. An angry Rory goes back into the pub and tells Logan "[Jess's] doing something." She realizes she is "doing nothing," that being waited on by a maid, "going to meetings and teas and cocktail parties," and hanging out with Emily is a waste of time. Rory ends the scene with Logan revealing that she thinks he is not appreciating his privileged position with "every door open to you," and we see a glimmer of what Jess says they used to say about douches who drive Porsches. Although this does not keep her from being with Logan, it does light a fire under her, and she begins the journey back to Yale, Lorelai, and remembering what she wants. Thank you, Jess.

WHEN YOU'RE OUT ON YOUR OWN

Throughout the series, the tensions created by money are key drivers of the major plot points, and that is frequently depicted in the tensions within relationships. Whether it is about getting face time or avoiding strings, the depiction of power and money in *Gilmore Girls* is a reflection of how money works in the world of access to privilege. Contrasting characters offer multiple sides to the story, from Logan and Marty, to Rory and Lorelai, to Emily and Luke, and even to Luke and Christopher.

What is particularly fascinating about the series is how it reveals the contradictions within many depictions of money, rank, and status. When Emily finds out she was not the preferred choice for Richard and that Lorelai the First actively campaigned to keep him from marrying her, instead of recognizing how her actions to keep Luke and Lorelai apart or Richard's opinion of Dean might be construed as similar, she throws social and familial obligation out the window (Episode 4.16, "The Reigning Lorelai"). High-class status is about repression of desire to fit into an expected behavior (we get this message full throttle in the ten-years-later reboot on Netflix), but Emily embraces these expectations because it is part of being a Gilmore. When she finds Gran's letter to Richard, she shirks her duties out of spite and Lorelai finds her smoking in the house, drinking, wearing a housecoat, and reading for her book club in the mid-

Emily flouting Gran's wishes. *The WB / Photofest © The WB, Photographer: Patrick Ecclesine.*

dle of the day instead of preparing for the wake later that evening. This is not the Emily that Lorelai grew up with, and what it suggests is how much of the Emily we know so far is a presentation for others. Similarly, when she decides to go to Europe, she tells Richard she will have "two glasses of wine with lunch," and Richard blusters, "Only prostitutes have two glasses of wine at lunch" (Episode 5.1, "Say Goodbye to Daisy Miller"). When Emily does not care what her husband thinks, she reveals those buried desires and flouts social expectations.

As a series, *Gilmore Girls* offers us a compelling version of tensions created by access to wealth, "unabashedly embracing elitist values and affinities"[9] while celebrating the simple pleasures of autonomy and independence. Themes of pulling yourself up by your bootstraps are mixed with messages about appreciating family networking and privilege when you have it. Us/them, autonomy/connection, weakness/power, misfortune/privilege—instead of resolving those tensions, *Gilmore Girls* magnifies the complex (and sometimes fun) push and pull between these themes as they intersect with money and social status. Although that tension may not be as gritty as real life would demand, it nonetheless provides important social commentary on the nature of childhood, adulthood, and the relationships forged along the way. At the very least, the show provides a good definition of a rich douche. Sorry, Logan.

8

SMALL-TOWN LIVIN'

"babette ate oatmeal!"

Stars Hollow is a tiny town, but how nice, and increasingly rare, it is to be part of a fictional world so vivid and intense.

—Ken Tucker[1]

Stars Hollow is an impossibly quaint, quirky place where neighbors help water each other's lawns, hold fall festivals, and even join together in loving mockery of one another. The town is like a macrocosm of what we all want a loving family to be.

—Maura Quint[2]

While writing this book, we stumbled upon the "Gilmore Girls Fan Fest" that proclaims on its website, "Stars Hollow means something to all of us. We can't quite articulate it & we can't exactly get there. It isn't just one place because it doesn't actually exist, but the idea definitely does."[3] In several discussions between us, Lara has frequently indicated to Rachel, "I want to live in Stars Hollow" (especially when she dreaded going to work every day at a corporate job). And while viewing the series, Rachel's husband, John, asked, "Why is this show so comforting?" It is apparent that part of the appeal of *Gilmore Girls* is the fictional small-town story line, where "civic pride wafts through every shabby-chic street."[4] Both off and on the screen, small towns say something about the world we live in, where "to erode small-town culture is to erode the culture of the nation."[5] This was an idea advanced in 1942 by Arthur

Morgan, who argued that "the social good of such places" was being "dissolved, diluted, and submerged by modern technology, commercialism, mass production, propaganda, and centralized government."[6] Since Morgan's writing, small towns have struggled in the United States, where the "rural population is declining, from more than half of the US population in 1910 to just 20% in 2010. The abandoned main streets show the wear and tear of an economy that has shifted away from rural people, and of public policy that has forgotten to pay attention."[7] In contrast, Sherman-Palladino's Stars Hollow main street is impeccably maintained, managing to sustain "twelve stores . . . devoted entirely to peddling porcelain unicorns" (Episode 2.5, "Nick & Nora/Sid & Nancy"). In 2004, Sherman-Palladino "joked that in Stars Hollow, Al Gore was president. An idealized liberal bubble . . . quaint yet progressive, cozy but not narrow-minded, accepting of strangers and its own native eccentrics."[8]

In this chapter, we suggest that Stars Hollow is appealing because it allows viewers to escape from and into something. We explore how the series' creators built an idyllic backdrop for *Gilmore Girls* and how watching the series allows viewers to escape both from the everyday realities of a changing American culture as well as into a small-town utopia; one that is colorful in character yet never perfect.

ESCAPING INTO STARS HOLLOW

Many small towns in Connecticut have capitalized on the popularity of *Gilmore Girls* by offering fans ways to experience the inspiration for Stars Hollow. The Connecticut Office of Tourism promotes a "Gilmore Girls Getaway" where fans can "visit the 'real' Stars Hollow, Connecticut." The website states, "Towns like Washington, New Milford, Bantam and Litchfield inspired the creators of the show, and they continue to draw fans looking to capture a little of the *Gilmore Girls* magic."[9] Stars Hollow, fictional or not, is a popular destination fantasy.

Part of the quaintness of Stars Hollow is that it is seemingly untouched by modern-day American capitalism. There are no chain restaurants or franchised businesses (despite Richard's pursuit to franchise the Dragonfly Inn and Luke's Diner). Instead, there is Gypsy's Garage as opposed to a Jiffy Lube; the Hungry Diner and Luke's Diner instead of Denny's; Antonioli's Restaurant (the business that tried to make the world's largest pizza for Lorelai's birthday in Episode 3.18, "Happy Birthday, Baby") instead of Pizza Hut; Stars Hollow Video instead of Red Box; Doose's Market as opposed to Kroger; two bookstores (Stars Hollow Books and Black & White & Read Bookstore) instead of Barnes & Nobles. Additionally, Stars Hollow had Le Chat Club, the Stars Hollow Beauty Shop, the Independence Inn, Miss Patty's School of Ballet, Al's Pancake World (which "has the best Chinese food in Stars Hollow"), Weston's Bakery, Kim's Antiques, Taylor's Olde Fashioned Soda Shoppe, and the Dragonfly Inn. These one-of-a-kind businesses are adored by fans who create lists about the "best" Stars Hollow businesses[10] and have even inspired writers to reflect on the "business lessons" offered by the show.[11] A Reddit thread posts the question, "If you could visit any business in Stars Hollow, which would it be?"[12] Part of the appeal of Stars Hollow is the absence of anything familiar to what one might find in any major metropolitan town in the United States. Stars Hollow seems to offer through its businesses a small-town quaintness that hearkens back to soda shops (which Taylor decides is missing and eventually opens) and mom and pop stores in early Americana.

A significant portion of Lorelai and Rory's interactions are set in Luke's Diner. *Thrillist Entertainment* writer Maura Quint explains, "Perhaps the biggest wish-fulfillment element in the show is the existence of Luke's Diner. . . . While he might grumble about their food choices, if the Gilmores want a cheeseburger in the middle of the night, Luke's magically opens for them."[13] Luke's is small and focuses on a more mainstream palette than Sookie's kitchen, and the owner knows you by name. In fact, there is a possibility (via at least one previous example) that the owner, Luke, might even flirt with you over the course of eight years, until you realize he's pined for you and you fall in love, and then the two of you can break up/make up/get engaged/break up/make up again. If that is not appealing, then the old-fashioned aspect of Luke's Diner offers one part of Stars Hollow's quaintness.

The Stars Hollow town square is often depicted in idyllic ways. The opening of the second season demonstrates this by showing every townie carrying at least one of Lorelai's one thousand yellow daisies given to her by Max in his wedding proposal (Episode 2.1, "Sadie, Sadie"). In this episode, everyone in town seems to be on the same page, with all of them waiting to know if Lorelai said yes to Max (and also, to spy on her telling Luke about the engagement). Sookie and pals also coordinate an amazing surprise wedding shower in the middle of town for Max and Lorelai (Episode 2.2, "Hammers and Veils"). The town square is host to many of Stars Hollow's special events including, but not limited to, Liz and T.J.'s wedding (Episode 4.21, "Last Week Fights, This Week Tights"), the Firelight Festival (Episodes 1.16, "Star-Crossed Lovers and Other Strangers"; 4.12, "A Family Matter"), and the Stars Hollow Winter Carnival (Episodes 3.10, "That'll Do, Pig"; 6.12, "Just like Gwen and Gavin"). During these festivals, people participate, interact, and sometimes enjoy Grant, the town troubadour (played by musician Grant-Lee Phillips), never letting the "snow nor cold weather [keep] him from making Stars Hollow a more musical or enlightened place to live."[14]

Although the town is idyllic to fans, it isn't always presented as such to all of the characters within the show. Luke frequently bashes the town "charm," although he ends up helping with the majority of events in the end. And when Jess first arrives to town, the song "This Is Hell" plays in the background while he observes what looks like Pleasantville (before Reese and Toby ruined it), implying Stars Hollow is not going to be his cup of tea (Episode 2.5, "Nick & Nora/Sid & Nancy"). He is dressed in jeans and a camo shirt in contrast to the sunny attire (the mother/daughter matching neon pink muumuu outfits are hysterical) of the Stars Hollow natives. Similarly, Paris holds a negative attitude about Stars Hollow throughout the series. In one episode, Paris says to Miss Patty: "Look, I understand the whole 'Mystic Pizza,' small-town, 'we don't let a clock run our lives' thing, but I come from the city where money talks, and I'm paying good money for this place, and I have a schedule to keep" (Episode 2.9, "Run Away, Little Boy"). In a slightly later episode, Paris is delighted to uncover the "seedy underbelly of Stars Hollow" in hopes that *The Franklin* can win the Oppenheimer award (Episode 2.12, "Richard in Stars Hollow"). The series' creators use these characters as a way to demonstrate that although Stars Hollow is idyllic, it is not revered by all.

Another part of the quaintness of the town is the idea that Stars Hollow has an interesting history, and the writers remind us of that past in various moments across all seasons of the series. Several episodes are devoted to establishing the colorful and sometimes humorous history of Stars Hollow. For example, Episode 1.16 ("Star-Crossed Lovers and Other Strangers") opens with Miss Patty telling a story about true love and "how Stars Hollow came to be." In her description of this story to her young dancers, Stars Hollow is described as a fairy-tale story. In "Women of Questionable Morals" (Episode 5.11), viewers learn about a "lady of the night" who distracted a Revolutionary War general to stop a battle from happening. Not only do we learn about this recently uncovered part of Stars Hollow history, but it is then re-created by the reenactors with costumes, the involvement of the local elementary school, and Kirk playing the part of the "Town Whore," thus providing another opportunity to highlight that the historical aspect of the town is enthusiastically embraced by those who live there. Relatedly, in "To Live and Let Diorama" (Episode 5.18), after Old Man Twickham dies and leaves his historic home to the town, Taylor and other Stars Hollow volunteers turn the house into the Stars Hollow Museum, which contains a diorama of the Jebediah family—the first family in Stars Hollow. The artifacts of the museum hold vague historical significance, and an even looser connection to Stars Hollow in some cases, but the deep desire to hang onto these potential scraps of historical significance is humorous and appropriate for such an eccentric town. In episode 6.6 ("Welcome to the Dollhouse"), Taylor has an idea (that uncharacteristically is supported without reservation by Lorelai and others) to boost the charm and thus the economy of Stars Hollow by going back to the original Stars Hollow street names. This does not actually work out well for Lorelai, Sookie, and Michel when the Dragonfly is given historic "Sores and Boils Alley," but the intention is overwhelmingly embraced by the townspeople, including Luke at first.

Part of Stars Hollow's history includes the traditions that are embraced by the town. Over seven seasons, many episodes center around a Stars Hollow tradition, including: the basket-bidding auction (Episode 2.13, "A-Tisket, A-Tasket"); a farmers market (Episode 2.17, "Dead Uncles and Vegetables"); the Revolutionary War reenactors (several episodes); the annual showing of *The Yearling* in the park (Episode 2.19, "Teach Me Tonight"); and the dance marathon (Episode 3.7, "They Shoot Gilmores, Don't They?"). Stars Hollow hosts the Edgar Allan Poe Society (Episode 3.17, "A Tale of Poes and Fire"); night yoga on the town square (Episode 3.21, "Here Comes the Son"); the Festival of Living Pictures (Episode 4.7, "The Festival of Living Art"); Stars Hollow Loves Pasquale Week and Miss Patty's fortieth anniversary party (Episode 5.10, "But Not as Cute as Pushkin"); a Revolutionary War reenactment with the first snow of the year (Episode 5.11, "Women of Questionable Morals"); and the short-lived Stars Hollow Museum (Episode 5.18, "To Live

Rory and Lorelai pouring coffee at the dance-a-thon. *The WB / Photofest © The WB, Photographer: Mitchell Haddad.*

and Let Diorama"). Some of these traditions are displayed within the narrative, and others are just talked about. Regardless, what these examples indicate is that *Gilmore Girls* emphasizes and idealizes the small-town quaintness that Stars Hollow embodies through its businesses, events, and traditions. Although the thought of getting out of our pajamas to run an errand is sometimes enough to make us cry, in theory, the events of Stars Hollow seem fun, quirky, and like something we would participate in . . . at least in our fantasies.

QUIRKY PERSONALITIES

Gilmore Girls' "Stars Hollow is a smallville of eccentrics"[15] where part of the series' appeal is the people who populate the town. The colorful characters create an added dynamic to the *Gilmore Girls*' narrative; a dynamic that provides small-town exemplars in community involvement and friendship.

One of the most unique (ahem . . . annoying but mostly sweet) characters on the show is Kirk. Finding Kirk and his job in each episode is like playing Where's Waldo, and this character quirk of his was an homage to Sherman-Palladino's actor father, who played a different character every week, donning many different hats.[16] Viewers look forward to seeing what Kirk is doing professionally (and for fun) next. Over seven seasons, Kirk (as Mick) is a DSL installer (Episode 1.2, "The Lorelais' First Day at Chilton"), a swan delivery guy (Episode 1.3, "Kill Me Now"), a mechanic (Episode 2.7, "Like Mother, Like Daughter"), a pest control worker (Episode 2.11, "Secrets and Loans"), a store clerk at Stars Hollow Video (Episode 2.12, "Richard in Stars Hollow"), a filmmaker (Episode 2.19, "Teach Me Tonight"), a mail carrier (Episode 3.16, "The Big One"), a one-of-a-kind mailbox maker (Episode 4.6, "An Affair to Remember"), a dog walker (Episode 4.15, "Scene in a Mall"), and a companion to really old women (Episode 6.1, "New and Improved Lorelai"). And this is only a small sampling of Kirk's sixty-two jobs.[17] Kirk delivered many of the best lines chosen for this book (see "An Opinionated Compendium" for our "Sophie's choice" decisions). Paige Gawley writes, "From his awkward nature to his love for Lulu to his tendency to name animals after himself, Kirk is certainly one of a kind,"[18] and his character is part of what makes Stars Hollow such a fun place to escape to. In real life, Kirk would not fare well with most people; customers tend to like mechanics who know what they are doing. But in a town of eccentrics, he is the King of Weird. Perhaps this is what makes his character so beloved; in a town like Stars Hollow, weird is embraced. Most importantly, Kirk's active involvement and willingness to throw himself into every opportunity in Stars Hollow represents an exemplar in what community involvement could and should look like.

Another character that models community-minded yet unusual behavior is Taylor Doose. Taylor also has multiple roles in the goings-on of Stars Hollow, but he tends to be the one in charge (frequently self-appointed). He is the love-to-hate (or, according to Babette, a "big anal creep" [Episode 5.14, "Say Something"]) owner of Doose's Market and the Olde Fashioned Soda Shoppe. He is member of the Town Beautification Committee, a Revolutionary War reenactor, and the town selectman (except in season 5 when he is ousted by citizens of Stars Hollow in favor of Jackson). Taylor calls town meetings at 3:12 a.m. (Episode 6.12, "Just like Gwen and Gavin"), raises concerns during a town meeting about

Lorelai and Luke's relationship (Episode 5.3, "Written in the Stars"), and passes out blue and pink ribbons to townspeople when Lorelai and Luke break up the first time (Episode 5.14, "Say Something"). And the thing is, although the town finds him annoying, they show up at 3:12 a.m. and they wear the ribbons. Taylor knows everything happening in Stars Hollow and is another major part of what makes Stars Hollow eccentric while modeling community involvement.

In general, and especially through characters like Taylor, the series does not shy away from presenting the pros and cons of living in a small town. One of the cons relates to dealing with the nosiness of your neighbors (the community service exemplars previously mentioned—Kirk and Taylor—are included in this con). Stars Hollow is populated with nosy people, but for some reason, it is still charming. For example, the entire town gives Lorelai a hard time for going out with Paul, the younger-than-she-realized man/boy she meets at business school (Episode 2.9, "Run Away, Little Boy"). We find out that Miss Patty keeps a picture of Lorelai in her purse to show potential suitors because Lorelai isn't good at dating (Episode 2.13, "A-Tisket, A-Tasket"). Miss Patty and Babette are frequently shown gossiping about the townspeople. In one episode, viewers witness Miss Patty saying to Babette, "So, you heard that Marilyn Horne is actually a man?" (Episode 5.3, "Written in the Stars"). Miss Patty and others know about Luke's "dark day"—the day he disappears on the anniversary of his father's death (Episode 5.10, "But Not as Cute as Pushkin"). In season 6, Miss Patty and Babette inform Lorelai that they already know about April, as they snoop through the window between Taylor's Olde Fashioned Soda Shoppe and Luke's Diner (Episode 6.13, "Friday Night's Alright for Fighting"). (To be fair, Lorelai is also snooping.) The town's nosiness is emphasized when Luke leaves Lorelai at her parents' wedding after a fight about Christopher (Episode 5.14, "Say Something"). Lorelai runs into both Babette and Kirk, who sense something is amiss between Lorelai and Luke. Even Caesar questions why they are not together. Lorelai stumbles into the video arcade where Kirk is dancing, and Kirk asks, "Nothing's up with you two, is there?" The townspeople, although funny and frequently lovable, tell the story of the cons of living in a small town. In short, small-town living means no privacy, for better or for worse.

Gilmore Girls also emphasizes the pros of small-town living, where the community is a family. Despite the sometimes annoying nosiness of the Stars Hollowers, the town comes together in times of crisis or need. When there is a fire at the Independence Inn, the town rallies to help Lorelai (Episode 3.17, "A Tale of Poes and Fire"). Sookie takes over Luke's Diner to feed the guests. Rory entertains the children of the guests. Miss Patty offers her dance school as a home base for the inn. The town also comes together to support each other when a fellow Stars Hollower, Stan, dies; it seems like the entire town goes to the funeral (Episode 4.11, "In the Clamor and the Clangor"). Miss Patty sings at the ceremony; Rory cries and says, "I'm going to miss him." Sookie reminisces about Stan coming to the inn to eat even though he "couldn't eat dairy or salt or meat." Or when Old Man Twickham apparently thinks he is dying and the townspeople line up to say farewell (Episode 5.18, "To Live and Let Diorama"). We find out this is a yearly queue. What seems like the majority of town even shows up to Babette and Morey's cat's funeral, squeezing into their diminutive house in a show of solidarity (Episode 1.5, "Cinnamon's Wake").

In addition to coming together in times of need, the town also helps Lorelai parent Rory. This relationship is addressed in direct and humorous ways. For instance, in the first season when Rory shows Christopher around Stars Hollow, they run into Miss Patty. She says to Christopher, "You know, Christopher, we're all like Rory's parents around here, and I'm one of her mothers. And since you're her father, well, that would make us . . . a couple" (Episode 1.15, "Christopher Returns"). Later, Rory and Christopher come up behind Jackson, who is describing Christopher's George Clooney-ness to a gathered crowd of townspeople. Christopher threatens to kidnap Rory and take her away from the town, but Rory just laughs it off.

Even when the entire town doesn't come together collectively, there are moments when the show highlights Stars Hollowers caring for each other in times of need. For example, when Lorelai breaks her house window and it is cold outside, Babette lets Lorelai and Rory sit in front of her stove, although they tell her it is to catch up (Episode 4.13, "Nag Hammadi Is Where They Found the Gnostic Gospels"). Stars Hollowers also create alliances with Lorelai and Rory even when they don't need to. In the same episode, Babette wants to make sure Rory is doing OK even though Jess has come back to town. She says, "He went into Weston's? That little bastard" (Episode 4.13, "Nag Hammadi Is Where they Found the Gnostic Gospels"). In a separate example, after Lorelai realizes that she is supposed to be throwing a bachelorette party for her mom, she throws a spontaneous one at her house and Gypsy, Miss Patty, Babette, and Sookie come, even though some of them have never met Emily (Episode 5.14, "Say Something"). After Rory leaves for Yale, Stars Hollowers care for Lorelai in their own ways. Kirk installs a security alarm system without her permission (Episode 4.4, "Chicken or Beef?"). In the next episode, Babette gives Lorelai a bag of bulbs to plant at the house to distract her from Rory's absence (Episode 4.5, "The Fundamental Things Apply"). Such examples illuminate the positive aspects of small-town living.

IT'S TAKES AN IMPERFECT VILLAGE

Rory and Lorelai are deeply rooted in the small town even as they pursue passions that could take them away from Stars Hollow. After Rory moves to Yale, she frequently goes back to Stars Hollow and keeps up on town news as a regular subscriber to the *Stars Hollow Gazette* (Episode 4.3, "The Hobbit, the Sofa and Digger Stiles"). In fact, in one episode, she says to Lorelai, "I'm going to do nothing but hang out in town. Read, veg, drink coffee, and have the perfect Stars Hollow day" (Episode 4.4, "Chicken or Beef?"). Viewers are asked to identify with the idyllic backdrop of the show in a similar way that Rory does despite its lack of Starbucks or Applebee's and its quirky, nosy, and sometimes annoying residents.

We are at a moment in American history where its citizens are divided across gender, race, class, and especially across political party lines. Although *Gilmore Girls* predates this division, we can look to Stars Hollow as a model for what might be missing from our current sociopolitical climate, or at least for the comfort that the fantasy provides. Stars Hollow is imperfect in character and in its residents. However, Stars Hollow thrives because of public involvement in the town's events, interaction between each other at those events, public debate on important aspects that are relevant to the town, and all the while respecting each other and what their (limited) diversity brings to the town. It is these imperfections that make Stars Hollow a perfect place to escape into. All we can say is, should the apocalypse be upon us, we adamantly hope Netflix continues to stream *Gilmore Girls* till the bitter end.

CONCLUSION

"Do I look shorter?"

> If I don't come back or they don't want me back, they can keep it going with other people, but . . . it would f--ing kill me to not close out the show. I've known what the finale should be since I pitched the pilot. . . . The show should at least go through [Rory's] college graduation. I just don't want to be sitting at home watching with a bottle of vodka and a bottle of Demerol crying when [the new writers] decide Rory is going to be a pole dancer at a strip club in Chicago, and I'm like, "NO! She was going to be Christiane Amanpour!"
>
> —Amy Sherman-Palladino[1]

As you have likely noticed from the notes for each chapter, *Gilmore Girls* has received much attention from scholars, writers, and fans since the show debuted in 2000. So, at this point, you might be asking why we felt it was necessary to contribute *more* to this already existing body of scholarship and thought on the beloved series. In many ways, and as documented throughout some of the existing literature, *Gilmore Girls* is culturally significant to explore because it reflects and reproduces the prevailing social norms of gender, race, class, and political thought, yet, as we hope to have shown throughout each chapter, it simultaneously offers countercultural attitudes on parenting, popular culture, friendship, socioeconomic status, and political ideology. The revivial on Netflix is at once a testiment to the popularity and panache of the series and also a significant sign of a changing television-watching culture and fandom, which we find interesting. The fact that *Gilmore Girls* continues to gather new viewers almost two decades after it first aired tells us it is as relevant, entertaining, and well written as it was when we first watched it. In all, we hope our analysis contributes nuanced (and fun) interpretations on the cultural significance of *Gilmore Girls* as well as elaborates on reasons for the show's cult following and its continued success with a new generation.

A REVIVAL: MAKING UP FOR LOST TIME?

When people found out we were writing a book about *Gilmore Girls*, the first question frequently posed to us was: "What did you think about the revival?" This was a difficult question for us to answer because the text that we have been studying for this book has been the first seven seasons of the series, not the revival. However, we did not like season 7, so the revival offered a new possibility, a do-over, and a glimpse at a parallel universe that could not completely ignore how the other universe had handled things. How many writers get a second chance like Amy Sherman-Palladino to tell her version of the end of a story? Because of this, we have intentionally attempted to keep our interpretations in perspective and save our thoughts on the revival for the end. We have had to cut ourselves off in many ways to the revival and discussions about it. However, we do have some opinions (oh boy, do we have opinions) about it and now we will attempt to more directly address those here.

When talks began about a *Gilmore Girls* revival, as poetically written by Emily Yahr of *The Washington Post*, "the Internet . . . lost its mind."[2] One fan/*Bustle.com* writer opines, "When I found out about the series revival, I cried. I cried as hard as I cried when Rory and her mother sat in Luke's diner one last time in 2007 before she left to be the next Christiane Amanpour."[3] After the announcement, fans speculated on possible story lines and many superfans proposed "Gilmore Girls revival theories."[4] Yahr reasons, "The reaction was understandable: The much-loved WB series never wrapped up in a way that was satisfying to fans, because creator Amy-Sherman Palladino and executive producer Dan Palladino left before the final season in 2007."[5] The news of a revival was met with much enthusiasm from *Gilmore Girls* superfans.

The Internet hype over the news of a revival was fulfilled when *Gilmore Girls: A Year in the Life* was released on Netflix. "Netflix's November 2016 revival of the beloved series was so popular," writes Nicole Villeneuve, "that it set a record for how many people watched all four feature-length new episodes within 24 hours of their release. (Netflix now calls this 'binge racing.')"[6] Since *Gilmore Girls* "went off the air in 2007," the series has "reached cult status with a combination of the WB-turned-CW show's original fans yearning for more and new fans who discovered it later and binged their way through the seven seasons."[7] The rediscovery made by new fans was only possible due to the rise of Netflix and its unique direct-to-consumer business model. Since the conclusion of the original series, there has been "a major competitive shift in the TV industry"[8] because of "the rise of the global internet firms and changing viewing habits, especially among young viewers."[9] The success of the revival, then, had much to do with contemporary advances in technology and TV consumption.

Because of the unique Netflix platform, the new revival could deviate from its original TV format. And deviate it did. Instead of the made-for-network-TV, forty-ish-minute dramedy, the revival includes four ninety-minute movie-like episodes themed around winter, spring, summer, and fall—an order that, as pointed out by Lauren Graham in her 2016 autobiography, follows the same order as another song from the same singer who gave us the *Gilmore Girls'* theme song, Carole King. Graham reflects on the day of filming the revival when King jumped on a piano and began to play "You've Got a Friend" for the cast:

> And just then Carole goes to the part of the song I sort of forgot was coming, even though I've heard it a million times: "Winter, spring, summer, or fall, all you've got to do is call . . ." . . . Later, as everyone is filing out, Amy and Dan find me and tell me that what's funny is that Carole doesn't even know the episodes are named after her song, or that they're in that very order because of it.[10]

Additionally, without needing to be quite as censored on Netflix, we get new classic lines, like when Babette complains that Lorelai "clam-jammed" her from talking to a cutie.

Although the new format and the rise of Netflix opened the door for new fans to enjoy the show, the revival of the series was created for fans. Emily Yahr writes, "Netflix's *Gilmore Girls: A Year in the Life* revival (theoretically) had one major purpose: to provide closure to fans who wanted to see how creator Amy Sherman-Palladino envisioned the end of the series, given that she exited the original show before the final season in 2006."[11] It has been frequently documented that "Sherman-Palladino used to tell interviewers that she knew exactly how the very last episode of *Gilmore Girls* was going to end, down to the final four words. Those four words have now acquired a kind of legendary status."[12] Through the creation of the *Year in the Life* revival, fans were finally able to "find out the last four words Amy Sherman-Palladino had always planned for the 'Gilmore Girls' series finale and never got to use."[13]

Fans seemed to appreciate the nostalgic allusions made to the first seven seasons, including Lorelai "smelling snow," Kirk's odd jobs, and the familiar look of Stars Hollow. However, some critics complained about aspects of the narrative. For example, some found the idea of Lorelai hiking alone to find herself a bit of a stretch. Patricia Garcia of *Vogue* writes, "The only place Lorelai would go off for some cathartic awakening would be the mall, or perhaps a Bangles reunion tour."[14] Jennifer Maas, contributor to *The Wrap*, offers a critique about the moral compass of Rory's character arguing, "At the end of Season 4, Rory slept with her married ex-boyfriend Dean and fans, understandably, freaked out. She seemed to have learned from the misstep during the original series, but in the revival she is having a full-blown affair with Logan. WTF?"[15] And it's not just Logan she's cheating with; she has a one-night stand with a Wookiee while researching an article, all while still with unforgettable Paul (is this a case of amnesia, Rory, as the *Real Housewives* might say).

However, perhaps the biggest complaint about the revival has to do with those legendary last four words. The lack of closure left some fans feeling dissatisfied. Samantha Highfill of *Entertainment Weekly* sums up this sentiment:

> Heading into Netflix's *Gilmore Girls* revival, Rory fans were divided into Team Dean, Team Jess, and Team Logan. Everyone wanted to know which of Rory's exes, if any, would be the one to ultimately steal her heart. Well, now that all four episodes of *Gilmore Girls: A Year in the Life* have been released, we still don't really know the answer, though we have a good idea.[16]

At the same time, many fans are asking for more epsisodes, dying to find out who Rory ends up with and how a baby changes the relationship between Rory and Lorelai. Does she stay in Stars Hollow? Does she tell Logan he's the father? (He's clearly the father.) Does Lorelai have a late-in-life miracle baby and they both end up pregnant together? This, without a doubt, is what was successful about the revival; we were left with enough to wonder about the future.

After analyzing all seven seasons of the original series and watching them through for what is a combined thirteen times, we can tell you that the parts people were critical about were actually not the ones we had issues with. Lorelai did not end up hiking and pretty much did everything possible to self-sabotage to keep herself from having to hike. She chose the hike based on a pop-culture reference, specifically the book version of *Wild*, which, in a series devoted to literature, is not that off the mark to us. The fact that she bought all the stuff to go hiking—and look cute hiking—is definitely within character as well, considering she did the same for the fishing date with Alex Lesman (Episode 3.12, "Lorelai out of Water"). And then she finds herself while seeking out coffee. It is completely appropriate to us and we found it funny.

As for Rory, we know fans were upset about her sleeping with Dean at the end of season 4. Even Alexis Bledel remarked on *The Tonight Show Starring Jimmy Fallon* that it was a bit of an extreme way to show that Rory is not so perfect, but that all made sense to us too. Rory says it to Lorelai; she felt Dean was her first. And why would Logan be any different? Rory has daddy issues. As well-intentioned as Christopher was, he was absent, and at the end of her first year at Yale, she felt alone and slept with Dean, a man who loved her even after he was married to someone else. And lest we forget how Dean and Rory break up the second time? She strings him along while she sorts out her feelings for Jess, somebody she kissed behind the inn while Dean waited in the audience for Sookie's wedding to start, and then it is Dean who ultimately breaks up with her; not Rory with him. It does not make us particularly happy about her choices, but it is fitting for who Rory has always been. It also makes sense that she would be too embarassed or defensive to tell Lorelai about it, even though that disconnect also made us sad.

In an interview with *The Hollywood Reporter*, Sherman-Palladino was asked about her choice to leave the father of Rory's baby unresolved. Sherman-Palladino explains:

> It really wasn't about the father; it was about the event. . . . Their love lives were a part of their lives but these were women really grappling with who they were as people and when they talked about their paths forward, especially Rory, it was usually about getting in *The New York Times* or breaking into journalism so it felt like the moment was on Rory and her future and not on, "Gee, which boy is this?" That's always taken a backseat when we've broken stories on Gilmore.[17]

We love this response because it is exactly a summation of our overall thoughts about the cultural significance of the original series. It is a show about imperfectly perfect women. Demanding that Rory and Lorelai have become perfect role models of the modern woman misses the point. The point is that by 2016, we shouldn't be striving for perfection or answers to be resolved. It is still the in-between that is the story, not a perfect conclusion with a shiny red bow.

Gilmore Girls as a series was about the progression of their relationship. Fans were similarly disappointed in season 4 when Lorelai and Rory disconnected a bit, but Sherman-Palladino said that was necessary because it was a time of change for both Rory and Lorelai. She needed time to "build it up again" including "an interim year for Lorelai if I wanted to get her to Luke."[18] The fourth season also represents more autonomy for both Rory and Lorelai from each other. This is when Lorelai builds toward opening the Dragonfly, a dream that will be fulfilled at the start of her life as an empty nester. The big fight of season 6 was also tortuous but necessary to fulfill Sherman-Palladino's goals.

Since the revival, and because of the long-anticipated reveal of the legendary last four words, fans have asked and pondered if new episodes are possible. Part of the reason is that the last four words offered a cliffhanger of sorts and left open the possibility of the continuation of the *Gilmore Girls*' story line. Eleanor Bley Griffiths of *Radio Times* reports, "Creator Amy Sherman-Palladino has negotiated the 'freedom' to make a sequel when the timing is right."[19] Some of the cast members have even weighed in on the possibility of reprising their role in future episodes. Keiko Agena, "who played Lane Kim on the hit show, says there's enough material for another *Gilmore Girls* revival" and that she "would love to work on another installment of *Gilmore Girls*."[20] Lauren Graham, however, feels "satisfied" with the way the revival ended and "revealed . . . that there may never be anymore installments."[21] Hopefully we can all agree that if they do come out with more episodes, somebody

Lorelai and Rory holding hands in doorway at Yale—the first goodbye. ***The WB / Photofest © The WB, Photographer: Mitchell Haddad.***

will help them trim down the portion with a musical (jeez Louise—oh, and get Louise and Madeline to come back for an appearance—Francie was not enough).

Amy Sherman-Palladino, we know there's a lot of discussion about more episodes. *Brit + Co* writer Nicole Villeneuve discusses the popularity of the revival and that "Sherman-Palladino said that a continuation was 'definitely possible,'"[22] and we also know that your Amazon contract for *The Marvelous Mrs. Maisel* includes time to devote to more episodes of *Gilmore Girls*, so you are thinking about it. As fans, we hope it will happen, and we want to let you know: This thing we're doing? You and us. We're in. We're all in. Copper boom!

THE EPISODES

An Opinionated Compendium

Episode 1.1: "Pilot" (October 5, 2000)

Writers should study this opening scene where we find out Lorelai is a young mom, with a sixteen-year-old daughter, and a magnet for men. She's quirky, with a bag full of lip gloss in flavors that resemble "breakfast cereal," and rattles off one-liners about Kerouac and is obsessed with coffee, and there might be some sexual chemistry with Luke, the diner owner. Three minutes in and this pretty much sums up the plot of the entire series. This is the episode where Rory gets accepted to the prestigious private school Chilton, Friday night dinners become a staple in the Gilmore girls' lives, and Rory meets Dean. It beautifully sets up relationships between mothers and daughters that become the central theme of the series and hints at complex layers of familial tension and romantic love.

Best Line: "OK, look, I know you and me are having a thing here, and I know you hate me, but I need you to be civil, at least through dinner, and then on the way home you can pull a Menendez. Deal?"

Episode 1.2: "The Lorelais' First Day at Chilton" (October 12, 2000)

Rory and Lorelai have a bad first day at Chilton. First, Lorelai's fuzzy alarm doesn't purr on time, and rushing madly around the house while a furious-about-being-late-for-the-first-day-of-school Rory pronounces the time by the minute, she soon realizes all of her Chilton-acceptable attire is at the cleaners. Lorelai tromps down the stairs in Daisy Duke cut-offs, a tie-dye, baby-doll shirt, and cowboy boots, begging the question, why didn't she just stay in her jammies? To make matters worse, once they finally make it to Chilton, they find Emily Gilmore sitting in Headmaster Charleston's office. After being forced to reveal her wildly inappropriate outfit ("laundry day"), Lorelai is further embarrassed as her mother steamrolls the conversation. Rory doesn't fare much better when she meets a jealous, competitive, and inhospitable Paris Geller, as well as Tristan Dugray, who insists on calling her (Virgin) "Mary." The episode ends with an important moment when Rory forbids Lorelai to consider dating Luke.

Best Line: "It would be all work and no play. Have you not seen *The Shining*, Mom?"

Episode 1.3: "Kill Me Now" (October 19, 2000)

Rory starts to get to know and like her grandparents, and Lorelai struggles with the emotions these budding relationships bring to the surface. Emily is thrilled that Richard gets to show off Rory at the club, telling him, "It means a great deal to my happiness, and yours, that this day go well. Are we clear?" And it does go well, much to Richard and Lorelai's surprise. On the golf outing with Richard, Rory gossips with him about the "most odious woman alive" and they make a connection over books and travel. Lorelai has a hard time sorting out her feelings and ends up yelling at Rory about who has the bigger bra-cup size. This episode in the first season sets up important themes about where Rory fits in with Richard and Emily versus Lorelai's world and what it means to dream of a better life for your children.

Best Line: "You can use your mother's old golf clubs. They're upstairs gathering dust along with the rest of her potential."

Episode 1.4: "The Deer Hunters" (October 26, 2000)

Rory gets a D, Sookie gets an A but obsesses over the +, and Lorelai meets Max Medina. Rory desperately tries to catch up after starting late in the semester, cramming for an upcoming important test worth a large portion of her semester grade. Lorelai and Rory oversleep the morning of the test and a panicked, half-dressed Rory races to Chilton only to get hit by a deer on the way. A furious Lorelai rails against Headmaster Charleston and Max Medina but later, alone with Rory, attempts to make sure the dream of Harvard is what Rory wants. Rory assures her mother that Harvard is her dream. Sookie tracks down a critic and persuades him to retry her famous risotto. A smitten Max leaves a message for the Gilmore girls.

Best Line: "I wouldn't want you to get in trouble with Il Duce here. I thought this place was going to be so great and now I guess this goes on the boy-was-I-wrong list. Right above gauchos but just below the Flashdance stage."

Episode 1.5: "Cinnamon's Wake" (November 2, 2000)

To date or not to date? Both Rory and Lorelai struggle with an attraction to their respective suitors. After some delightful repartee, Max convinces a hesitant Lorelai to go on a date with him (technically two, but they don't seem to count the coffee date). Lorelai is worried about hurting Rory by dating her teacher and does not tell her that Max is in the picture socially. Dean pursues Rory . . . onto her bus. Then Babette's cat Cinnamon dies and Lorelai forgets her date with Max. Rory sees Max at their front door and sulks off to stew about Lorelai not telling her, where she is forced to voice her feelings for Dean when he tells her he gets the message and will back off. In the end, Rory gives Lorelai permission to date Max.

Best Line: "I'm just so mixed up though. This is a real crossroads situation. It's like to perm or not to perm. I'm really confused."

Episode 1.6: "Rory's Birthday Parties" (November 9, 2000)

Unwilling to cancel Friday night dinner, Emily insists on throwing Rory a birthday party and crosses all kinds of boundaries by inviting her classmates without her permission. Emily calls Lorelai to help her find a gift for Rory, and because Emily served pudding at dinner, Lorelai wants to encourage the behavior that shows her Emily is thinking of what Rory wants, not what she wants. Lorelai does not know about the invites, and Rory, who likes seeing Lorelai and Emily get along, doesn't tell her. Embarrassment builds when Paris wants Rory to know she is only there out of obligation, Tristan makes nice with Richard, and Rory yells at Emily in the middle of the party. Rory feels terrible and invites Emily and Richard to the Stars Hollow party the next night. They show up, and we find out this is the first time they have ever visited Lorelai's house. Emily finds out Lorelai broke her leg, and Lorelai sees Dean give Rory a birthday gift. Emily and Lorelai both have moments where they wonder how well they know their daughters.

Best Line: "No, Mom, I'm shopping for Rory. You're shopping for your imaginary granddaughter, Barbara Hutton."

Episode 1.7: "Kiss and Tell" (November 16, 2000)

Cornstarch officially becomes romantic—and evidence of a felony—when Dean kisses Rory at Doose's Market. Rory says, "Thank you," and runs away to tell Lane, but not Lorelai. Mrs. Kim tells Lorelai, who ruminates over why Rory didn't tell her, spying on Dean at Doose's. Luke wrestles her out of the store and tells her Rory is growing up. Lorelai tries to control herself, but eventually (and quite casually) asks Rory, "So, kissed any good boys lately?" Through an awkward encounter at the market, Lorelai invites Dean over for a (chaperoned) first date to watch *Willy Wonka and the Chocolate Factory*. Rory is horrified and panicked, eventually revealing that she didn't handle the kiss well. Lorelai and Dean have a chat ("She's not going on your motorcycle"). Dean knows the score and wants to get along with Lorelai.

Best Line: "That Lothario over there has wormed his way into my daughter's heart—and mouth—and for that he must die!"

Episode 1.8: "Love & War & Snow" (December 14, 2000)

Due to a winter storm, Rory's on her own for Friday night dinner with Richard and Emily. She charms her grandparents into heating a frozen pizza for dinner and then promptly makes things frosty all around by reminding them that Lorelai ruined her life to have Rory. Lorelai finally gets a first date with Max when his car breaks down in Stars Hollow. (Anybody else think Max may have planned this, taking a hint from the teenage girls he teaches on how to conveniently break down right outside the cute boy's house?) Lorelai doesn't seem to mind, but Luke does. When Lane feels ignored and abandoned by Rory in favor of Dean, she cops a feel of Rich Blumenfeld's hair and then runs away to listen to the Cure. In the end, we see a (lucky for the casting agent) slightly blurry picture of Christopher, Lane and Rory make up, and Rory comes to terms with her teacher sleeping on her couch.

Best Line: "Rory, are you in any way malnourished or in need of some international relief organization to recruit a celebrity to raise money on your account?"

Episode 1.9: "Rory's Dance" (December 20, 2000)

One step forward, two steps back, cha-cha-cha. Rory asks Dean to the Chilton formal, and Lorelai pulls a muscle making her dress. An intrusive Emily insists on taking care of Lorelai, who's laid up on the couch, while Rory goes to the dance. At the dance, Rory starts to make "friends," Paris has to bring her cousin as her date, and we start to suspect that Tristan may have learned that pulling a girl's braid means you like them. He tries to fight Dean, and Dean defends his woman's honor and himself. Rory and Dean define the relationship and then fall asleep (for real, nothing happens) at Miss Patty's. After a night of sweet moments between Lorelai and Emily, both awaken to find Rory gone. An epic fight and nasty words ensue, and an eavesdropping Rory is grateful for her mother's defense, until Lorelai turns the tables and yells at Rory.

Best Line: "It is not a drive-thru. She is not fried chicken."

Episode 1.10: "Forgiveness and Stuff" (December 21, 2000)

At the beginning of the episode, Rory and Lorelai have not made up, and neither have Lorelai and Emily. Emily un-invites Lorelai to Christmas dinner and then lies to her guests about why she isn't there. A bored and hungry Lorelai finds a six-foot-two-beautiful boy tapping at Rory's window, and she kind of forgives him after telling him all the ways she fantasized about killing him. 'Tis the season! Richard falls ill at dinner, and a caring Luke drives a distraught Lorelai to the hospital. Lorelai has a hard time confronting her daddy issues in this episode, but Richard pulls through. We find out Emily and Richard are deeply in love when she demands to die first and he grants her request (try not to cry at this scene, you heartless bastard). Luke and Lorelai share a special moment in the dark.

Best Line: "He went to work, he came home, he read the paper, he went to bed, I snuck out the window. Simple."

Episode 1.11: "Paris Is Burning" (January 11, 2001)

Things are going well with Max (Norman), until Rory indicates that she likes him, jarring Lorelai because she sees that Rory is getting attached. Sookie astutely argues it is Lorelai who is nervous about getting too attached, prompting Lorelai to act like a "witch with a b" when she tells Sookie to get a date (aka a life). Lorelai decides to break up with Max but instead ends up passionately kissing Max in his classroom on Parents' Day. Paris, who is tired of all the rumors at school being about her parents' divorce, sees the kiss and plays telephone until the whole school knows. Rory is furious with Lorelai, and they fight in the Chilton stairwell. It is Max who later tells Lorelai that maybe they need to take a break. The episode concludes with the first time we see the recurring image of Rory comforting her crying mom—a nice bookend to an episode that focused on the mother/daughter role switcheroo in the beginning. Sookie asks out Jackson.

Best Line: "It's the best tiny weird bird I've ever eaten."

Episode 1.12: "Double Date" (January 18, 2001)

Lane and Rory (especially Lane) have excellent taste in obscure and artsy music—XTC, Blondie, Kraftwerk, and Yoko Ono. Lane claims to be in love with Dean's (only?) friend, *Beethoven* (the movie)–loving Todd. Rory reluctantly sets up Lane with Todd, and they go on a double date. Jackson's cousin Rune is disappointed in his date, Lorelai Gilmore, who is second choice next to the Bearded Lady. The "mom-packet" gets the missing info at the last minute, and both Lane and Rory get in trouble for lying. Overall, Lorelai is a comedian, Mrs. Kim is strict, Lane is boy crazy, and Rory should have listened to Dean.

Best Line: "They're at the movies. There are no drugs there. They don't even have the real Red Vines!"

Episode 1.13: "Concert Interruptus" (February 15, 2001)

The Bangles episode, or what we like to call the Bandana episode. Viewers get the cool mom vibe from Lorelai as she wears bandanas (twice in the episode), pilfers (er, purchases) a rhinestone sweatshirt that makes Luke go nuts, and invites Paris, Madeline, and Louise to the Bangles concert. This episode also previews Lorelai's love interest in Luke when she becomes curious—and slightly jealous (as Sookie's raised eyebrows tell us)—when she finds out that Luke had a previous love, Rachel, who looked like supermodel Elle Macpherson and broke Luke's heart. Madeline and Louise go off with two strange guys in New York City (girls, have you not seen even one after-school special?). Lorelai pounds down doors until she finds them and then verbally spanks the overaged guys and underaged girls. Paris and Rory share a moment or two.

Best Line: "No, no—you and I have bonded already. In fact, if we bond any further, we will be permanently fused together."

Episode 1.14: "That Damn Donna Reed" (February 22, 2001)

The Troubadour's first appearance! Rory and Dean have their first argument, and it's about feminism (of course) thanks to a Gilmore viewing of *The Donna Reed Show*. Rory exudes "academic" as she argues with Dean about women's roles and expectations in the home but then does some research and plans a secret (she doesn't tell Lorelai) throwback dinner, complete with big skirt and pearls, while babysitting Babette's kitten. Lorelai babysits Rory's midterm project, a baby chick named Stella. When Stella gets loose, Lorelai calls Luke, a move that, Sookie later tells Lorelai, was suggestive. The episode ends with Christopher, Rory's biological father, riding into town on a motorcycle and telling Lorelai to take her shirt off. Ah, Christopher.

Best Line: "When standards slip, families flee and in comes the seedy crowd."

Episode 1.15: "Christopher Returns" (March 1, 2001)

Although presented as extremely likeable and heart-throbby (Stars Hollow residents compare Christopher to Brad Pitt, George Clooney, and a more obscure hottie—Billy Crudup), Christopher's immaturity is at the forefront of the episode during his first visit to Stars Hollow . . . ever. A dinner at the Gilmore house that includes Christopher's parents ends up a disaster as Christopher's father, Straub, is still bitter that Lorelai is "responsible" for Chris's failure. Richard Gilmore has some snobby shortcomings, but this episode shows his true character as a father who will not put up with others attacking his daughter or the Gilmore name. Back to the (im)maturity theme, Christopher and Lorelai rekindle their sixteen-year-old passion and make whoopie on her parents' balcony. It's a heck of a morning the next day when Lorelai realizes she forgot to show up at Luke's to help him paint his diner (at her insistence) and then gets a marriage proposal from Christopher—all before coffee. The episode concludes with Lorelai surprising Luke with a fully painted diner.

Best Line: "In this parade of stupid and dumb, I am the one twirling the flaming baton."

Episode 1.16: "Star-Crossed Lovers and Other Strangers" (March 8, 2001)

A dreamy one about love and the magic that is Stars Hollow, including an appearance from the Troubadour and a Miss Patty story about "true love."

The "dreamy" tone includes lots of oddball happenings, like Emily uncharacteristically allowing Rory to miss Friday dinner so that she can celebrate her three-month anniversary with Dean and later Dean giving Rory a car that he built (!), albeit one that does not yet run, as an anniversary present. This episode develops Dean's character as a hands-on, blue-collar, rough-around-the-edges young man. Lorelai and her father agree that her blind date (invited by Emily) is boring, and Richard allows her to escape through her bedroom window. Although the episode begins with dreamy allusions about love and small towns, it ends rather bleak. When Dean tells Rory he loves her, she responds with "I love the car." They break up.

Best Line: "If there was a runoff between what Emily Gilmore would care about less, a two-for-one toilet paper sale at Costco or your three-month anniversary, your anniversary would win. Hands down."

Episode 1.17: "The Breakup, Part 2" (March 15, 2001)

Rory is unusually guarded with Lorelai in this episode. Lorelai is dying for Rory to wallow, watch movies, and eat ice cream in the aftermath of her breakup with Dean, but Rory prefers to make a to-do list a mile long. Lorelai goes out of her way to accommodate not talking about it, shooing away Luke, Babette, and Kirk as well. In another ongoing plot point, Luke shows his fatherly instincts with Rory when he literally puts Dean in a headlock in front of the diner. Lane meets Henry, a Korean boy her mom would love (his only drawback). After Tristan kisses Rory at a Chilton party, Rory runs out crying and decides it is time to wallow, starting with a gallon tub of Ben and Jerry's ice cream.

Best Line: "Unbelievable, she's here five minutes, she has a date. I've been going to this school nine years and I'm the French soda monitor."

Episode 1.18: "The Third Lorelai" (March 22, 2001)

Gran (Trix) comes to visit for the first time in more than twenty years and Emily gets rattled. Lorelai revels in her mother's discomfort. Lorelai's young taste in clothes is apparent when, after Rory sets up Paris and Tristan (aka the first GG iteration of Logan, albeit a younger, dumber version), Paris borrows some of Lorelai's clothes for her date. Upon finding out Lorelai borrowed money for Chilton from Richard and Emily, Gran offers to give Rory her trust fund of $250,000 early. Emily fears she will lose Lorelai, so she makes Lorelai fear she will lose Rory. After a public argument between Lorelai and Emily during tea, Gran rescinds the offer. The lesson for viewers in this episode: It's OK to have a pet name for your mom.

Best Line: "My mother says the color pink makes my head look small."

Episode 1.19: "Emily in Wonderland" (April 26, 2001)

More is revealed in this episode about Lorelai and Emily's less-than-ideal mother/daughter relationship when Emily learns where Lorelai ran to sixteen years ago: the potting shed at the inn. Lorelai is really trying to avoid coal in her stocking this year when she agrees to give Rune a job at the inn, albeit reluctantly. The similarities between Rory and Lorelai continue to be part of this show's narrative. In particular, the Gilmores' coolness factor is apparent as Rory, a sixteen-year-old, proudly rattles off the names of the original Charlie's Angels; the actresses, not their character names. Rachel seems a little intense with Lorelai and reveals to her that she is interested in settling down with Luke.

Best Line: "I don't want Boo Radley touching my rosebud wallpaper."

Episode 1.20: "P.S. I Lo . . ." (May 3, 2001)

Lorelai's commitment issues are at the forefront of this episode. Red flags are revealed when Max is weirded out that Lorelai is not telling anyone about their rekindled romance. Lorelai and Rory's mother/daughter relationship is developed as a functional one, even though they get in a bad fight that pushes Rory to Emily and Richard's house. After confronting Dean and finding out Rory didn't say "I love you" back, Lorelai makes up with her daughter and tells her that she (Lorelai) has great taste in music and movies but not in commitment. Another red flag occurs when Rachel walks in on Lorelai helping Luke get dressed. (Although it doesn't sound like it, it was completely platonic, Rach. She was helping you get a cooler birthday gift than a potholder.)

Best Line: "Oh no, she'll hate you forever. It's just nothing personal."

Episode 1.21: "Love, Daisies and Troubadours" (May 10, 2001)

This episode opens in what might be a dream with Luke fixing something on the Gilmores' porch. The dream question is not resolved until later, when it turns out Luke is avoiding Rachel by doing work on Lorelai's house. It's the end of Luke and Rachel, which turns the notch up slightly on the simmering attraction between Luke and Lorelai. And then Max proposes with one thousand yellow daisies. Rory finds the Dean box and finally gets up enough courage to tell him how she feels, crushing Tristan's hopes in the process.

Best Line: "Today, I am suffering from ennui."

Episode 2.1: "Sadie, Sadie" (October 9, 2001)

The second season opens with sunny imagery of Stars Hollow, where every townie carries at least one of Lorelai's one thousand yellow daisies. Lorelai is still unsure about marrying Max although everyone else in town (even Luke!) seems certain that she is going to say yes. Lorelai decides to say yes but does not tell her parents. The Gilmore family snobbery is later apparent when Richard snubs and is disrespectful to Dean after Rory invites him to her celebration for making the "top 3 percent at Chilton." Sookie plans a surprise engagement party for Lorelai and invites the Gilmores, inadvertently informing Emily of Lorelai's big news. Just when you think Emily is only all about Rory, this thirty-second moment shows viewers that Emily loves her daughter and is truly crushed that Lorelai did not share the news of her engagement.

Best Line: "I'm being mysterious. . . . That's what women do."

Episode 2.2: "Hammers and Veils" (October 9, 2001)

"Hammers and veils" is a metaphor for the complex mother/daughter narrative that continues to be told through Emily and Lorelai. The cliffhanger from the previous episode gets resolved when Lorelai finds out why Emily is cold to her after revealing her engagement to Max—that's the "hammer." Lorelai's hurt manifests itself into tears and anger, which she unloads on Emily in a drive-by yelling, and then she realizes that she is the one at fault. Rory freaks out about her lack of volunteerism and chooses school over Dean . . . on her summer break. The episode concludes with a sweet moment when Lorelai goes to see her mom about a veil. Emily accepts Lorelai's apology in her own unique way—"Your head is much too big for a veil"—and suggests that Lorelai consider wearing a tiara, like she did for her wedding.

Best Line: "I have hit a level of perfection that has rarely been seen outside of a Victoria's Secret catalog."

Episode 2.3: "Red Light on the Wedding Night" (October 16, 2001)

Anybody else think this story line moved waaayyy too fast? Wedding plans, a double date, and drag. This episode does a lot of work to contrast the different and sometimes opposing lifestyles of Max and the Gilmore girls. Max orders slowly and he wants to have a "role" and guidelines for dealing with Rory and Dean, and the conversation about the rules highlights Max's seriousness and Lorelai's silliness. In one of the best scenes in the second season, Lorelai, Rory, Sookie, Michel, and Emily go to a drag club for Lorelai's bachelorette party where Emily makes the group sentimental after she tells everyone how excited she was about her wedding to Richard. This prompts Sookie to call Jackson, Rory to page Dean, and Lorelai to call . . . Christopher . . . red light. The episode closes with Lorelai planning an impromptu road trip. She tearfully reveals to Rory that she isn't going to marry Max.

Best Line: "If eating cake is wrong, I don't want to be right."

Episode 2.4: "The Road Trip to Harvard" (October 23, 2001)

There is one major difference between the Gilmore girls: Lorelai is spontaneous and doesn't want to plan, whereas Rory tries to sneak in a map. While accidentally staying at the Cheshire Cat (a bed and breakfast), the ladies decide to forgo food because they want to avoid chatting with the other guests. While holed up in their room, they get into a big argument about Max. Lorelai doesn't love him. Sookie doesn't get mad when Lorelai calls her to say the wedding is off, even as the finishing touches are being put on "Clyde," their five-tiered wedding cake. Luke finds out the news and has a great day. And Rory and Lorelai visit Harvard.

Best Line: "We are not going to have this fight in a flowery bedroom with dentists singing "Gypsies, Tramps, and Thieves" in the background. . . . It's too David Lynch."

Episode 2.5: "Nick & Nora/Sid & Nancy" (October 30, 2001)

The key players in this episode are: Jess, the bad-boy new love interest who drinks beer and smokes but understands and appreciates Rory's reference to *Oliver Twist* and is the nephew of Luke, the non-great communicator, a reluctant father figure who pushes Jess in a lake out of frustration but later buys Nicorette gum and patches to help his nephew kick the habit. Rory, the sixteen-year-old with a heart of gold who can see past Jess's bad-boy image and pulls through an awkward interview with Max Medina. And Lorelai, the experienced mother who attempts to get to know Jess with some straight talk and then Luke with advice on parenting. She should have visited Weston's before dinner to pick up two pies.

Best Line: "Jackson grows fruit and then scares people with it."

Episode 2.6: "Presenting Lorelai Gilmore" (November 6, 2001)

Rory's open for business when she agrees to come out to society to make her grandma happy. There are several LOL moments as Lorelai explains how to be a lady to Rory, always with a twist. Christopher is a changed man who shows up for the ball and does his fatherly duty. Lorelai likes what she sees, but it turns out he has a girlfriend named Sherry. You were getting a little flirty with Lorelai for having a girlfriend at home, Chris. Dean is a trooper. And Richard and Emily are fighting in public.

Best Line: "You saved me. I love you. I want to have your baby. Too late."

Episode 2.7: "Like Mother, Like Daughter" (November 13, 2001)

The episode opens with lots of popular-culture love from Barry Manilow to Dido and Olivia Newton-John to the Shins. Most central to this episode is the full circle that Lorelai and Rory complete when they let "society" guilt them into becoming something they are not; respectively, a fashion model and a "Puff" sorority girl. These new roles, however undesired by the Gilmore girls, advance the narrative along in two ways. First, at the fashion show, a Chilton mom shows interest in Luke and Lorelai gets jealous, which reveals much insight about Lorelai's feelings for Luke. Second, Rory's unlikely new friendship with the Puffs makes Paris jealous but also reveals the beginnings of a budding friendship between the ladies. Girls just wanna have fun . . . breaking into Headmaster Charleston's office. Rory tells him off, and he finally agrees she is right. By the end of the episode, she gets to eat alone at lunch again.

Best Line: "I like the new look. It was very high-class substitute teacher."

Episode 2.8: "The Ins and Outs of Inns" (November 20, 2001)

In this episode, viewers witness an uncharacteristically mean Lorelai. She's mean to Emily (per the usual) but also to Sookie. She's moving to a new part of her life: leaving the Independence Inn, where Rory "took her first steps," and trying to open a new inn with Sookie, but that makes her start to panic and lash out. Jess stages a murder, and while Rory finds it funny (he checks), she tells him Luke is going out of his way to stick up for him and he needs to show his appreciation. Jess meets Dean; he's not impressed. Jess fixes Luke's toaster, though won't admit to his good deed. Emily meets Mia and tells her she should have sent Lorelai home; then she asks for pictures.

Best Line: "Sweet little Fran the cupcake lady, not some cigar-chomping city slicker."

Episode 2.9: "Run Away, Little Boy" (November 27, 2001)

Fernando, pre-transition Paul, and Paris as Romeo. After hearing that Lorelai named the late wedding gift—a Musso Lussino 480 ice cream maker—"Fernando," Sookie expresses her concern that Lorelai is not moving forward after Max. So Lorelai decides to accept a date with Paul, a student in her business class. After Paul visits Luke's Diner with his parents, and his youthfulness is apparent, the entire town, including Rory and Luke, begin making fun of Lorelai. This is a pivotal moment, however, as Luke ends up getting jealous, and the episode makes a little more explicit the romantic chemistry between Luke and Lorelai. The Chilton deviant Tristan is thrown in Rory's group for the re-creation of *Romeo and Juliet*, and Rory panics because she never told Dean about the kiss. Tristan toys with her—and Dean—for the week but then has to bail on the performance on his way to military school. Paris and Rory "kiss."

Best Line: "This is incredible. I go on one stupid date, and suddenly I'm the female Jerry Lee Lewis."

Episode 2.10: "The Bracebridge Dinner" (December 11, 2001)

The Bracebridge group gets snowed out of the inn, and the elaborate dinner and performance Sookie and Lorelai had planned gets turned into a town affair. This episode previews a jealous side to Lorelai when she is confronted with having to share Rory with a much-more-involved Christopher and Rory's new "stepmommy," Sherry. Jess continues the slow insertion of himself as a wedge between Dean and Rory, asking if Dean knows Björk and wondering what they talk about. This episode focuses on developments in romantic relationships. Although Emily and Richard fight about his sudden retirement, their functional relationship is apparent; Jess and Rory are flirtatious with each other, and Dean starts to notice; and Lorelai invites Luke on a sleigh ride with her.

Best Line: "Things have been so hectic, you know, with the Bracebridge dinner and, um, building a snowwoman, and planning the ugly baby gag, that took time."

Episode 2.11: "Secrets and Loans" (January 22, 2002)

Termites and picture pajamas . . . strange but a related pairing in this episode. A termite infestation prompts Lorelai and Rory to crash at Sookie's in the middle of the night, catching Jackson in his wrestling picture pajamas. Termites also help the show advance the relationship between Lorelai and Luke, as well as Lorelai and Emily. When Lorelai cannot afford the $15,000 termite damage bill, she turns to Luke for a second opinion. Although Luke offers a "temporary exchange of money," Lorelai calls it a loan and refuses his offer. But what a sweet gesture and moment between the pair. After Rory spills the beans about the termite problem to Emily, Lorelai is furious and does not want her mother's help because she thinks her mother will expect something in return. This leads to a blowup between mother and daughter, and Lorelai leaves feeling guilty for this thought until the concluding moments of the episode when Emily accepts Lorelai's apology and quickly says, "By the way, I've moved my DAR meetings to the Independence Inn." The strings have attached.

Best Line: "You're not torturing me, you know. I don't care. My scores were great. I'm very, very happy with my scores. And I hate looking at a sunset, so my standard for happiness is high."

Episode 2.12: "Richard in Stars Hollow" (January 29, 2002)

This episode reveals death is not a taboo topic for the Gilmore family. The episode opens with Emily asking if Lorelai thinks she will ever get married as there is not enough space in the family mausoleum if she does. Emily wants Richard out of her hair, so she sends him to Stars Hollow, where Rory accidentally becomes the town hero for censoring the local video store. Paris is delighted by this turn of events, as she wants to uncover the "seedy underbelly of Stars Hollow" so that Chilton can win the Oppenheimer award. This episode defines Lorelai's relationship with her dad when we get insight into Richard's perspective after he seems to be hurt that he has only been invited to Lorelai's house once and also realizes that retirement is not all it is cracked up to be. Rory owes Jess an eggroll.

Best Line: "It is not going to be fine. It's gonna be horrible. It is going to be a bad, depressing Lifetime movie, and Nancy McKeon will be playing me. I'm Jo."

Episode 2.13: "A-Tisket, A-Tasket" (February 5, 2002)

Two Pop-Tarts and a Slim Jim . . . the contents of Lorelai's basket for the Stars Hollow Basket Auction. This annual tradition leads to an argument, and later a proposal, between Sookie and Jackson, the first "unofficial" date between Rory and Jess, and another opportunity for Luke to swoop in and save Lorelai from several potential "suitors" arranged by Miss Patty. This episode clearly aligns Jess with Rory over Dean, as their basket date leads to discussions about Hemingway and Ayn Rand. Lorelai and Emily have a rare moment of agreement, which causes Lorelai to loosen up on Rory hanging out with Jess. Lane and Henry "break up." Jess keeps a souvenir from the picnic.

Best Line: "He seems cool because he's got this dangerous vibe and this problem with authority and he's seen a lot of Sylvester Stallone movies."

Episode 2.14: "It Should've Been Lorelai" (February 12, 2002)

Doctor-assisted suicide and leftover Halloween candy . . . two things that drive the narrative in this episode. Christopher is invited to Rory's debate on doctor-assisted suicide and brings his girlfriend, Sherry. Lorelai and Rory invite the duo to their house and offer them apple juice "with a very respectable expiration date" and leftover Halloween candy. After Sherry insists on spending some quality time with Rory on Friday night, Emily is furious that Lorelai allowed Rory to spend the evening with "that woman." Viewers witness a first-time conflict between Christopher and Lorelai after she reveals to him that she thinks she's been sabotaging her relationships with men because she always thought she'd end up with him. He does not like this revelation, yells at her in front of everyone at Luke's Diner, and storms out.

Best Line: "She's a chic, good-haired, wrinkle-free, no-hose-wearing witch."

Episode 2.15: "Lost and Found" (February 26, 2002)

Viewers learn that Lorelai wants Mel Brooks's face tattooed on her booty and that she called Luke "Duke" for two years, just to make him mad . . . and it worked. This episode, though, focuses on the unraveling of Dean and Rory. At a book fund-raiser, Rory is in her happy place, but Dean is miserable. Dean also notices that Rory's bracelet is gone. When Jess overhears Rory panic about finding the bracelet, he plants it under her bed for her to find. Jess and Lorelai try to bond over gutters and Chinese food, but the episode ends with a heated argument after she catches him in Rory's bedroom. Lorelai accuses Jess of stealing the bracelet. Luke makes more living space.

Best Line: "That's your room. Finish up. We'll hold hands and skip afterwards."

Episode 2.16: "There's the Rub" (April 9, 2002)

Vicious Trollop . . . the name of the lipstick color that bonds Emily and Lorelai and the nickname we give Rory as she continues to avoid her feelings for Jess and treats Dean poorly. Emily wins a spa weekend for two and tricks Lorelai into joining her. Emily tries very hard to bond, but Lorelai is annoyed with her mom . . . who is being annoying. The two share the start of a lovely dinner, but then Emily accuses Lorelai of getting her 60/40'd and all is ruined. Emily finally reveals her motivation for the weekend by asking Lorelai, "Why can't we have what you and Rory have?" Lorelai tries to "fix" the situation by persuading Emily to steal the spa's bathrobes. Paris helps Rory out of a jam with Dean.

Best Line: "Rory, you have to do something bad when Mommy's out of town. It's the law. You've seen *Risky Business*, right?"

Episode 2.17: "Dead Uncles and Vegetables" (April 16, 2002)

Lorelai is adorable to both viewers and patrons at Luke's Diner when she and Rory fill in for Luke, who is making preparations for his Uncle Louie's funeral. Lorelai relishes in the "diner lingo." Luke worries he is going to turn into his uncle. Other episode touchpoints include an appearance by the Revolutionary War reenactors, a talking role for the Stars Hollow Troubadour as he briefly discusses writing a song about Taylor, and Sookie requesting "midgets" and "mushrooms" from Prague for her wedding, based on Emily's urging. This episode also portrays a daughter-like Rory, angry at Jess for not helping Luke while he is planning the funeral.

Best Line: "I made love to my wife that night like I never have."

Episode 2.18: "Back in the Saddle Again" (April 23, 2002)

Richard helps Rory and her Chilton friends develop and market "tricked-out first aid kits," and Lorelai helps Sookie (er, Susie?) deal with a misprint on her wedding invitations. Michel is very excited to have his mom, Giselle, in town until Lorelai informs her that he does not eat carbs, and everything is ruined. Lorelai continues to see that Rory is interested in Jess and tries to work as a mediator between Dean and Rory. She tells Dean to give Rory some space, and she tells Rory to understand that Dean is feeling insecure about their relationship. The episode closes with Dean sulking on the Gilmore porch saying to Lorelai, "She likes Jess, doesn't she?" Richard misses work.

Best Line: "Working moms are so '90s."

Episode 2.19: "Teach Me Tonight" (April 30, 2002)

Lorelai is annoyed that Taylor plans to show *The Yearling* again for the annual Stars Hollow film festival, and fed up, he relinquishes his movie-choosing crown to her. She is very excited until she realizes that she must pick from an approved binder full of movies and ultimately concludes that *The Yearling* is the best option. We also discover Kirk is an amateur filmmaker, among his other professions, and the episode ends with a David Lynch–esque short film starring himself. Luke asks Rory to tutor Jess so that he doesn't flunk out of eleventh grade, and she accepts, much to Lorelai's disapproval. Jess doesn't take the tutoring seriously (why does he know magic tricks?) and convinces Rory to leave the session for ice cream. We later find out that Jess crashes her car swerving to miss an animal, sending Rory to the hospital with a fractured wrist. Luke and

Lorelai have a blowout fight, and he puts Jess on a bus back home. Lorelai calls Christopher.

Best Line: "I can edit out two of the 'hell's. But I have to keep all of the 'damn's. It's a street-cred thing."

Episode 2.20: "Help Wanted" (May 7, 2002)

Lorelai tries to minimize her fight with Luke to Rory, and Rory is certain that Luke went "fishing" because of her car accident with Jess. Lorelai and Rory have to find a new food establishment for coffee and breakfast, and they choose the Hungry Diner. In this episode, Lorelai also offers to fill in as the new "Margie" for Richard's new business venture. Richard is hesitant to hire an office assistant because he's enjoying his time with Lorelai, and she is so competent. This is also the episode where Sophie's Music opens in Stars Hollow and Lane discovers her passion to play drums. The episode concludes with a mother/daughter argument between Lorelai and Rory because Rory gets fed up that everyone is blaming Jess for the accident when she feels equally responsible.

Best Line: "You're like the tiny fellow on that *M*A*S*H* program, always anticipating."

Episode 2.21: "Lorelai's Graduation Day" (May 14, 2002)

The episode where Lorelai graduates from business school and Rory plays hooky to see Jess in New York. Lorelai emphatically does not want her parents to attend her graduation ceremony, but Rory invites them anyway. Lorelai is annoyed at first by her parents' presence and the hired cameraman in her face as she walks across the stage; however, Lorelai is emotional when she sees Emily tear up as Lorelai is given her degree. Rory gets on a bus to New York and finds Jess on a park bench reading. They grab a hot dog and take the subway to a cool record store where Rory finds the perfect graduation gift for her mom—a signed Go-Go's album. However, Rory's bus does not get her home in time for her mom's graduation and she misses it. Rory tries punishing herself for her out-of-character behavior. Lorelai tells her, "My best friend should have been there." Rory likes Jess.

Best Line: "Child, what be your name?"

Episode 2.22: "I Can't Get Started" (May 21, 2002)

In this season ender, Sookie invites Emily and Richard to her wedding at the last minute, aka a "pity invite." Luke continues to be upset with Lorelai. Paris convinces Rory to run with her for student council because people like Rory. Rory gets "Castie"—Lorelai's pet name for Rory's cast—off, and Christopher surprises them by showing up at the doctor's office. Lorelai invites him to Sookie and Jackson's rehearsal dinner. They have a great time and quickly rekindle their romance. At the wedding, Christopher receives a phone call from Sherry informing him she is pregnant. Christopher immediately leaves the wedding. Meanwhile, Jess finds Rory at the wedding where she impulsively kisses him, tells him not to tell anyone, and then runs away yelling, "Welcome back." Paris and Rory go to Washington.

Best Line: "Oy, with the poodles already."

Episode 3.1: "Those Lazy-Hazy-Crazy Days" (September 24, 2002)

The season opener begins with a cutesy dream of Luke fixing Lorelai breakfast in her kitchen and then kissing her and her belly . . . pregnant with his twins. Upon waking up, Lorelai calls Rory in Washington to ask her to analyze her dream. Paris scores a date with Jamie, although she doesn't realize it is a date until Rory tells her. Sookie decides to redesign her house to be more "manly" for Jackson, which he does not like or want. Lorelai and Rory get into a fight when Rory reveals she kissed Jess. Lorelai tells her to pick: Jess or Dean. She goes with Dean when she sees Jess sucking face with a blonde. Lorelai has to tell her parents that she and Christopher are not dating, causing a fight, after which Lorelai goes into Luke's and says she is "Mimi, a new customer," and then proceeds to vent to Luke about whether she'll find someone. This is not Lorelai's best side, as she only goes to Luke's because Sookie is busy, and she complains about love even though multiple people have told her he carries a torch for her. A little self-absorbed. However, it works and they make up. As she leaves, Luke tells her, "Come again, Mimi."

Best Line: "I decided if you wanted to date Jess . . . I would help you . . . get vaccinated."

Episode 3.2: "Haunted Leg" (October 1, 2002)

Kirk asks Lorelai on a date (two weeks in advance so that the cold virus she has can get out of her system). Rory starts her last first day of high school. Emily and Lorelai are still fighting. Emily invites Lorelai to lunch at Luke's, but Lorelai ends up leaving her there after finding out that she called Christopher. Francie, leader of the Puffs, threatens Rory in the bathroom to make sure that Paris addresses the hemline length as her first issue as student body president. Paris doesn't want the "hemline" issue to be her first issue as president and says, "It would be my gays in the military." The episode ends with Christopher's interruption at Friday night dinner. Christopher yells at Lorelai, and Rory yells at Christopher. In the end, Emily firmly asks Christopher to leave.

Best Line: "Was the tuna inquiry too personal?"

Episode 3.3: "Application Anxiety" (October 8, 2002)

Rory receives her Harvard application in the mail while watching the *Brady Bunch Variety Hour* and considers this a negative sign. Emily, Lorelai, Rory, and Paris freak out about getting into Harvard. Lorelai and Rory are put at ease after they arrange a dinner with a Harvard alum, Darren Springsteen. An awkward family dinner ensues as Darren quizzes his Harvard-bound children, Jack and Jennifer, on Shakespeare, Polish composers, and the Mesozoic era. He forces a reluctant Rory and Lorelai to participate as well. The meeting goes well when Darren leaves a message on their voicemail telling Rory to "pack her bags" for Harvard. Dean questions how their relationship will work when Rory goes off to college. Lane meets Dave Rygalski.

Best Line: "And now it's the in thing for young Hollywood celebrities to go to universities. What do they call themselves, the Brat Pack?"

Episode 3.4: "One's Got Class and the Other One Dyes" (October 15, 2002)

Spoiler alert! Zack, Lane's future husband and baby daddy, is introduced in this episode, though Lane only has eyes for Dave Rygalski. This episode has some timing issues; it is a lot to accomplish in one day. Rory dyes Lane's hair purple to help her rebel but later dyes her hair back to black when Lane panics and realizes her impulsiveness will have bad repercussions with Mrs. Kim. Debbie (not Deb) invites Lorelai and Luke to talk to high school students about their business experiences. Lorelai prepares for the occasion thoughtfully only to be bombarded with questions about being a pregnant sixteen-year-old, and she chooses to answer honestly. Debbie and her similar-haired friends are furious. Rory is rude to Jess's girl, Shane.

Best Line: "If you meet Jesus crossing the street, what three questions would you like to ask?"

Episode 3.5: "Eight O'Clock at the Oasis" (October 22, 2002)

The Jon Hamm episode. At the Society Matron's League Antique Auction, Lorelai has a brief encounter with the man carrying paddle #17 (played by Jon Hamm). Lorelai asks Emily to put her in contact with paddle #17, which she later finds out is Peyton Sanders. When the date turns out to be "kind of a dud," according to Lorelai, Emily and Richard grapple with the social implications of Lorelai refusing to go on their second date (a David Bowie concert!). Meanwhile, Lorelai waters Dwight's lawn, the new neighbor who purchased "Beenie Morrison's old place." When Lorelai makes Rory water Dwight's lawn, the sprinkler breaks; in a panic, Rory sends Dean a page, but he doesn't respond due to his "Unabomber tendencies." She runs into Jess (literally), who helps her fix the sprinkler, and they share a moment.

Best Line: "If my wife wants the first cup of tea, she is going to have the first cup of tea. That's it!"

Episode 3.6: "Take the Deviled Eggs . . ." (November 5, 2002)

All of Stars Hollow seems interested in Jess and his new car. Luke is amused when he finds out that Jess is a Walmart employee. Rory (by choice) and Lorelai (not by choice) go to Sherry's cheesy baby shower where they find out that "green is the new pink" and that Christopher is an attentive and concerned father-to-be to Sherry. Lorelai rearranges Sherry's medicine cabinet. Sherry insists that Rory and Lorelai take home the deviled eggs, which they later rearrange on Jess's car. The episode concludes with Jess discovering that his car has been "devil-egged," and he says to Luke, "Someone prepared deviled eggs to throw at my car?!"

Best Line: "Man, that car's a honey."

Episode 3.7: "They Shoot Gilmores, Don't They?" (November 12, 2002)

Lorelai wants a great dance partner for the Stars Hollow dance marathon. After Stanley Appleman cancels on her because his wife thinks Lorelai looks like "Elizabeth Taylor," she convinces Rory to be her partner. Sookie finds out Jackson wants four kids in four years and blames Lorelai for thinking it is crazy. Jess and Shane join other spectators, which distracts and infuriates Rory. Dean recognizes this, and he publicly breaks up with her on the dance floor. Lorelai and Luke share a moment while he fixes her shoe. Jess finds Rory on their bridge, and she admits she has feelings for him. The episode ends with Kirk taking a victory lap around the gym to the *Rocky* theme song after winning (again) the Stars Hollow dance marathon, as a confused Lorelai holds a sobbing Rory.

Best Line: "You would kick Tiny Tim's crutch out from under him, wouldn't you?"

Episode 3.8: "Let the Games Begin" (November 19, 2002)

Kirk is still gloating from his dance marathon win. Jess and Rory say "hi" to each other . . . a lot. Viewers learn that Richard used to take Yale girls to see art and mastered the "frown, step back, wrinkle, and sigh" move. Richard invites Rory and Lorelai to Yale and arranges a secret meeting with the dean of admissions. Rory takes the meeting but is upset, as is Lorelai . . . and Emily. Jess and Rory work on their PDA. Rory apologizes to Dean, but he is not forgiving to her.

Best Line: "You're not gonna do anything to her because when you're at her place, there's Lorelai, and when you're here, there's me, and when you're out there, there's Taylor."

Episode 3.9: "A Deep-Fried Korean Thanksgiving" (November 26, 2002)

Christian guitar players, Cat Kirk, and PDA. This episode, centered around Thanksgiving, extends the plot line of the romantic relationship building between Lane and Dave, whom Mrs. Kim hires as the "Christian guitar player" for their Thanksgiving dinner. Meanwhile, Kirk buys a scratch-happy cat and names him (Cat) Kirk. Rory is still uncomfortable with PDA with Jess and thinks the "whole town is watching." Lorelai and Rory attend FOUR Thanksgiving Dinners: the Kims', Sookie and Jackson's, Luke's, and the Gilmores'. Rory reveals to the Thanksgiving table at Emily and Richard's that she applied to Yale, unbeknownst to Lorelai. Rory kisses Jess (sort of) passionately in public. Jess is pleased but runs squarely into Dean.

Best Line: "My arms are too short to box with Mrs. Kim."

Episode 3.10: "That'll Do, Pig" (January 14, 2003)

Lorelai offers her garage as practice space to Lane and her band, with a caveat: Lane is never allowed to pose naked on the cover of *Rolling Stone*. Paris continues to be distracted and less high-strung because Jamie "loves" her. Dean runs into Rory (literally), and they decide to be friends. Jess is jealous that Rory and Dean are "buddy-buddy." Trix manages a surprise visit on Richard's sixtieth birthday and informs them, to Emily's dismay, that her previous tenants (the band Korn!) are moving out of her house in the States and she is moving in. Lorelai gives Emily advice on how to deal with Trix. Rory runs into Dean and Clara on the way to the Stars Hollow Winter Carnival, and Dean likes that Jess feels threatened by him.

Best Line: "Actually, I scare them with my Minnie Pearl impressions."

Episode 3.11: "I Solemnly Swear" (January 21, 2003)

Richard and Emily get sued for wrongful termination of a maid, and Emily wants Lorelai to make a deposition on her behalf. Lorelai gets "coaching" from Rory on how to "not lie" about her mother in her deposition. Emily reads part of the deposition to Rory and Lorelai before dinner, highlighting where Lorelai compares her mom to Ben-Hur. Lorelai and Sookie attend a class on starting an inn and run into Joe, an old friend of Sookie's, and Alex, who plans to open a coffee shop. Sookie does not realize Joe is romantically interested in her and guiltily tells Lorelai, "I'm a whore!" Jackson comes home to his favorite food and favorite music playing in the background and screams, "You cheated on me!" to Sookie. Paris tries to fence Rory to death after Francie convinces her of friendship foul play.

Best Line: "If you see Fat Sal, give him a kiss for me."

Episode 3.12: "Lorelai out of Water" (January 28, 2003)

Gilmore niceness is emphasized in this episode that begins with Rory and Lorelai cleaning out their hoarder-like garage so that Lane's band can have practice space. Zack hits on Lorelai, and Dave and Lane pretend to dislike each other in front of the band. Alex and Lorelai have a good first date sampling coffee, and he invites her to go fishing for their second one. Luke's niceness is also emphasized as he volunteers to teach Lorelai how to fish for her date. Lorelai has fun with Alex and brings home a beautiful (live) fish she names Jayne Mansfield. Paris and Rory are still arguing and get called into the headmaster's office. Luke asks Nicole Leahy, Taylor's lawyer, on a date. She accepts.

Best Line: "Peeled to death. That's a bad way to go."

Episode 3.13: "Dear Emily and Richard" (February 4, 2003)

Graduation must be near because we start hearing about Rory and Lorelai's European backpacking trip. Emily and Richard think they are joking. Dean (wearing a turtleneck) is working for a construction crew for Taylor's new business. The backstory of Lorelai's pregnancy and Rory's birth is paralleled with Sherry's labor. We learn that sixteen-year-old Lorelai is resentful toward Emily and Richard for deciding her future without consulting her or Christopher. She goes into labor and takes herself to the hospital, listening to "99 Luftballons" on her Walkman. Unlike the birth of Rory, Christopher is present for Sherry's labor. We also learn how Lorelai runs away from home after Rory's birth, leaving her parents a letter. Present-day Lorelai sets up a DVD player for her mom.

Best Line: "Dear Mom and Dad. I'm in labor. See you later."

Episode 3.14: "Swan Song" (February 11, 2003)

Emily finds out that Rory is no longer with Dean and is currently dating Jess. Emily invites him to Friday night dinner. Jess continues to be insecure about Dean and Rory's friendship. Lorelai becomes worried about Rory and Jess consummating their relationship while she's out of town for the weekend. Jess shows up to Friday night dinner with a black eye, and Rory is upset because she assumes he was in a fistfight with Dean. Jess abruptly leaves dinner. We later learn that Jess was beaked by a swan and he was embarrassed to admit it to Rory. Emily is great with Rory about Jess but goes off on Lorelai. Mrs. Kim warns Dave that Lane has a crush on him. Zack and Brian learn that Dave is a Christian but assure him "Christians can still rock." Jess and Rory make up, but he continues to lie about the cause of the black eye. Rory promises Lorelai she will tell her before she has sex for the first time.

Best Line: "You and Dean have mutual friends in common that Rory and I don't? Who would that be? The Talbots or that senior partner at Deloitte & Touche?"

Episode 3.15: "Face-Off" (February 18, 2003)

Trix makes another appearance in this episode, and we see Emily reach out to Lorelai for support. Rory makes the dangerous mistake of comparing a previous boyfriend to her current boyfriend. When Jess doesn't call again, Rory goes to the Stars Hollow High hockey game and finds out Dean has a girlfriend, Lindsay. Dave and Lane continue to scheme to figure out how to get Mrs. Kim to let them date. Yiung Chui is part of the plan. Yiung Chui takes Lane to the hockey game and Dave looks on, jealous. Emily walks in on Trix kissing a man in a purple tracksuit. After Emily reveals this in front of Trix's friends, they make amends over tea. In the end, Richard jokes with Lorelai, "I guess I've got a new daddy!" Rory leaves a furious message on Jess's answering machine at the hockey game, but as she walks out of the game, he is waiting for her with tickets to a concert. She tells him not to listen to the message when he gets home.

Best Line: "Just remember, there's cute jealous and there's Othello."

Episode 3.16: "The Big One" (February 25, 2003)

Lorelai encourages Rory to practice her "speeching" skills, and Paris and Rory find more to argue about in their speech competition for the Chilton bicentennial. Lorelai runs into Max, who is back for the Chilton bicentennial, and after an impulsive kiss, he declares, "And, apparently, I'm not over it." After Headmaster Charleston insists that Paris and Rory combine their speeches into one for the bicentennial, Paris shows up for an impromptu practice and reveals that she slept with Jamie and wants to have a "healthy debate" about it with Rory. Lorelai overhears and finds out that Rory is still a virgin. Lorelai secretly gloats, "I have the good kid." Paris angrily reveals to the C-SPAN televised audience that she didn't get into Harvard. Rory gets three of the big envelopes at the end of the episode. We also find out that Sookie is pregnant and Jackson is going to be a protective husband and daddy . . . oh, boy.

Best Line: "I can't believe Nicole made you take off the Monte Cristo. She's got you menu-whipped."

Episode 3.17: "A Tale of Poes and Fire" (April 15, 2003)

Harvard, Princeton, and Yale—three college acceptance letters that Rory received. Lorelai and Rory start a pro/con list for each school, which Luke sees as a waste of time. Paralleling Rory's good news, Luke shares with Lorelai that Jess was chosen as Walmart's Employee of the Month. Being a supportive "father figure" for Jess, Luke goes to the "ceremony" and finds out that Jess has been working forty-plus hours, which means he is not always attending school. Meanwhile, Stars Hollow is hosting the Edgar Allan Poe Society, and during a reading of "The Raven" at Miss Patty's, Nicole and Lindsay, separately, give a stink eye to Lorelai and Rory, respectively. A fire at the Independence Inn sends the guests to various homes in Stars Hollow, including Lorelai's. Being displaced herself, Lorelai seeks out a bed at Luke's, then proceeds to tell him about the dream she had where she was pregnant with his babies. Luke shares that Lorelai is a "sore spot" with Nicole. The episode closes with Lorelai realizing the pro list for Yale greatly outweighs the others and Rory finds Yale paraphernalia covering her bedroom walls.

Best Line: "Poes are very testy people."

Episode 3.18: "Happy Birthday, Baby" (April 22, 2003)

Richard cooks his favorite childhood meal, Johnny Machete, for Friday night dinner. Rory announces that she is going to Yale. Emily and Richard pretend to be unenthused, until Lorelai tells them she is on board. Jess looks at a map. We meet Tobin, the night manager, and find out that Michel hates him. It is Lorelai's birthday week and she gets lots of wonderful gifts: the "world's" largest pizza from Rory; five hours of free handyman work from Luke; a Joe Strummer leather jacket from Tobin; and a $75,000 investment birthday gift from Richard. Lorelai uses part of the money to repay her Chilton loan to her parents. Emily is very upset; so is Rory.

Best Line: "Well, it may seem extreme, but these candy people are shifty characters."

Episode 3.19: "Keg! Max!" (April 29, 2003)

Lorelai has to lay off employees at the inn. Michel welcomes two new Chow puppies to the family: Paw Paw and Chin Chin. Lorelai runs into Max at the Booster Club meeting, and she is bothered that he doesn't make a big deal out of it. Later, she confronts him in his office, where he demands at least ten feet between them and ultimately tells her he doesn't want to see her again. Jess can't take Rory to the Stars Hollow prom because he gets kicked out of school. Lane's band has a gig and needs a band name: the Harry Potters . . . We Are the We . . . Follow Them to the Edge of the Desert (FTTEOTD). Lots of romantic problems happen at the party: Dave gives Lane the cold shoulder because of Yiung Chui; Lane drinks beer, calls her mom, and vomits outside of the house; Rory gets upset that Jess wants to consummate their relationship in an upstairs bedroom; Dean punches Jess, and they tear up the house.

Best Line: "Don't call plants by their specific names. It's very not rock 'n' roll."

Episode 3.20: "Say Goodnight, Gracie" (May 6, 2003)

Lorelai is proud that Rory went to her first cop-raided party and even prouder when she finds out Rory "started the raid." Fran, owner of Weston's and the Dragonfly Inn, passes away. Sookie worries that they killed her through the power of their minds. At Fran's funeral, Lorelai and Sookie score a meeting with Fran's lawyer about buying the Dragonfly Inn. Jess's biological dad, Jimmy (aka loser coffee guy, according to Jess), comes to Stars Hollow. Jimmy and Jess bond (kind of) over David Bowie's "Suffragette City," then Jimmy runs out of the diner. Dave goes to see Mrs. Kim, reveals his crush on Lane, and asks for her permission to take her to prom. Mrs. Kim eventually agrees but says that they "cannot get married." When Luke proposes that Jess quit his job to focus on school next year, Jess refuses; Luke then tells Jess he has to leave. On her way to school, Rory notices Jess sitting at the back of the bus. He does not tell her that he has been kicked out of school or Luke's apartment. He just tells her that he can't take her to prom and that he'll call her.

Best Line: "Are you sure she's gonna want that back? It's been left alone all night at a keg party. There's no getting it over that. That backpack is permanently scarred. That backpack is Zelda Fitzgerald."

Episode 3.21: "Here Comes the Son" (May 13, 2003)

Filmed as the pilot episode for an almost spin-off, Luke tells Lorelai that Jess is gone. Rory doesn't know. Jess goes to California to see his dad and meets his partner, Sasha, and her daughter. Jess wants to crash at Jimmy's house for a while but Jimmy doesn't want that; however, Jimmy reluctantly agrees. Miss Celine styles Emily for Rory's upcoming graduation. Miss Celine calls Rory "Audrey Hepburn in *Sabrina*" and says to Lorelai, "Oh my God, it's Natalie Wood." At the end of the episode, Lorelai finds out (anticlimactically) that Rory has been named valedictorian.

Best Line: "You need to stop looking at my boobs."

Episode 3.22: "Those Are Strings, Pinocchio" (May 20, 2003)

Rory and Lorelai prepare for their Europe trip by backpacking around Stars Hollow. At Luke's, Lorelai finds out that Luke is taking Nicole on a romantic, Loveboat-style cruise. Luke checks out the Dragonfly Inn and tells Lorelai and Sookie that it will need some work but "it's a steal." Lorelai goes to Sookie and Jackson's house to "celebrate" the bad news: that the inn is closing and she doesn't have enough money for her part of the Dragonfly investment. Rory gives Dean unsolicited tips on planning his wedding to Lindsay and tells him to pick out a gift from a catalog . . . their first wedding gift. Dean appreciates the gesture. After Rory finds out that Lorelai cannot afford the Dragonfly Inn because of Yale, Rory asks Richard and Emily for a loan to pay for Yale. They happily agree, with the condition of continuing the Friday night dinners. Rory informs Lorelai, and Sookie buys the Dragonfly Inn during the ceremony. Luke has a dream that Lorelai tells him not to get engaged on the cruise. Try not to cry at Rory's graduation speech.

Best Line: "I've seen you dance and you jump around like a duck."

Episode 4.1: "Ballrooms and Biscotti" (September 23, 2003)

Upon returning from Europe, Lorelai schedules a fun and productive mother/daughter week before Rory's Yale move-in day. Their plans get thwarted when Rory realizes she wrote the date down wrong in her planner (how 2003) and she is actually moving in two days. Their week of festivities is condensed to days. Sookie is having a boy, but Jackson and Rory don't want to know the sex. Luke avoids talking about the cruise until pressed by Lorelai. He reveals that he and Nicole got married on the cruise and are now getting divorced. A jet-lagged Lorelai and Rory spend their last night together at Emily's watching taped ballroom dancing competitions.

Best Line: "I'm gonna go take a shower and leave you alone to make out with your sock drawer."

Episode 4.2: "The Lorelais' First Day at Yale" (September 30, 2003)

Luke's truck and Rory's Yale mattress have central roles in this episode. Lorelai borrows the truck to move Rory into Yale, but she doesn't know how to drive a stick. Lorelai purchases a new mattress for Rory but has to make arrangements for the old mattress; she doesn't make arrangements so it stays in Luke's truck until Luke brings it back to Rory's suite. After Lorelai leaves Rory at Yale, Rory pages Lorelai to "Come back!!!!" so she asks to borrow Luke's truck again. Lorelai is just one of the girls and spends the night with Rory on her first night at Yale.

Best Line: "You didn't socialize me properly. You made me a mama's girl. Why don't I hate you? Why don't I want to be away from you? It's going to be very hard to be Christiane Amanpour broadcasting live from a foxhole in Tehran with my mommy."

Episode 4.3: "The Hobbit, the Sofa and Digger Stiles" (October 7, 2003)

Emily breaks into Rory's dorm to measure for $25,000 worth of furniture and Lorelai "smells" her presence. Meanwhile, Sookie asks Lorelai if she wants to start a catering business until the Dragonfly Inn begins generating income. Their first job is a Lord of the Rings birthday party. Lorelai plans activities and Sookie takes care of the food but doesn't consider her audience. When Lorelai sees the green mac 'n' cheese Sookie prepared, she sends one of the chefs to Doose's to buy frozen pizzas and cupcakes. A suddenly panicked Sookie reveals that she thinks she will be a bad mom. Jason "Digger" Stiles wants to go into business with Richard to get revenge on his dad. Richard loves this, but Emily does not. Paris convinces Rory to throw a dorm party and wants their room's identity to be the "meaningful conversation room." Rory meets Marty ("the naked guy") sleeping in the dorm hallway.

Best Line: "It smells like guilt and Chanel No. 5."

Episode 4.4: "Chicken or Beef?" (October 14, 2003)

No one tells Lorelai anything! Kirk installs a home security system without telling Lorelai, and Rory cuts her hair . . . without telling Lorelai. On Rory's "Perfect Stars Hollow Day," she bumps into Dean and finds out he's getting married that weekend (not so perfect). Rory and Lorelai plan to go until Luke tells them not to after hearing a drunk Dean at his bachelor party saying that he misses Rory and her "shiny hair." Viewers find out that Dave went to college in California (probably somewhere in *The O.C.*), so the band (still nameless) needs a new guitar player.

Best Line: "Lorelai, please don't sneak up on me like that. I almost blew my emergency whistle."

Episode 4.5: "The Fundamental Things Apply" (October 21, 2003)

The town continues to take care of Lorelai in Rory's absence. Babette gives Lorelai a bag of bulbs to fill the gaping hole in her heart. Rory almost misses breakfast because, in an argument between Janet and Paris, Paris turns off Rory's alarm. In her fuzzy slippers and robe, Marty finally has the confidence to approach Rory, thank her for the robe, and introduce her to "The Breakfast Crew." Lorelai encourages Rory to date because she's only been in relationships. Lorelai invites Luke over for movie night, but they are interrupted by Rory's phone call asking for advice about her awkward first date with Trevor. Luke gives good advice. Traci Lords makes an appearance as interior designer Natalie Zimmerman.

Best Line: "Sweet means bad butt."

Episode 4.6: "An Affair to Remember" (October 28, 2003)

Richard and Jason "Digger" Stiles sign important paperwork to solidify their partnership. Emily is excited to plan a "Russian-themed launch party" and hires Lorelai and Sookie to cater. When Jason finds out about the launch party, he says he wants to do something new and exciting and informs Emily and Richard that he has a trip planned to Atlantic City. Richard agrees with this approach and does not notice that Emily is hurt. Emily confides in Lorelai (kind of), motivating Lorelai to confront Jason Stiles in his office. After a hilarious scene that reveals a braless Lorelai's camp name was "umlaut," Digger, er, Jason almost convinces Lorelai to go on a date with him because "Emily would hate it." Lorelai starts to "dig" it. Kirk has a good first date with Lulu.

Best Line: "You know how many kids in India would love to come home to a room full of quiche?"

Episode 4.7: "The Festival of Living Art" (November 4, 2003)

Nick Offerman stars as Beau, Jackson's brother, who is visiting and waiting for the impending birth of Davey. Sookie reveals to Lorelai that she is having a home birth with a midwife, a woman named Bruce. In this episode, viewers are introduced to the new guitarist in Lane's band, Gil, played by Sebastian Bach. The band is uncomfortable with his "old age" (approaching forty!). Zack says, "Dude rocks, but dude's too old." When Lane hears his backstory at the Festival of Living Pictures, she makes an executive decision and tells him he's in the band. Meanwhile, Stars Hollow prepares for the Festival of Living Pictures and Lorelai worries that she'll have another flinch moment as she did seven years ago while playing the Renoir Girl. Even though Sookie's baby pager goes off during Lorelai's posing as Renoir Girl, she doesn't flinch. Nicole proposes to Luke that they put a hold on the divorce and start dating again.

Best Line: "There were no CDs when he was born."

Episode 4.8: "Die, Jerk" (November 11, 2003)

Lane and Dave are still dating, Davey says his first word ("Ah oopah"), and Rory mistakenly calls Jason Stiles "Scooper." Lane gets in her first (completely unnecessary) fight with Dave over her "marriage jug." Later, Mrs. Kim tells her that was just something she said to Lane when she was little to get her to stop crying. Rory is writing for *The Yale Daily News* (not on staff yet), but Doyle, the editor, thinks her work lacks opinion and is a bit of a yawn. Inspired by this advice, Rory writes a scathing review of a Yale ballet performance. Rory consequently receives death threats ("Die Jerk") on her dorm door.

Best Line: "I can assure you, Emily, there are no belly shots in our future."

Episode 4.9: "Ted Koppel's Big Night Out" (November 18, 2003)

This episode introduces viewers to Brennon Lewis, Asher Fleming, and Pennilyn Lott. Luke's new hired help at the diner is not on Stars Hollow's good list due to butt napkins and fog brain. In fact, regular Luke's Diner goers eventually go elsewhere for coffee and food. Asher Fleming, a college buddy of Richard's and current Yale professor, is introduced to Rory and Paris, and the end of the episode concludes with Rory seeing Paris and Asher making out. Finally, at the Harvard–Yale football game, Emily finds out Richard has been having an annual lunch with his Yale girlfriend, Pennilyn Lott, every year for the past thirty-nine years. Meanwhile, Lorelai agrees to go out with Jason and they have the weirdest first date ever. They walk out of a fancy Chinese restaurant, blow through a Taco Barn drive-through, and eventually have their first (perfect) date at a café table in front of a grocery store.

Best Line: "You are a honey-tongued devil, aren't you, Dick?"

Episode 4.10: "The Nanny and the Professor" (January 20, 2004)

Tobin makes another appearance as Davey's nanny, and Michel finally reveals to Lorelai that he hates Tobin. Out of jealousy, Michel offers to babysit Davey and calls Lorelai panicked to ask for help getting Davey unstuck from under the bed. Jason is back from Australia, and Lorelai finds out he is quirky. After having sex for the first time, Jason proceeds to ask her to stay in his very nice guest room without him. Lorelai reluctantly agrees and has a wonderful visit. Lorelai tells Jason she does not want to tell her parents about their relationship. Paris is still seeing Asher, and Rory begrudgingly covers for her at the Yale newspaper.

Best Line: "Don't flirt with me. I'm finding you very weird right now."

Episode 4.11: "In the Clamor and the Clangor" (January 27, 2004)

The episode opens with Stan's funeral, where we find out he wore a fedora and Hush Puppies and wanted to restore the Stars Hollow church bells. The bells are beloved at first but then become a town annoyance and even Little Davey begins crying in anticipation of them. Lane's band gets booked at CBGB, though they get bumped because only two people are in the audience—Brian's parents. Lane wasn't sure how to tell her mom she had a gig, so she didn't. When Lane finally comes home, Mrs. Kim has uncovered her secrets from her room. They have a brief conversation where Lane reveals her desires to be in a band and not go to school. Mrs. Kim tells her she can move out and live that life somewhere else. Lorelai and Luke have a fight but reconcile to break the church bells (*Hart to Hart* style). Lane goes to Yale.

Best Line: "A little more Stones, a little less Kraftwerk."

Episode 4.12: "A Family Matter" (February 3, 2004)

Lane has moved in with Rory at Yale, and Paris is dodging Jamie. Rory covers for Paris again and then confronts her to demand that she let Jamie go. She does, "with all of the tact of a Nazi storm trooper," according to

Rory. Jason takes the morning "off" to spend with Lorelai in Stars Hollow. Jason can't get off his phone and keeps calling Luke "Duke" after tailgating him that morning. Liz, Luke's sister, comes to town for her twentieth high school reunion. Luke finds out that she is selling jewelry on the Renaissance fair circuit. After Luke reveals to her that he stole Jess's car, Jess shows up to take it back, although it breaks down on the interstate. Rory and Lorelai see Jess sleeping in the backseat of his car; Luke leaves him a key.

Best Line: "What's 'chasing the dragon?'"

Episode 4.13: "Nag Hammadi Is Where They Found the Gnostic Gospels" (February 10, 2004)

Lorelai's solution to a broken window in her house is plastic wrap and Band-Aids. Luke meets T.J. (aka Gary), Liz's boyfriend. Luke is skeptical of him at first but decides he is an OK guy in the end, to which T.J. responds, "You're a dick." Jess tells Luke that he is a "pain in the ass" because he tries to "fix" everything even if people don't want his help. Luke is hurt, gets drunk, and then tries to fix Lorelai's window. Jason and Lorelai have to "pretend" to be a couple at a fund-raiser dinner. Jason's father, Floyd, is also at the fund-raiser and asks about Jason's golf game. Richard is convinced that Floyd has an agenda. Jess and Rory keep running into each other in Stars Hollow, and Jess keeps fleeing, which infuriates Rory. The last time, Rory says it is her turn. Jess catches up to her, says "I love you," then runs off again.

Best Line: "I skipped obscure manuscript humor 101."

Episode 4.14: "The Incredible Sinking Lorelais" (February 17, 2004)

Both Rory and Lorelai struggle in this episode. Although things seem to be coming together at the Dragonfly, Sookie finds out they are running out of money. Rory goes to see one of her professors expecting to hear how great her essay was, but instead he advises her to drop the course because it is a D paper and he thinks she is taking too many classes. Rory is upset and tries to find her mom at the inn but finds Dean instead. He comforts her. Lorelai, upset after Friday night dinner with Trix, finds Luke to reschedule their date. She cries about not having a partner during times like these and says she was going to ask him to borrow $30,000. He puts his arm around her to comfort her. Rory and Lorelai need each other but can't seem to connect.

Best Line: "And all I asked for was just one hour to get my hair done, and then two seconds into the shampoo, I get a phone call from a guy who sounds like a *Kids in the Hall* character telling me I have to get to the inn to okay a sink that I wouldn't know how to okay because I don't know what makes it okay."

Episode 4.15: "Scene in a Mall" (February 24, 2004)

Lorelai and Rory decide to play hooky and go window shopping. At the mall, they run into Emily, who makes them buy a bunch of things they don't need. Emily has a breakdown, and Lorelai and her mom share a touching moment in the food court. Luke gives Lorelai a check for $30,000; they write the terms of the loan on a napkin. Lane finds an apartment with Zack and Brian. Luke sees Dean still pining over Rory while at the arcade.

Best Line: "I thought my mom was harsh, but your mom makes the guy from Joy Division look like one of the Teletubbies."

Episode 4.16: "The Reigning Lorelai" (March 2, 2004)

Gran/Trix dies and Sookie makes mock turtle soup for a devastated Richard. After Trix's death, Emily finds a note to Richard from Gran dated just before their wedding day begging him to leave Emily at the altar. Out of anger, Emily stops planning Trix's funeral, so the responsibility falls on Lorelai and Rory. Lorelai forgets to buy Gran fresh underwear. Lorelai and Rory learn that Gran married another Gilmore, her second cousin . . . ew. Richard tells Emily that Gran's ashes will not be on their mantel, despite Gran's wishes.

Best Line: "It didn't end. It was the hug that wouldn't end, and he was wearing a robe."

Episode 4.17: "Girls in Bikinis, Boys Doin' the Twist" (April 13, 2004)

After their failed attempt to petition for political prisoners in Burma, Rory and Paris decide to catch a late ride with Glen and Janet to Florida for spring break. The pair make themselves do "spring break-y" stuff—they dance, drink, drunk dial Dean, and Paris kisses Rory. Jason makes an unclear statement to Lorelai about moving forward in their relationship with a "talking key" to his condo. Luke finds out Nicole is cheating on him after finding someone else's socks at the townhouse. Luke gets arrested after kicking the "sock man's" car and calls Lorelai, who subsequently bails him out of jail.

Best Line: "In Burma you'd be married or brutally killed."

Episode 4.18: "Tick, Tick, Tick, Boom!" (April 20, 2004)

At Friday night dinner, Lorelai wants to know where all of the anvils have gone. The town smells like skunks after Kirk failed to find fifty-nine Easter eggs left over from the Stars Hollow Easter Egg Hunt. Town volunteers find all but twelve eggs, throwing Kirk into a sleepless, dizzying hunt for them. Luke finds the final twelve eggs and tells Kirk to take credit and "be the hero." Jason's father, Floyd, informs Jason and Richard that he is suing their firm. Even though Jason tells Richard he's going to figure it out, the episode closes with Richard and Floyd playing golf, indicating that Richard is double-crossing Jason. Rory is upset that Dean drops out of school to work and blames Lindsay. Dean informs Rory that Lindsay doesn't want them talking, although he says he doesn't want that to happen.

Best Line: "Do you know how long cuticle damage takes to heal?"

Episode 4.19: "Afterboom" (April 27, 2004)

Lane's band has a gig. Paris thinks Asher Fleming's book dedication to a "wise, willful, and wonderful woman" is about her, and Rory thinks it's kind of "vague." Doyle tells Rory that Fleming has a new young girlfriend every year. Lane thinks Mrs. Kim is replacing her after seeing a young Korean foreign exchange student staying in her old house and wearing her clothes. Lane feels alone after the concert because her bandmates have loved ones in attendance and she has no one. Lorelai and Rory think Emily might be staying somewhere else. Jason reveals he is suing Richard, and blood is thicker than water.

Best Line: "Luke, that is a Mailboxes, Etc. It's not dignified."

Episode 4.20: "Luke Can See Her Face" (May 4, 2004)

Lorelai is overwhelmed with work and can't sleep, and Luke buys a self-help book and sees "her face." Lorelai and Sookie overhear Dean and Lindsay arguing. Liz and T.J. inform Luke that they are having a Renaissance wedding (wheat stalks, horses, costumes, and turkey legs) in Stars Hollow. Luke finds Jess living on a mattress in New York and pleads with him to come to the wedding. Jess agrees because of Luke. When Lorelai realizes Jackson is literally "sleeping with the zucchini" to make sure the crop is safe for Sookie's famous zucchini soup, she, along with Sookie and Michel, have a meeting about the Dragonfly and agree to remove something from their to-do lists. All of them fall asleep in the zucchini patch. Inspired by the book of love, Luke asks Lorelai to go with him to Liz's wedding. Affirmed by her positive response, Luke gifts the book to Jess.

Best Line: "I need bare-ass stalks."

Episode 4.21: "Last Week Fights, This Week Tights" (May 11, 2004)

Paris is going to England with Asher for the summer. Emily and Richard still have not revealed their separation. Mrs. Kim visits Lane's apartment and is horrified by the boys, the broken window, and the mess, subsequently running out of the apartment, but gets advice from Lorelai and Brian and Zack become "girls." Lorelai fixes Liz's wedding dress at Miss Patty's and spots Jess's love book in his bag. Later, she tries to laugh about it with Luke and he becomes defensive. After making up, Luke asks Lorelai to dance and she finds out that he can waltz! Emily sets Rory up with a Yale student, Graham Sullivan. She meets him and his friends at a bar but is turned off by their drunken behavior. They leave the bar; she stays but has no way home so she calls Dean to pick her up. Inspired by the book, Jess goes to Yale and finds Dean and Rory together. Rory asks Dean to leave, and Jess implores Rory to run away with him and she says no, firmly.

Best Line: "It's commonly known that James Madison liked big knockers."

Episode 4.22: "Raincoats and Recipes" (May 18, 2004)

Kirk convinces Luke to stay in the room next to his and Lulu's at the Dragonfly's test run just in case Luke needs to pull him off of Lulu in one of his violent night terrors. Rory calls Graham "James Spader in *Pretty in Pink*" and reveals to Lane that she was uncomfortable with Jess's unpredictability but comfortable with Dean as a safety net. Jason shows up at the test run and will not leave. He tells Luke that he and Lorelai are together. Luke confronts Lorelai, and they (finally!) kiss after Luke tells her to "just hold still." Unfortunately, this is when the Luke and Lorelai relationship stops being fun—boo. Rory confronts Dean to ask why he is mad, and he reveals that he does not want her to be with Jess. Rory loses her virginity to Dean. Lorelai finds out and Rory says, "I hate that you're ruining this for me."

Best Line: "I think Kirk wants you to go upstairs and make love to him."

Episode 5.1: "Say Goodbye to Daisy Miller" (September 21, 2004)

This episode begins by showing viewers what happened between Rory and Dean before Lorelai walks in. They say they love each other and Rory decides that Sammy Davis Jr.'s "Candy Man" is "their song." They hear Lorelai enter the house and scramble to get dressed. Emily and Richard continue to fight. Emily finally tells Rory and Lorelai that they are separated and she reoffers Rory a chance to travel Europe with her. Lorelai thinks this is a great idea. Rory thinks Lorelai is shipping her off to Europe to keep her away from Dean, but she wants to go to get away from Lorelai, so she goes. Meanwhile, Lorelai and Luke agree that they liked the kiss and want to meet again in the evening. However, Luke receives a call from Liz and T.J. and they need his help in Maine. He goes but gets a cell phone so that he and Lorelai can still talk.

Best Line: "Only prostitutes have two glasses of wine at lunch."

Episode 5.2: "A Messenger, Nothing More" (September 28, 2004)

Seven weeks pass in the *Gilmore Girl* world, where Rory and Emily spent the time in Europe and Luke spent the time helping Liz and T.J. at the Renaissance fair. Lane is working at Luke's. Near the end of the Europe trip, Rory calls Lorelai to apologize and asks for help in delivering a note to Dean. Lindsay finds the note and throws all of Dean's items out of their townhouse window in front of all of Stars Hollow. Lindsay and her mom run into Rory and Lorelai. Lindsay's mom yells at Rory. Finally, Lane asks Rory, "Am I in love with Zack?"

Best Line: "What's that, Lucy, a football for me to kick?"

Episode 5.3: "Written in the Stars" (October 5, 2004)

Emily and Richard are still separated, and Lorelai and Rory split time at Friday night dinners: drinks in the pool house with Richard and dinner with Emily in the main house. The first weekend back in the new school year, Paris holds a wake in their new Yale suite for Asher Fleming, who died in Oxford over the summer. Rory meets Logan during two random encounters; once with Marty and the second when Logan and pals mistakenly go to Rory's room looking for a girl. Luke takes Lorelai on a date where she finds out that he has kept the horoscope she gave him on the day they first met in his wallet for eight years. Lorelai and Luke consummate their relationship, and she wonders why the town isn't gossiping about them until their relationship is the subject at a town meeting. Taylor thinks their relationship (and potential breakup) could be bad for the town (Team Lorelai or Team Luke) so Luke agrees to leave town if they break up.

Best Line: "No, Rory. This great man was not brought down by my vagina."

Episode 5.4: "Tippecanoe and Taylor, Too" (October 12, 2004)

When Taylor tells Jackson that he has to move his new greenhouse six inches, Jackson says he's running for Taylor's job as town selectman. Hep Alien is officially named at Jackson's campaign rally, and they play his favorite song, the theme song from *Greatest American Hero*. Jackson wins in a landslide but immediately seems miserable about his new job. Dean and Rory are dating but encounter obstacles in getting together: Dean is still sharing a car with Lindsay, Dean's mom and dad are weird to Rory when she goes to his house, and her car is too small for them to make out in. Lane tells Zack that she likes him more than a bandmate and she doesn't think the feeling is going away.

Best Line: "Don't hate the tick messenger, hate the tick."

Episode 5.5: "We Got Us a Pippi Virgin" (October 19, 2004)

Richard and Emily are still separated, but both seem to be uneasy about the situation. Richard is spending his nights reading the sixth and final volume of *The Decline and Fall of the Roman Empire*—a book that took him thirty-six years to read—and Emily buys a panic room. At Friday night dinner, while Richard is out of town, Emily, Lorelai, and Rory snoop around the pool house. Emily is appalled to find a sequin vest. Richard later informs her that he joined a barbershop quartet. Luke, Lorelai, Rory, and Dean go on a double date to see the *Adventures of Pippi Longstocking*. Lorelai finds out that Luke is a "Pippi Virgin," and Kirk tells Rory and Dean that it is a great "make-out movie." Lane tells Zack that she changed her mind and only wants to be roommates and bandmates. Later, Zack confronts Lane to tell her it takes him a while to adjust to things but she knows him better than anyone (even his parents have not seen him cry during *Dances with Wolves*).

Best Line: "It's reminding me of Billy Dee Williams and cancer."

Episode 5.6: "Norman Mailer, I'm Pregnant!" (October 26, 2004)

Norman Mailer becomes an iced-tea-drinking, non-food-consuming patron at the Dragonfly. When it is advised that the Dragonfly drop lunch because they are losing money, Sookie blames Norman Mailer. Sookie later finds out that she's not really mad at Norman Mailer but that she is cranky because she is pregnant. Rory panics that she is not doing enough professionally after hearing that Glen got published in *The New York Times* and Doyle spent the summer in Muncie, Indiana, working for the *Muncie Messenger*. Rory discovers "gorilla girl." Christopher calls Lorelai panicked because Gigi keeps crawling out of her crib. Lorelai finds out that Sherry moved to Paris, leaving Christopher to care for Gigi alone. Rory finds out that Christopher called Lorelai for help, and she confronts Christopher. She tells him not to contact her mom for fear he'll screw up her relationship with Luke.

Best Line: "Technically, I'm a giant wiener."

Episode 5.7: "You Jump, I Jump, Jack" (November 2, 2004)

Emily finds out from Kirk that Lorelai is dating Luke and wants to "re-meet" him. Luke and Lorelai have dinner at Emily's, where she passive-aggressively insults Luke and his diner. Not to be outdone by Emily, Richard invites Luke to play golf with him, hoping to franchise his diner and make him an acceptable mate for Lorelai. Zack tells Lane that he is ready to date her now. Rory gets invited to a Life and Death Brigade event by Logan. Logan persuades Rory to jump off a seven-story platform, and Rory gets champagne, her camera, and a gorilla head left at her door as a reward. She worries she has been too sheltered, and there is something about Logan . . . according to Rory because we think he's a douche.

Best Line: "Charming . . . slang for doggy poopy. The word 'beer,' backhand slang for nitwit juice."

Episode 5.8: "The Party's Over" (November 9, 2004)

After finding out Dean and Rory are back together, Richard and Emily hold a "Yale Alumni Event" where Rory is the only girl. Emily dresses her up like a princess, including diamonds and a tiara. Logan saves Rory from slimy Jordan, who wants to make sure she is "legal" before they continue their discussion. Logan and friends start a "sub-party" in the pool house, where they drink champagne and Rory loses track of the time. She is fifteen minutes late to meet Dean. When Dean sees her stumble out of the house, dressed like a princess surrounded by boys in suits, he says, "I don't belong here." Rory lets him leave and cries, and Logan consoles her. T.J. and Liz decide to move to Stars Hollow. They find a house and TJ tells everyone he is "in Esk-erow." T.J., upset after a fight with Liz, crashes Luke and Lorelai's dinner date. Lorelai watches Rory from the window.

Best Line: "You dirty, filthy devil boy. . . . You are a wild pig of filth!"

Episode 5.9: "Emily Says Hello" (November 16, 2004)

Sookie has crazy pregnancy cravings and sobs over the 2000 breakup of Elizabeth Hurley and Hugh Grant. Lorelai realizes Christopher never called her back after she helped him with Gigi. Lorelai invites Christopher, Gigi, and Rory to the Dragonfly for lunch but doesn't tell anybody else about the guest list and Rory gets mad at Christopher. Lorelai assures Rory that Christopher will not come between her and Luke. However, she lies to Rory when she says Luke was OK with the lunch. She did not tell Luke. She does tell Luke, later, though awkwardly. He is jealous but says it's OK. Emily seems to have a good time on her date with Simon McLane but comes home and cries after she shuts the door.

Best Line: "I helloed him today and he's taking me to dinner."

Episode 5.10: "But Not as Cute as Pushkin" (November 30, 2004)

Lorelai discovers that Luke has a "dark day" once a year when he grieves on the anniversary of his dad's death. Lorelai buys the items in Mrs.

Thompson's garage in order to save Luke's dad's boat. Life coach Terrance makes an appearance during this episode because Paris is having trouble getting "back out there" after Asher's death. Headmaster Charleston asks Rory to host Anna Fairchild, a sixteen-year-old Yale-bound Chilton student. Logan, Colin, and Finn stage a fight over Rory during one of her classes. The class applauds and Anna is impressed, but Rory is not. Rory loses Anna and later finds out she was picked up by Yale police at a party. An annoyed Marty tells Rory that she's part of Logan's group now.

Best Line: "Could we sit down? The doctor says the screw in my hip is loose."

Episode 5.11: "Women of Questionable Morals" (January 25, 2005)

Emily and Richard find a stray dog on their porch and bond over the caring of the dog until it gets picked up by its owner. The first snow of the season hits Stars Hollow and creates several annoyances for Lorelai. First snow means the Stars Hollow Revolutionary War reenactment. There is a new plot to the story: Taylor uncovers that a "lady of the night" distracted a war general to stop a battle. The reenactors try to find a woman to play the role of the lady. The decide on Lulu, who later gets sick. Unbeknownst to Taylor, who is playing the distracted general, Kirk stands in for his sick girlfriend. Christopher drops by Yale to visit Rory. He apologizes, but she is cold to him. Later, Rory and Lorelai find out that Christopher's father, Straub, has died, but Christopher did not tell them. Separately, they visit Christopher. Rory brings him milk and cookies. Lorelai brings a bottle of tequila. She is hungover the next day but does not tell Luke where she was. Concerned about Lorelai's strained relationship with the snow, Luke builds Lorelai an ice rink in her front yard.

Best Line: "We have a pool house for stray dogs? Love the innuendo, Emily."

Episode 5.12: "Come Home" (February 1, 2005)

Rory offers to help Logan write a story for the newspaper. While she is helping him, she discovers he is going to a Seymour Hersh party and Rory is visibly intrigued. She thinks he might invite her to attend with him, but he does not. Lorelai uncovers the ghost stealing Toblerones from the rooms: a pregnant Sookie who wants some guilt-free alone time. Zack and Mrs. Kim develop an unexpected bond over wanting Lane to wear her glasses. After seeing Simon talk with Emily, Richard rear-ends her and insists on taking her to the hospital, telling Simon not to call. Emily and Richard decide to renew their vows on their fortieth anniversary and ask Lorelai to be Emily's maid of honor and Rory to be Richard's best man. The episode concludes with Emily seeking out Christopher, imploring him to pursue Lorelai.

Best Line: "Were you bitten by some kind of rabid animal?"

Episode 5.13: "Wedding Bell Blues" (February 8, 2005)

Lorelai throws a spontaneous bachelorette party for Emily, with Gypsy, Sookie, Miss Patty, and Babette in attendance. Rory tells Logan that she wants to have "stringless fun." Christopher attends the party and drinks too much. Lorelai has to reveal to Luke that she lied about being hungover and spending time with Christopher. Lorelai walks in on Rory and Logan making out (getting ready for more?) at the wedding. Luke and Christopher both have words with Logan and then argue over who has "been there" for Rory. Christopher says, "Lorelai and I belong together. Emily told me it's not too late." Luke flees the scene, and when Lorelai is grabbed for wedding pictures with the wedding party, she whispers to her mom, "You and me, we're done."

Best Line: "I will kick your ass, you little weasel."

Episode 5.14: "Say Something" (February 15, 2005)

Lorelai and Rory deal with the aftermath of the wedding. Rory goes back to Yale looking for a message from Logan, but there is none. Lorelai rushes to Stars Hollow to find Luke, and she finds him at the Black &

White & Read movie theater watching an old movie. Although she finds him, Luke tells her he needs time to think and process. She pushes him; they break up. The town quickly catches on, and Taylor creates pink ribbons for Team Lorelai and blue ribbons for Team Luke. Lorelai is distraught and Rory comes over to console her (with the help of Logan's limo driver, Frank). The episode concludes with Lorelai leaving an embarrassing message for Luke, breaking into his apartment and stealing the message, and then apologizing to Luke and accepting the breakup.

Best Line: "I'm not calling you a hooker or nothing."

Episode 5.15: "Jews and Chinese Food" (February 22, 2005)

Rory runs into Marty and invites him over for *Duck Soup*. He reluctantly agrees. Logan interrupts their night and insists that they go to get Chinese food with him. At dinner, it is clear that Marty doesn't fit in and feels uncomfortable, as he sees Logan playing with Rory's hair. His lack of comfort is emphasized when he has to borrow $75 from Rory to pay for the dinner. After dinner, Marty reveals to Rory that he likes her and she says she likes Logan. Luke is cranky at the diner until Lulu comes in reminding him that Lorelai signed him up to help with the set for the elementary school's production of *Fiddler on the Roof*. He continues to ask Lulu, "Where are all the adults?" because he wants to run into Lorelai, who is helping with the costumes. Rory and Logan have sex.

Best Line: "Well, it's too good. You built me a twenty-first-century dairy cart."

Episode 5.16: "So . . . Good Talk" (March 1, 2005)

Emily and Richard come back from their second honeymoon, and Emily calls Lorelai, who keeps hanging up on her. Luke continues to be grumpy at the diner and is literally throwing patrons out the front door. Sookie is worried that Lorelai is becoming a "couch potato girl" and insists on having a girls' night out that doesn't include dancing, drinking, or movie watching; they decide to order pizza and compare and contrast three versions of *A Star Is Born*. Rory goes to Friday night dinner and clearly snubs Emily. Richard calls Lorelai to tell her to talk to Rory, but she declines and then seeks out her dad for help with insurance at the Dragonfly. He enthusiastically accepts, and Emily is jealous because he is "the favorite." Emily visits Luke at the diner and says that he "won" and to get back together with Lorelai. He immediately goes to Lorelai's house and passionately kisses her when she opens the door.

Best Line: "You're my only daughter, that I know of . . . "

Episode 5.17: "Pulp Friction" (March 8, 2005)

Logan's 1-percent status is further explored when Rory finds out that Tony Kushner plays canasta with his mom. Rory sees Logan having lunch with another girl while shopping for a "back-together-with-Luke dress" with Lorelai. Rory gets invited to Finn's Quentin Tarantino–inspired birthday party by Robert "Grimaldi," and Logan is jealous, even though he attended the party with another date. The Dragonfly is chosen as one of the top ten inns in Connecticut, but the outdoor photo shoot gets sabotaged by Michel's *Price Is Right* prize: a $100,000 RV that he does not want. After Luke inspires Kirk to move out of his mom's house, Lorelai and Luke find Kirk in Lorelai's garage, sleeping nude in Luke's boat. Lorelai is still not attending Friday night dinners even though Emily thinks she "fixed" the problem. Emily confronts Luke at the diner because she assumes he did not understand her first appeal to him. Lorelai dispels this assumption by coldly telling her mom to shut up.

Best Line: "When you look in the mirror, do you see Reggae Fever?"

Episode 5.18: "To Live and Let Diorama" (April 19, 2005)

After Old Man Twickham really dies this time and leaves his home to Stars Hollow, Luke throws himself into the effort to turn it into the Stars Hollow museum. Lorelai and Taylor are skeptical of his motives until Luke reveals to Taylor that he has always loved that house and he wants it. Lorelai asks her interviewer to pull the "Emily stories" from the piece. Paris, Rory, and Lane drown their boy problems in Miss Patty's Founder's Day punch. Lane finds out that Zack is playing banjo in a bluegrass band on the side (in Sophie's music store). The episode concludes with Lorelai comforting a crying Rory on the bathroom floor in front of a toilet.

Best Line: "Taylor's Taylorness can now break glass."

Episode 5.19: "But I'm a Gilmore!" (April 26, 2005)

Rory and Paris nurse their hangovers from Miss Patty's punch. Paris finds out that Doyle was not avoiding her but rather he was sick. She brings over her former nanny to help nurse him back to health. Rory confronts Logan to tell him she is a "boyfriend person," not a casual dating person. He interprets this as an ultimatum and agrees to try to be her boyfriend. Sookie is ordered to go on bedrest, and Lorelai, in a panic, calls Luke to run the kitchen at the Dragonfly. Logan's sister, Honor, gets engaged to Josh and begs Logan and Rory to join them for dinner to diffuse the potentially stressful situation. At dinner, Logan's grandfather and mother publicly share their disappointment in Logan for choosing Rory because she will not be suitable for the Huntzberger family. The end of the episode concludes with Logan's dad visiting Rory in the newsroom, apologizing first and then offering her an internship at one of his newspapers.

Best Line: "How dare you take a ladle from a pregnant woman!"

Episode 5.20: "How Many Kropogs to Cape Cod?" (May 3, 2005)

Rory informs Lorelai about her internship with Huntzberger's *Stamford Eagle Gazette* . . . a few days later. Rory does some research on Mitchum and finds out that Logan doesn't know much about his father. Emily and Richard invite Logan to dinner in a panic after hearing that the Huntzbergers invited Rory to dinner. Lorelai invites herself to dinner because she doesn't think it's right that her parents get "first dibs." Richard thinks they should get acreage at Cape Cod for the next phase of their family: weddings and children. Emily and Richard love the idea of Rory and Logan together and think Lorelai is paranoid and crazy when she expresses her doubts.

Best Line: "I've just won the spaz of the year award."

Episode 5.21: "Blame Booze and Melville" (May 10, 2005)

Lorelai and Rory plan a surprise baby shower for Sookie that gets foiled when she goes into labor early. After Sookie delivers a baby girl (name TBD), she arranges for Jackson to get a vasectomy while they are at the hospital. Lorelai and Luke have unprotected sex, and Lorelai worries she might be pregnant because she eats an apple and "likes it." Luke tries to buy the Twickham house only to find out Kirk, who has had fifteen thousand jobs over eleven years, put in a competing offer. They talk to the town elders in a sauna, and they grant the house to Luke. Lorelai brings the printed magazine article to her parents' house. Emily is excited until she begins to read, but she doesn't react as negatively as Lorelai thought. Lorelai apologizes to her . . . through the safety of a door. Mitchum Huntzberger tells Rory that, although she'll make a great assistant one day, she doesn't have what it takes to be a journalist. Rory meets Logan at Honor's engagement party, and instead of telling him what his father said, she asks him to steal another yacht with her and take it out for a joy ride. The episode concludes with Lorelai receiving a call from Rory to pick her up.

Best Line: "Mom, it was meant as a joke. The Pol Pot, the walking anthrax. I was just being edgy like Chris Rock."

Episode 5.22: "A House Is Not a Home" (May 17, 2005)

Lane is worried the band is breaking up because it doesn't seem to be a priority to anyone. Mrs. Kim organizes a two-month "Christian Crusade Tour." We learn that Rory called Lorelai from a police station. Lorelai picks her up and overhears Colin and Finn discussing Logan's penchant for stealing. Lorelai and Luke assume that it was Logan who got Rory arrested. Rory tells Lorelai what Mitchum told her to try to explain why she stole the yacht. Weirdly, Rory defends Mitchum when Lorelai gets upset. Rory is embarrassed and asks that her mom not inform Richard and Emily. However, when Rory later reveals that she is not returning to Yale, Lorelai seeks out Richard and Emily for help. They agree to help, but then change their minds after Rory visits Richard. Richard and Emily decide that Rory needs a break from school and will move into their pool house. Lorelai goes to Luke to vent. After he insists that he's "not going to let this happen," Lorelai asks, "Luke, will you marry me?"

Best Line: "Eternal damnation is what I'm risking for my rock 'n' roll."

Episode 6.1: "New and Improved Lorelai" (September 13, 2005)

Luke says yes! And with no hesitation. Taylor finds out first, only because they need him to open the market after hours to find a beverage to toast the moment. They find an old case of Zima that Taylor was saving for Babette and toast their engagement under the Stars Hollow gazebo. Richard arranges for Charlie Davenport to represent Rory in court, and he assures her that the punishment will be light. To everyone's surprise, Rory gets three hundred hours of community service that she must complete in six months. Rory seems more upset that her mom was not at her sentencing than she is about the punishment (a glimmer of hope). Rory tells Paris that she is not returning to Yale. Paris blames Logan and seeks out Lorelai. Logan throws a getting-out-of-jail party for Rory at a bar (ugh).

Best Line: "I befriend really old women."

Episode 6.2: "Fight Face" (September 20, 2005)

Lorelai meets Cocoa, the dog, whom she renames Paul Anka (we love this choice). Although Luke and Lorelai have plans to move to the Twickham house, Lorelai tells Luke that she wants to keep her house . . . and not to rent to anyone else . . . just for her. Luke picks up on this hint and decides to renovate Lorelai's house instead of buying the Twickham house. Rory starts to officially work for the DAR. Emily drops Rory off at her first community service job and gives her tips on "how to interact with fellow prisoners," which includes Rory bartering with cigarettes. Rory visits Luke, and he tells her about his engagement with Lorelai. She's understandably upset. Lorelai sees Rory doing community service on the highway and stops to talk (i.e., argue) with her about who hurt the other more.

Best Line: "Hole! Dirt, bed, dirt hole."

Episode 6.3: "The UnGraduate" (September 27, 2005)

Lorelai becomes chummy with the construction crew, and T.J. thinks he is the head contractor on the job, which is good because, according to Tom, he has "terrible instincts with zero follow-through." Rory seems to be enjoying community service and gossips with Emily about fellow DAR member Constance's prescription drug problem. Rory gets inducted into the DAR. Sookie pushes Lorelai to tell her the wedding date because she is worried that Lorelai is not going to follow through with the wedding. Without Rory around, Paris begins having lunch with Lorelai at the Dragonfly, which drives Sookie and Michel (and Lorelai) crazy. Hep Alien wraps up their successful tour, and Lane informs them she saved $9,000 so that they can record an album. Lorelai tells Luke that she doesn't want to set a wedding date until things are right with Rory.

Best Line: "Only pet the dog with your non-watch hand."

Episode 6.4: "Always a Godmother, Never a God" (October 4, 2005)

Rory continues to get socialized into Emily and Richard's high society ways. When Emily can't get back from Helsinki in time, Rory steps in to help her with a DAR function. Jackson's family comes into town and stays at the Dragonfly for Davey's and Martha's (and Jackson's) baptisms. Sookie schemes to get Lorelai and Rory back together by asking each of them to be godmother to Davey and Martha (good plan). Sookie presses Luke for a wedding date. Lorelai tries to call Rory, but her number is disconnected. Lorelai is hurt because she thinks Rory gave Sookie her new number before her. Rory continues to be attracted to Logan's spontaneity. The end of the episode concludes with Logan telling Rory to meet him at the airport to go on a last-minute helicopter trip to New York.

Best Line: "Thanks. This is the suit they buried my dad in."

Episode 6.5: "We've Got Magic to Do" (October 11, 2005)

Lorelai calls herself a "firestarter" after finding out about a kitchen fire at the Dragonfly. Luke and Jackson diagnose the problem, but when insurance gets involved, Lorelai is forced to call Richard for help. When Richard visits, she asks him how the big plan is going (awkward). Rory has big ideas about a failing DAR event. Emily is worried about Rory's approach, but the newly themed USO event is a raving success. Paris informs Rory that she is broke, and Rory offers her a job as a server at her event. Kirk performs an interpretive dance called "A Journey of a Man" at Miss Patty's annual dance recital—a performance he created twenty years ago. Richard has a turning point at the USO event after Mitchum Huntzberger confirms Lorelai's accusations and he sees Rory on stage as the "architect" of the event. He knows she can do better.

Best Line: "We're screwing the pooch, Emily, and we've got to go balls out."

Episode 6.6: "Welcome to the Dollhouse" (October 18, 2005)

Phineas and Zebediah (played by Kirk and Andrew) interrupt the town meeting to persuade the town to return to Stars Hollow's old street names. Everyone, including Lorelai, is excited about this prospect until the Dragonfly Inn receives the street name "Sores and Boils Alley." Richard's concern over Rory deepens in this episode. He asks Logan if Rory has any "big plans," which Logan misinterprets as "wedding plans." Emily is only concerned about Rory's romantic plans but is comforted when Logan gives Rory a Birkin bag, which Emily perceives as a great sign that their relationship is going well. Emily calls Lorelai to pick up her old dollhouse before Goodwill picks it up (classic Emily manipulation). When Lorelai refuses to pick it up, Richard brings it to Lorelai and then says, "We need to talk about Rory."

Best Line: "What could a girl possibly want with a drawer full of Tootsie Rolls?"

Episode 6.7: "Twenty-One Is the Loneliest Number" (October 25, 2005)

The one where Rory has a dream that Madeleine Albright is her mom. Richard continues to be worried about Rory and seeks out Lorelai to come up with a plan. Lorelai refuses to bribe her child to go back to Yale (we agree!). Lorelai wants to create a new Halloween tradition with Luke—a skit where she is a mad scientist and she electrocutes, cuts open, and pulls out sausages from Luke's body. He declines. Emily and Richard arrange for Reverend Boatwright to talk to Rory about sex, which backfires when Rory tells him that "the ultimate-gift ship has sailed." Separately, Lorelai and Rory reminisce about their plan for Rory's twenty-first birthday: go to Atlantic City, sit a Blackjack table and play twenty-one, buy twenty-one things, and then do something inappropriate with twenty-one men. Emily throws a twenty-first birthday party for Rory, and Richard sulks in his den. When Emily confronts him, Richard says he wants more for Rory than tea parties and DAR functions. Emily interprets this as an insult to her identity, and she's kind of right.

Best Line: "I paid 40,000 dollars to redecorate her sex house. I bought her her sex mattress, her sex box springs."

Episode 6.8: "Let Me Hear Your Balalaikas Ringing Out" (November 8, 2005)

Luke agrees to sponsor the middle school girls' soccer team but is uncomfortable with the violence or, as Lorelai puts it, "*Scarface* on the soccer field." Rory gets annoyed with her high-society peeps: Logan and his drunk friends, as well as Emily. Jess is waiting for her at the Gilmore house and he brings her a book, *The Subsect*, that he has just written and published. They make plans to catch up the next night, but when Logan pulls up, he foils their evening. Logan interrogates Jess to the point that Jess leaves. When Rory follows Jess, he forcefully questions her, "What the hell is going on with you?" Rory goes back into the bar and gets into a public fight with Logan about their way of life. She crashes at Lane's, worrying Emily. Emily and Rory get in an argument at the Russian-themed tea party.

Best Line: "He's very anal when he misbehaves."

Episode 6.9: "The Prodigal Daughter Returns" (November 15, 2005)

Lorelai and Luke have Sookie and Jackson over for a housewarming post-renovation dinner. Christopher calls in the middle of dinner and leaves a message on the answering machine. Luke thinks Lorelai is hiding something so they argue in front of their guests. Colin and Finn move Rory's things out of the Gilmore house and into Lane's apartment. Lane tells Lorelai that Rory moved in. Rory hits the pavement, determined to find a job, and she begins by returning to the *Stamford Eagle Gazette*. She is persistent with the editor and gets a job by the end of the episode. The first person she calls: Lorelai. She's going back to Yale, and Lorelai and Rory reunite (yay!). Luke meets a twelve-year-old girl, April, who pulls a hair off of his head at the diner to do a DNA test. Congrats, Luke, you're a father!

Best Line: "When I was in fifth grade, I told everyone that Erik Estrada was my boyfriend and we made out on his motorcycle."

Episode 6.10: "He's Slippin' 'Em Bread . . . Dig?" (November 22, 2005)

Rory meets Paul Anka (the dog) and Lorelai tells her to let him lick sugar off of her toes. Lorelai kept a hatbox with notes of things she wanted to discuss with Rory over the five months that they weren't talking (it felt like longer . . . thank God they made up). Lorelai "(re)introduces" Rory to Luke's Diner and to Sookie at the Dragonfly. Lane is a little bothered that Zack writes songs using other girls' names and not hers. In response, Brian writes a song called "Lane," which makes Zack jealous . . . so jealous that he starts a fight on stage during their label performance. Luke confides in Liz about April but still does not tell Lorelai. Christopher inherits a large sum of money and wants to take care of Lorelai and Rory. Lorelai says no thank you, but Rory asks him to pay for Yale. He agrees. Honor calls Rory and informs her that she and Logan have broken up . . . yikes, not the way you want to find out that your boyfriend has broken up with you.

Best Line: "She is such a Rolo whore."

Episode 6.11: "The Perfect Dress" (January 10, 2005)

Lorelai and Rory go to Atlantic City for the "best belated twenty-first birthday trip." Rory moves in with Paris and Doyle. Rory has to meet with the Yale school psychologist, and after she unexpectedly cries in his office, he recommends that she make weekly sessions with him. Sookie informs Luke that she is the BFOTB (Best Friend of the Bride) and that he doesn't have to worry about planning the wedding. On a wedding planning trip, Lorelai spots the perfect dress on sale (and in her size), which leads to the rest of the wedding plans falling perfectly into place in one day . . . invitations, date, church, and so on. Lorelai later worries it might be too perfect. After the band breaks up, Lane moves in with Mrs. Kim and is still very upset with Zack. Luke contacts April's mom, Anna, and says he wants to know his daughter and have a relationship with her. Lorelai tries on her dress for Luke who says, "It's perfect."

Best Line: "If you need some love, get a hooker."

Episode 6.12: "Just like Gwen and Gavin" (January 17, 2006)

Taylor calls a town meeting via Skype (or the 2006 version of it) to tell everyone that he is snowed in and can't get back to Stars Hollow for the Winter Carnival. He thinks they need to cancel until Miss Patty suggests that Kirk take over. Logan pursues Rory by sending her flowers, renting her a coffee cart for the day, and even going to see Lorelai for advice. Luke meets April in the park, and she says that she wants to hang out at the diner. She fills his salt and pepper shakers. Lorelai unexpectedly goes to the diner, and April tells her that her "biological father owns the place"—whoops . . . probably not the way Luke wanted Lorelai to find out. *The Yale Daily News* writers want to oust Paris. Luke wants to postpone the wedding and Lorelai says OK.

Best Line: "You've known a strangler for fifteen years?"

Episode 6.13: "Friday Night's Alright for Fighting" (January 31, 2006)

The wedding is postponed, unofficially. In hopes that Luke will change his mind, Lorelai tells Sookie that she will wait for a week to cancel all of the perfect plans. Paris goes nuts and faces the prospect of being the editor during the "first time in history that *The Yale Daily News* does not come out." Determined, Rory takes charge, and with Logan's help, they get the paper out on time. Friday night dinners get "officially reinstated" after Lorelai, Rory, Emily, and Richard spend the evening in bouts of fights intertwined with laughter and "really good sorbet."

Best Line: "He had seed and he passed it around."

Episode 6.14: "You've Been Gilmored" (February 7, 2006)

The Gilmores are still mad at each other for various reasons but are making efforts to be civil at Friday night dinner. *The Yale Daily News* board votes out Paris, leaving the editor position open. They nominate and vote for Rory to be the new editor. She accepts, but the party is short-lived. When she arrives home, Paris has evicted her from the apartment, leaving all of her things in the hallway. After exhausting all other housing options, she calls Logan, who invites her to move in with him. She accepts. Lorelai encourages Rory to invite Christopher to Yale for lunch and a tour since he is paying for it. On the tour (the same day that she gets voted in as editor, gets evicted, and moves in with Logan), Christopher wants to see Rory's apartment. She hesitantly agrees and tells him about living with Logan. Christopher and Logan quickly bond over their similar private school pasts, and Christopher decides he likes him. Richard and Emily insist that Luke come over for Friday night dinner. They frighten Lorelai and Luke over insurance mishaps and the possibility that April might be a con man.

Best Line: "Fake stomach pain is my specialty."

Episode 6.15: "A Vineyard Valentine" (February 14, 2006)

We find out Luke loves lobster and is OK with Logan after he gifts a Valentine's present to him to give to Lorelai. Up until that point, Luke is very negative, annoyingly so, about "Rory's snotty boyfriend." Lorelai and Rory spend an amusing afternoon at the gym that ends with them getting massages by Ron and Jerry in laundry services. Logan makes enough lobster for a small army. The next day, Mitchum Huntzberger breaks up the party and demands that Logan fly to London, immediately. Lorelai gets home and finds out that Emily has put an engagement announcement in the paper.

Best Line: "You've got nice Mass ass."

Episode 6.16: "Bridesmaids Revisited" (February 28, 2006)

Lorelai continues to feel insecure about her relationship with Luke and generally left out when she finds out Lane knows April. Christopher and Lorelai attend Rory's Young Voices of Journalism panel. When Christopher reveals his single-parent frustrations, Lorelai offers to babysit Gigi if he's in a pinch. Christopher takes her up on the offer, and Lorelai endures a yelling, spiteful, permanent-marker-drawing-on-the-floor Gigi. Christopher doesn't take it too well when Lorelai decides to encourage him to apply a little discipline. Meanwhile, Zack tries to get Hep Alien back together. Gil and Brian take some persuading, but they are in if Lane agrees. Lane agrees to get the band back together and simultaneously accepts Zack's marriage proposal. Rory finds out that Logan slept with all but one of Honor's bridesmaids. She tells Logan she is moving out.

Best Line: "Just remember, if things don't go well, we will stop loving you."

Episode 6.17: "I'm OK, You're OK" (April 4, 2006)

Doyle and Logan show up at Paris's apartment, trying to win back their respective loves. It works for both. Rory goes back home with Logan; Doyle and Paris do what Doyle and Paris do. April asks Luke to chaperone a school trip to Philadelphia, and Lorelai encourages him to go.

When Zack asks Mrs. Kim for her blessing, she demands that he write a hit song before he can propose to Lane (whoops). Rory wants to spy on Anna Nardini, but Lorelai does not. Rory goes to Anna's shop anyway and sees a one-of-a-kind bag that later shows up at Luke's Diner. When asked, Luke tells Lorelai that Anna gave him the bag (good guy). Kirk, in his new position as realtor, accidentally reveals to Lorelai that Emily and Richard are looking for homes in Stars Hollow.

Best Line: "Well, since mine was a fake professional, I got to pay him in Monopoly money."

Episode 6.18: "The Real Paul Anka" (April 11, 2006)

Lorelai has a trippy dream starring Paul Anka, the dog, and the real Paul Anka. There is still tension between Rory and Logan. Logan accuses Rory of embarrassing him in front of his friends as they are planning the ultimate Life and Death Brigade stunt because she's still mad at him. Luke leaves for Philly with April, and he finds out she has a crush on Freddie. Luke is happy to overhear April tell a friend that "my dad's ridiculously overprotective." Luke takes April to see Jess at his company's open house. Rory decides to go to it as well. She meets April, and Jess kisses her. Then she tells him she is still in love with Logan (ugh). Mrs. Kim brings her wedding dress to Lorelai for alterations because she wants Lane to wear it. It has pants. Lorelai finds Emily and Richard in Stars Hollow. They say they are antiquing, but she thinks they are looking for a house.

Best Line: "It has great bones literally. There's an Indian burial ground underneath it."

Episode 6.19: "I Get a Sidekick out of You" (April 18, 2006)

Mrs. Kim finds out that her mother is coming to Lane's wedding, and the apple doesn't fall far from the tree. Mrs. Kim demands that Lorelai bring a male date because otherwise she'll look like a "tramp and possibly for sale." Lorelai (and maybe Rory?) organize a bachelorette party for Lane that ends up at Brian's aunt's basement, listening to records and playing foosball with the bachelor party. Christopher discovers texting and creates his own acronym when Rory asks him to go to Lane's wedding with Lorelai: TPTDI . . . Totally Psyched To Do It. Lane has two wedding ceremonies: one for her grandmother and the other in the church. Mrs. Kim gives Lane "the talk" and explains that she'll have to kiss Zack at the wedding and "do it with him" on her wedding night. Mrs. Kim leaves the wedding early, and the real party happens that evening. Kirk brings his "Yummy" bartenders and Hep Alien reunites. After Lorelai sees a picture of Rory with April, she drowns her sorrows in eight shots of tequila, subsequently giving a toast in front of the entire wedding announcing to not save the date for June 3rd. Rory gets a call that Logan has been in a terrible accident.

Best Line: "Prop her up; she hates to get pillow face."

Episode 6.20: "Super Cool Party People" (April 25, 2006)

Rory stays by Logan's side in the hospital and calls Mitchum to demand that he also come. Luke throws April a birthday party and thinks he has it covered, but it is a disaster, and Lorelai comes to save the day (and the party) with an impromptu makeover, Bonne Bell Lip Smackers, and the girls' first introduction to Molly Ringwald in the classic '80s film *Pretty in Pink*. When Anna finds out about the party, she is royally upset with Luke for letting a stranger (aka his fiancée, Lorelai) spend the night with all of the girls. Lorelai goes to see Anna to explain, but Anna doesn't want Lorelai in April's life until after she and Luke are married.

Best Line: "Jackson's so getting under my bra tonight."

Episode 6.21: "Driving Miss Gilmore" (May 2, 2006)

Emily gets botched Lasik eye surgery, and Lorelai comes to her rescue. Rory continues to be Logan's caretaker (aka his mom) when he leaves the hospital. Lorelai is avoiding Luke. Jackson finds marijuana in his garden but getting rid of it is more difficult than he and Sookie imagined. Liz informs Luke that she is pregnant but that T.J. left her. When Luke confronts T.J. and wants to fight him, T.J. informs Luke that Liz actually kicked him out of the house. Lorelai finds out that Emily and Richard are not looking for a house in Stars Hollow for themselves but as a wedding gift for Luke and her. Lorelai is touched and then reveals to her mom that the wedding is not going to happen.

Best Line: "Everyone knows ugly men make the best doctors."

Episode 6.22: "Partings" (May 9, 2006)

Taylor is bothered by the recent influx of traveling musicians playing in Stars Hollow trying to be discovered after the town's Troubadour is picked to open for Neil Young, even though he only made "$700 and got booed." Logan graduates from Yale and leaves for London. Lorelai is still avoiding Luke. At Friday night dinner, Richard and Emily reveal they have made a donation to Yale in Rory's name and Rory will have her own building: the Rory Gilmore Astronomy Building. Emily also invites Christopher and Carolyn (aka Lynnie) Bates to dinner as a setup. They do not hit it off, but Lorelai has an impromptu therapy session with her (Lynnie is a psychologist) in the backseat of Lynnie's car. Inspired by Lynnie's (good) advice, Lorelai asks Luke to elope with her, but he isn't ready because of April. She breaks up with Luke and finds her way to Christopher's for comfort and ends up in bed with him . . . of course.

Best Line: "Every now and then I just feel the need to reenact certain key scenes from *Purple Rain*, you know, for a captive audience."

Episode 7.1: "The Long Morrow" (September 26, 2006)

The start of the final season and the conclusion of our choosing a "Best Line." Lorelai does not regret her decision to cancel the wedding to Luke but does regret her booty call with Christopher. Rory tries to puzzle out a rocket riddle. Lorelai has particularly cute jammies in this episode.

Episode 7.2: "That's What You Get, Folks, for Makin' Whoopie" (October 3, 2006)

Luke punches Christopher and feels "better." Lane refuses to have sex ever again and then finds out she is pregnant. Rory finds out Lorelai slept with Christopher.

Episode 7.3: "Lorelai's First Cotillion" (October 10, 2006)

Emily starts a training school for little girls and throws a mini-cotillion, which Michel makes Lorelai take him to. Rory learns to sext . . . once Logan explains how her phone works. Good thing she's pretty. Lorelai calls Christopher.

Episode 7.4: "'S Wonderful, 'S Marvelous" (October 17, 2006)

Christopher plans a private drive-in movie date to watch *Funny Face*, and then Lorelai gets a call from Emily from jail. Rory meets Olivia and Lucy at the art show she's covering for the paper.

Episode 7.5: "The Great Stink" (October 24, 2006)

Stars Hollow is stinky from an overturned pickle truck. Christopher tells Lorelai that Sherry wants to reconnect with Gigi, and Lorelai suggests that Christopher reconsider the plan to make this happen. They fight; they make up. Logan surprises Rory with a visit, and Rory meets his coworkers. She gets jealous of the pretty one.

Episode 7.6: "Go Bulldogs!" (November 7, 2006)

Christopher and Lorelai attend Yale's Parents' Weekend, and he tries to overcompensate and make up for lost time, getting Rory's entire newspaper staff drunk before a big story breaks.

Episode 7.7: "French Twist" (November 14, 2006)

Christopher and Lorelai take Gigi to Paris and end up eloping. Rory starts to panic about her future. So do Lane and Zack, when they find out they are having twins. Mrs. Kim prepares to move in. Rory finds out Lucy's boyfriend is Marty, and he pretends not to know her.

Episode 7.8: "Introducing Lorelai Planetarium" (November 21, 2006)

Rory is upset when she finds out her parents are married. Logan invites her to a party, and Rory writes a mean story about it. They make up, but Rory decides to move out anyway. April gets appendicitis, and Luke calls Lorelai.

Episode 7.9: "Knit, People, Knit!" (November 28, 2006)

Lorelai worries that Stars Hollow is not warming up to Christopher. Christopher cuts a knit-a-thon short when he donates the remaining money. Rory confronts Marty, and Marty hits on her. Luke finally grows a pair.

Episode 7.10: "Merry Fisticuffs" (December 5, 2006)

Christopher sees Luke and Lorelai together. Logan is a jerk, this time because he gets jealous that Marty still has a thing for Rory and he tells Lucy that Rory and Marty have been lying to her. Christopher wants a baby, but Lorelai wants to talk about it first. Emily advises Lorelai to compromise. Luke and Christopher have a middle-aged man fight in the town square.

Episode 7.11: "Santa's Secret Stuff" (January 23, 2007)

Luke asks Lorelai to write a character reference, which she struggles with until she and Rory run into Luke with April at the mall. However, she hides it from Christopher. Lane comes to terms with becoming a mom.

Episode 7.12: "To Whom It May Concern" (January 30, 2007)

Jackson didn't get the vasectomy (Melissa McCarthy was pregnant in real life), so Sookie finds out she is pregnant with surprise baby number 3. Christopher finds the letter, and Luke wins his case. Richard falls to the floor in front of Rory's class.

Episode 7.13: "I'd Rather Be in Philadelphia" (February 6, 2007)

Richard has a heart attack and needs surgery. Logan shows up, Luke shows up, but no Christopher . . . until the end, when he sees Lorelai talking to Luke.

Episode 7.14: "Farewell, My Pet" (February 13, 2007)

Logan explains how crushes work. Seriously, how does this girl get dressed in the morning without instructions? Michel plans a funeral for Chin Chin. Christopher and Lorelai discuss their relationship, ultimately deciding on divorce.

Episode 7.15: "I'm a Kayak, Hear Me Roar" (February 20, 2007)

Lorelai breaks the news to Rory, who is not surprised. Lorelai avoids telling her parents about Christopher and helps Emily take care of Richard. Lorelai and Emily have a drunken heart-to-heart that goes better drunk than sober the next morning. Emily admires Lorelai's independence. Rory throws Logan every birthday party he missed out on.

Episode 7.16: "Will You Be My Lorelai Gilmore?" (February 27, 2007)

Lorelai mediates a fight between Mrs. Kim and Lane, prior to throwing the babies shower. Logan finally tells Rory that he lost everybody's money on the Internet company and then takes off to Vegas with Finn and Colin.

Episode 7.17: "Gilmore Girls Only" (March 6, 2007)

Lorelai and Rory decide to attend Mia's wedding, and Emily invites herself along. Emily continues to resent the close relationship Mia shares with the girls. Logan shows up unexpectedly and apologizes. Lane has the twins after asking Luke to be the godfather.

Episode 7.18: "Hay Bale Maze" (April 17, 2007)

Logan comes to visit Stars Hollow, and a maze acts as a metaphor for the various paths ahead for Rory, Logan, Lorelai, and Luke. Lorelai and Luke come to terms with one another, and Rory decides to take a risk and turns down a job at a paper to hold out for an internship that she hopes to get with *The New York Times*.

Episode 7.19: "It's Just like Riding a Bike" (April 24, 2007)

Luke helps Lorelai shop for a car, and they get into a fight. Rory does not get the internship. Doyle won't let Paris break up with him.

Episode 7.20: "Lorelai? Lorelai?" (May 1, 2007)

Lorelai sings her heart out to Luke in a karaoke song. Logan asks Lorelai for her permission to ask Rory to marry him.

Episode 7.21: "Unto the Breach" (May 8, 2007)

Logan proposes at the party Richard and Emily throw Rory prior to graduation, and Rory tells him she has to think about it. Lorelai isn't sure what to do about the karaoke serenade. At graduation, Rory turns down Logan's proposal.

Episode 7.22: "Bon Voyage" (February 22, 2007)

Rory gets a job reporting on Obama's campaign. The town gathers to say goodbye. Lorelai and Luke kiss after she finds out he saved the day to make the party happen.

NOTES

INTRODUCTION

1. Jennifer Crusie, "Introduction: Speaking of the Gilmore Girls . . ." In *Coffee at Luke's: An Unauthorized* Gilmore Girls *Gabfest*, ed. Jennifer Crusie with Leah Wilson (Dallas: Benbella Books, 2007), 1.

2. Amy Plitt, "10 Things You Need to Know about the Revival," *Rolling Stone*, 21 November 2016, http://www.rollingstone.com/tv/news/10-things-you-need-to-know-about-gilmore-girls-revival-w449485.

3. James Poniewozik, "How I Chose the List," *Time*, 6 September 2007, http://time.com/collection-post/3087799/how-i-chose-the-list/.

4. Alan Sepinwall, "Best of the '00s in TV: Best Comedies," *NJ.com*, 21 December 2009, http://www.nj.com/entertainment/tv/index.ssf/2009/12/best_of_the_00s_in_tv_best_com.html.

5. James Poniewozik and Jeanne McDowell, "Postnuclear Explosion," *Time* 156, no. 19 (6 November 2000).

6. Stacia Fleegal, "Like Mother-Daughter, Like Daughter-Mother." In *"Gilmore Girls" and the Politics of Identity: Essays on Family and Feminism in the Television Series*, ed. Ritch Calvin (Jefferson, NC: McFarland, 2008), 144.

7. Joy Press, *Stealing the Show* (New York: Atria Books, 2018), 76.

8. Press, *Stealing the Show*, 76.

9. Lauren Graham, *Talking as Fast as I Can: From* Gilmore Girls *to* Gilmore Girls *(and Everything in Between)* (New York: Ballantine Books, 2016).

10. Anna Leszkiewicz, "'People Are Born Evil': The Unlikely Cynicism of Gilmore Girls Creator Amy Sherman-Palladino," *New Statesman America*, 16 November 2017, https://www.newstatesman.com/culture/tv-radio/2017/11/amy-sherman-palladino-interview-dan-gilmore-girls-marvelous-mrs-maisel.

11. Miellyn Fitzwater, "My Three Dads." In *Coffee at Luke's: An Unauthorized* Gilmore Girls *Gabfest*, ed. Jennifer Crusie (Dallas: Benbella Books, 2007), 70.

12. Lili Loofbourow, "What *Gilmore Girls* Gets Right about Money and Love," *The Cut*, 3 October 2014, https://www.thecut.com/2014/10/what-gilmore-girls-shows-us-about-money-and-love.html.

13. Press, *Stealing the Show*, 87.

14. Bill Keveney, "Mailer's 'Gilmore Girls' Guest Shot Is a Family Affair," *USA Today*, 24 September 2004.

15. Crusie, "Introduction," 2.

16. Press, *Stealing the Show*.

17. Christina Radish, "Amy Sherman-Palladino and Dan Palladino on the Return of 'Gilmore Girls' and the Problem with Network TV," *Collider*, 24 November 2016, http://collider.com/amy-sherman-palladino-dan-palladino-gilmore-girls-a-year-in-the-life-interview/.

18. Press, *Stealing the Show*, 86.

19. Graham, *Talking as Fast as I Can*.

20. Lara C. Stache, *Breaking Bad: A Cultural History* (New York: Rowman & Littlefield, 2017).

21. Press, *Stealing the Show*, 97.

22. Graham, *Talking as Fast as I Can*, 85.

23. Press, *Stealing the Show*, 93.

24. Press, *Stealing the Show*, 81.

1. MOTHERS AND DAUGHTERS

1. Ginia Bellafante, "Mother and Daughter, Each Coming into Her Own," *The New York Times*, 17 May 2007.

2. Lili Loofbourow, "What *Gilmore Girls* Gets Right about Money and Love," *The Cut*, 3 October 2014, https://www.thecut.com/2014/10/what-gilmore-girls-shows-us-about-money-and-love.html.

3. Bellafante, "Mother and Daughter."

4. Mary Chase, "Gilmore Girls' Math," *AmyandMary.com*, 26 October 2018, https://amyandmary.com/2018/10/26/gilmore-girls-math/?fbclid=IwAR2ZbbPvGVKqr56-OvZsQ7s4iDhICERHVJoLkYdy0fMgjgBpN_YOa-t4Y48.

5. Anna Leszkiewicz, "'People are Born Evil': The Unlikely Cynicism of Gilmore Girls Creator Amy Sherman-Palladino," *New Statesman America*, https://www.newstatesman.com/culture/tv-radio/2017/11/amy-sherman-palladino-interview-dan-gilmore-girls-marvelous-mrs-maisel.

6. Leszkiewicz, "'People Are Born Evil.'"

7. Allison Hope Weiner, "Golden Girls," *Entertainment Weekly*, 22 March 2002.

8. Pamela Hill Nettleton, "Table for Two: *Gilmore Girls*' Lorelai and Rory Legitimize Single Mothers and Their Children as Family," *U.S. Catholic*, December 2016.

9. Bruce Fretts, "Happy Gilmore," *Entertainment Weekly*, 29 September 2000.

10. Lauren Valenti, "Lorelai Gilmore's 'Vicious Trollop' Lip Color Can Now Be Yours," *Marie Claire*, 3 November 2016, https://www.marieclaire.com/beauty/news/a23371/vicious-trollop-lip-color/.

11. Ken Tucker, "Gilmore Girls," *Entertainment Weekly*, 11 March 2007, https://ew.com/article/2007/05/11/gilmore-girls-2/.

12. Loofbourow, "What *Gilmore Girls* Gets Right."

13. Jessica Shaw, "Mother of Reinvention," *Entertainment Weekly* 806, 11 February 2005.

14. Janine Hiddlestone, "Mothers, Daughters, and Gilmore Girls." In *Coffee at Luke's: An Unauthorized* Gilmore Girls *Gabfest*, ed. Jennifer Crusie (Dallas: Benbella Books, 2007), 41.

2. FATHERHOOD

1. James Poniewozik and Jeanne McDowell, "Postnuclear Explosion," *Time*, 6 November 2000.

2. Miellyn Fitzwater, "My Three Dads." In *Coffee at Luke's: An Unauthorized* Gilmore Girls *Gabfest*, ed. Jennifer Crusie (Dallas: Benbella Books, 2007), 69.

3. John Fetto, "Wholesome Goodness: An Advertiser-Advocated, 'Family-Friendly' TV Show Manages Its Way into a Network's Fall Lineup," *American Demographics*, 1 August 2000.

4. Catherine Helen Palczewski, Victoria Pruin DeFrancisco, and Danielle Dick McGeough, *Gender in Communication: A Critical Introduction*, 3rd ed. (Los Angeles: Sage Publications, 2019), 142.

5. "Bringing Up Rory: Father Figures in Rory's Life," *Reddit.com*, https://www.reddit.com/r/GilmoreGirls/comments/52fm4z/bringing_up_rory_father_figures_in_rorys_life/.

6. Fitzwater, "My Three Dads," 70.

7. Heather L. Hundley and Sara E. Hayden, eds., *Mediated Moms: Contemporary Challenges to the Motherhood Myth* (New York: Peter Lang Publishing, 2016), 1.

8. Palczewski, DeFrancisco, and McGeough, *Gender in Communication*, 147.

9. Palczewski, DeFrancisco, and McGeough, *Gender in Communication*, 141–42.

10. Alysse Elhage, "Growing Up with a Single Mom Isn't like Life on *Gilmore Girls*," *Verily*, 4 November 2014, https://verilymag.com/2014/11/girlmore-girls-single-motherhood.

11. Elhage, "Growing Up."

3. ROMANCE

1. Allison Pittman, "Digger Stiles: A Man for One Season," *MelissaTagg.com*, 18 July 2014, http://www.melissatagg.com/giveaway/gilmore-guys-digger.

2. Mary Chase, "Gilmore Girls' Math," *AmyandMary.com*, 26 October 2018, https://amyandmary.com/2018/10/26/gilmore-girls-math/?fbclid=IwAR2ZbbPvGVKqr56-OvZsQ7s4iDhICERHVJoLkYdy0fMgjgBpN_YOa-t4Y48.

3. Jimmie Manning, "But Luke and Lorelai Belong Together! Relationships, Social Control, and Gilmore Girls." In *Screwball Television: Critical Perspectives on "Gilmore Girls,"* eds. David Scott Diffrient with David Lavery (Syracuse, NY: Syracuse University Press, 2010), 303.

4. In full disclosure, one of us (Lara) is Team Jess and one of us (Rachel) is Team Rory . . . no man (so far) is good enough.

5. Lili Loofbourow, "The Decline and Fall of the Gilmore Girls," *The Week*, 1 December 2016, https://theweek.com/articles/664566/decline-fall-gilmore-girls.

6. Actually about midway through season 1, because in the beginning of the series, Dean was written as more of a motorcycle-riding, leather-coat-wearing bad boy and someone who could recommend Hunter Thompson to Rory (Episode 1.8, "Love & War & Snow").

7. Joy Press, *Stealing the Show* (New York: Atria Books, 2018), 85.

8. Pittman, "Digger Stiles."

9. Virginia Heffernan, "A Series Changes Horses, and the Ride Gets Bumpy," *The New York Times*, 7 November 2006, https://www.nytimes.com/2006/11/07/arts/television/07heff.html.

10. Heffernan, "A Series Changes."

11. Esther Zuckerman, "*Gilmore Girls*: A Not-So-Modest Proposal," *Entertainment Weekly*, 24 October 2014.

12. Sabienna Bowman, "The One 'Gilmore Girls' Revival Series Theory about Rory's Love Life You Probably Haven't Considered," *Bustle.com*, 5 February 2016, https://www.bustle.com/articles/139829-the-one-gilmore-girls-revival-series-theory-about-rorys-love-life-you-probably-havent-considered.

4. FRIENDSHIP

1. Sabienna Bowman, "What Your Favorite 'Gilmore Girls' Friendship Says about You," *Bustle.com*, 26 April 2016, https://www.bustle.com/articles/156534-what-your-favorite-gilmore-girls-friendship-says-about-you.
2. Mary Chase, "Gilmore Girls' Math," *AmyandMary.com*, 26 October 2018, https://amyandmary.com/2018/10/26/gilmore-girls-math/?fbclid=IwAR2ZbbPvGVKqr56-OvZsQ7s4iDhICERHVJoLkYdy0fMgjgBpN_YOa-t4Y48.
3. Nathan Phan and Sania Syed, "Teens Aren't Fairly Portrayed in Media," *The Princeton Summer Journal*, 11 August 2014, https://princetonsummerjournal.com/2014/08/11/teens-arent-fairly-portrayed-in-media/.
4. Steven McCornack, *Reflect and Relate: An Introduction to Interpersonal Communication* (Boston: Bedford/St. Martin's, 2013), 357.
5. McCornack, *Reflect and Relate*, 357.
6. McCornack, *Reflect and Relate*, 357.
7. Phan and Syed, "Teens Aren't Fairly Portrayed."
8. McCornack, *Reflect and Relate*, 300.
9. Suzannah Weiss, "4 Problems with How We're Talking about 'Female Friendships,'" *Everyday Feminism*, 23 March 2016, https://everydayfeminism.com/2016/03/female-friendship-trope/.
10. McCornack, *Reflect and Relate*, 370.
11. Weiss, "4 Problems."
12. Stephanie Whiteside, "When Paris Met Rory." In *Coffee at Luke's: An Unauthorized* Gilmore Girls *Gabfest*, ed. Jennifer Crusie (Dallas: Benbella Books, 2007), 21.
13. McCornack, *Reflect and Relate*, 368.
14. McCornack, *Reflect and Relate*, 369–70.
15. McCornack, *Reflect and Relate*, 362.
16. Whiteside, "When Paris Met Rory," 22.
17. McCornack, *Reflect and Relate*, 370.
18. McCornack, *Reflect and Relate*, 362.
19. Catherine Helen Palczewski, Victoria Pruin DeFrancisco, and Danielle Dick McGeough, *Gender in Communication: A Critical Introduction*, 3rd ed. (Los Angeles: Sage Publications, 2019).

20. Abigail Radnor, "'It's Sunny and Safe': Why *Gilmore Girls* Is Perfect Comfort TV," *The Guardian*, 5 November 2016, https://www.theguardian.com/tv-and-radio/2016/nov/05/sunny-safe-gilmore-girls-comfort-tv.

5. FEMINISM

1. Meghan Giannotta, "'Gilmore Girls' Creator Amy Sherman-Palladino: It's Absurd to Say Show Isn't Feminist," *AMNetwork.com*, 15 November 2017, https://www.amny.com/entertainment/gilmore-girls-feminism-1.14989877.
2. James Poniewozik, "6 DVDs Great for a Chuckle," *Time*, 6 June 2005.
3. Episode 1.18, "The Third Lorelai."
4. Giannotta, "'Gilmore Girls' Creator."
5. "The Best and Worst of 2000: TV," *Time* 156, no. 25, 18 December 2000.
6. Lili Loofbourow, "What *Gilmore Girls* Gets Right about Money and Love," *The Cut*, 3 October 2014, https://www.thecut.com/2014/10/what-gilmore-girls-shows-us-about-money-and-love.html.
7. Sharon Ross, "'Tough Enough': Female Friendship and Heroism in *Xena* and *Buffy*." In *Action Chicks: New Images of Tough Women in Popular Culture*, ed. Sherrie A. Inness (New York: Palgrave Macmillan, 2004).
8. Joe Levy, "Gilmore Girls," *Rolling Stone*, 30 August 2001.
9. A. J. Jacobs, "*Gilmore Girls* is the Best Show on TV for Men," *Esquire*, October 2005.
10. Jennifer Baumgardner and Amy Richards, *Manifesta: Young Women, Feminism, and the Future* (New York: Farrar, Straus and Giroux, 2010).
11. Abigail Radnor, "'It's Sunny and Safe': Why *Gilmore Girls* Is Perfect Comfort TV," *The Guardian*, 5 November 2016, https://www.theguardian.com/tv-and-radio/2016/nov/05/sunny-safe-gilmore-girls-comfort-tv.
12. Ken Tucker, "A Literary Legend Pays a Visit to 'Gilmore Girls,'" *Entertainment Weekly*, 15 October 2004.
13. Chimamanda Ngozi Adichie, *We Should All Be Feminists* (New York: Anchor Books, 2014).
14. Roxane Gay, *Bad Feminist* (New York: Harper Perennial, 2014).
15. Episode 1.14, "That Damn Donna Reed."
16. Lara Stache, "Sexuality in Popular Culture: Is It 'All about That Bass'?" In *Contemporary Studies of Sexuality and Communication*, ed. J. Manning and C. Noland (Dubuque, IA: Kendall Hunt, 2016).
17. Danielle Nussbaum, "Lauren Graham: Why *Gilmore Girls* Is Feminist," *Entertainment Weekly*, 8 September 2016, http://www.ew.com/article/2016/09/08/lauren-graham-gilmore-girls-feminist/.
18. Gay, *Bad Feminist*, xi.

19. *Gilmore Girls: A Year in the Life*, Episode 1.4, "Fall."

20. Although, for us, the most anti-feminist part of the show revolves around when Lane Kim has a horrible experience the first time she has sex, vows never to have sex again, and then finds out she is pregnant with twins from that one awful sandy encounter. It is not this moment per se, but the fact that during the revival, she has no other kids and therefore there is no indication that she and Zack did ever have sex again. We suppose it is less "anti-feminist" and more just a huge bummer. We hope Lane and Zack are both happy with their sex life, whatever that may look like.

6. POPULAR CULTURE

1. Maura Quint, "Your Friend's 'Gilmore Girls' Obsession, Explained," *Thrillist Entertainment*, 22 November 2016, https://www.thrillist.com/entertainment/nation/gilmore-girls-why-are-your-friends-obsessed-with-an-old-wb-show.

2. Anna Leszkiewicz, "'People are Born Evil': The Unlikely Cynicism of Gilmore Girls Creator Amy Sherman-Palladino," *New Statesman America*, 16 November 2017, https://www.newstatesman.com/culture/tv-radio/2017/11/amy-sherman-palladino-interview-dan-gilmore-girls-marvelous-mrs-maisel.

3. Allison Hope Weiner, "Golden Girls," *Entertainment Weekly*, 22 March 2002.

4. Rose Maura Lorre, "*Gilmore Girls*' Pop-Culture References, by the Numbers," *Vulture*, 1 December 2015, https://www.vulture.com/2015/12/gilmore-girls-pop-culture-references-by-the-numbers.html.

5. Lorre. "*Gilmore Girls*' Pop-Culture References."

6. Lauren Graham, *Talking as Fast as I Can: From* Gilmore Girls *to* Gilmore Girls *(and Everything in Between)* (New York: Ballantine Books, 2016), 60.

7. Graham, *Talking*, 60.

8. Graham, *Talking*, 61.

9. Graham, *Talking*, 63–64.

10. *Media and Girls*, Media Smarts: Canada's Centre for Digital and Media Literacy, http://mediasmarts.ca/gender-representation/women-and-girls/media-and-girls.

11. Brenna Ehrlich, "11 Musical Moments That Prove 'Gilmore Girls' Was the Most Hipster Show on TV," *MTV.com*, 12 September 2014.

12. Sadaf Ahsan, "'It's a Lifestyle, It's a Religion': How Gilmore Girls Has Transcended Generations, Gender and Genre," *National Post*, 24 November

2016, https://nationalpost.com/entertainment/television/its-a-lifestyle-its-a-religion-how-gilmore-girls-has-transcended-generations-gender-and-genre.

13. Melissa Locker, "Monkey Gone to Heaven," *Rolling Stone*, 7 May 2012, https://www.rollingstone.com/music/music-news/monkey-gone-to-heaven-87722/.

14. Shannon Carlin, "23 'Gilmore Girls' Pop Culture References You Totally Forgot About," *Bustle.com*, 16 November 2017, https://www.bustle.com/p/23-gilmore-girls-pop-culture-references-you-totally-forgot-about-77015.

15. Meredith Ochs, "The New Pornographers, a 'Real' Supergroup," *NPR*, 25 October 2007, https://www.npr.org/templates/story/story.php?storyId=15630417.

16. Carl E. Pickhardt, "The Challenge of Mothering an Adolescent Daughter," *Psychology Today*, 6 December 2010, https://www.psychologytoday.com/us/blog/surviving-your-childs-adolescence/201012/the-challenge-mothering-adolescent-daughter.

17. Bruce Fretts, "Happy Gilmore," *Entertainment Weekly*, 29 September 2000.

18. Lily Kosner, "10 Musical Moments All 'Gilmore Girls' Fans Should Never Forget," *AXS.com*, 2016, https://www.axs.com/10-musical-moments-all-gilmore-girls-fans-should-never-forget-103603.

19. https://rateyourmusic.com/board_message?message_id=349472.

20. https://www.reddit.com/r/GilmoreGirls/comments/7x6jv8/music_you_like_that_the_gilmores_hate_music_the/.

21. Jeff Finkle, "5 Reasons 'Gilmore Girls' Isn't Just for Girls," *Goodmen-project.com*, 16 December 2016, https://goodmenproject.com/arts/5-reasons-gilmore-girls-isnt-just-for-girls-dg/.

22. Ehrlich, "11 Musical Moments."

23. https://www.rottentomatoes.com/m/moment_by_moment.

24. Carlin, "23 'Gilmore Girls' Pop Culture References."

25. Carlin, "23 'Gilmore Girls' Pop Culture References."

26. https://www.listchallenges.com/rory-gilmore-reading-challenge.

27. "Alexis Bledel," *Biography*, March 2003.

28. Emma Dibdin, "The Definitive Reading List for Each of Rory Gilmore's Boyfriends," *Elle.com*, 16 November 2016, https://www.elle.com/culture/movies-tv/news/a40817/gilmore-girls-boyfriends-reading-list/.

29. Kevin Porter, "The 15 Best Pop Culture References in 'Gilmore Girls,'" *Elle.com*, 1 November 2016, https://www.elle.com/culture/movies-tv/g29070/best-gilmore-girls-pop-culture-references/.

30. Carlin, "23 'Gilmore Girls' Pop Culture References."

31. Andrew Husband, "'Gilmore Girls' Celebrated Smart People as Celebrities When Other Shows Wouldn't," *UPROXX.com*, 23 November 2016, https://uproxx.com/tv/gilmore-girls-celebrity-cameos/.
32. Husband, "'Gilmore Girls' Celebrated Smart People."
33. Husband, "'Gilmore Girls' Celebrated Smart People."
34. Graham, *Talking*, 61.
35. Ahsan, "'It's a Lifestyle.'"
36. Pamela Hill Nettleton, "Table for Two: *Gilmore Girls*' Lorelai and Rory Legitimize Single Mothers and Their Children as Family," *U.S. Catholic*, December 2016.
37. Weiner, "Golden Girls."
38. A. J. Jacobs, *Man at His Best: Opinions* "*Gilmore Girls* Is the Best Show on TV for Men." *Esquire*, October 2005.
39. Jacobs, "*Gilmore Girls*."
40. Jonathan Dee, "The Myth of '18 to 34,'" *The New York Times*, 13 October 2002.
41. https://www.listchallenges.com/movies-mentioned-in-the-gilmore-girls.
42. https://letterboxd.com/lesaladino/list/every-movie-referenced-watched-in-gilmore/.
43. Husband, "'Gilmore Girls' Celebrated Smart People."
44. Abigail Radnor, "'It's Sunny and Safe': Why *Gilmore Girls* Is Perfect Comfort TV," *The Guardian*, 5 November 2016, https://www.theguardian.com/tv-and-radio/2016/nov/05/sunny-safe-gilmore-girls-comfort-tv.
45. Todd K. Platts, "Locating Zombies in the Sociology of Popular Culture," *Sociology Compass* 7, no. 7 (July 2013): 547–60.
46. Barry Brummett, *Rhetoric in Popular Culture*, 4th ed. (Los Angeles: Sage Publications, 2015.
47. Ahsan, "'It's a Lifestyle.'"
48. Ahsan, "'It's a Lifestyle.'"
49. Ahsan, "'It's a Lifestyle.'"
50. Ken Tucker, "Goodbye 'Girls,'" *Entertainment Weekly*, 18 May 2007.

7. ISSUES OF CLASS

1. Todd VanDerWerff, "*Gilmore Girls* Is Slyly Smart about Class and How Isolating Money Can Be," *Vox.com*, 1 December 2016, https://www.vox.com/culture/2016/12/1/13786732/gilmore-girls-netflix-year-life-class-money.
2. Lili Loofbourow, "What *Gilmore Girls* Gets Right about Money and Love," *The Cut*, 3 October 2014, https://www.thecut.com/2014/10/what-gilmore-girls-shows-us-about-money-and-love.html.

3. Loofbourow, "What *Gilmore Girls* Gets Right."

4. VanDerWerff, "*Gilmore Girls* Is Slyly Smart."

5. Emily Marcus, "*Gilmore Girls*' Matt Czuchry: Fans Called Me a 'Real A-hole' for Playing Logan Huntzberger," *US Weekly*, 18 January 2018, https://www.usmagazine.com/entertainment/news/gilmore-girls-matt-czuchry-i-was-called-an-a-hole-for-playing-logan/.

6. Jason Stiles is a big exception, which we talk about in the third chapter of this book (on romantic relationships), and Christopher shares a history and progeny with Lorelai, which will always cement them together.

7. Lili Loofbourow, "The Decline and Fall of the Gilmore Girls," *The Week*, 1 December 2016, https://theweek.com/articles/664566/decline-fall-gilmore-girls.

8. Loofbourow, "The Decline and Fall."

9. Ginia Bellafante, "Mother and Daughter, Each Coming into Her Own," *The New York Times*, 17 May 2007.

8. SMALL-TOWN LIVIN'

1. Ken Tucker, "The Good 'Girls,'" *Entertainment Weekly*, 4 April 2003.

2. Maura Quint, "Your Friend's 'Gilmore Girls' Obsession, Explained," *Thrillist Entertainment*, 22 November 2016, https://www.thrillist.com/entertainment/nation/gilmore-girls-why-are-your-friends-obsessed-with-an-old-wb-show.

3. https://www.gilmoregirlsfanfest.com.

4. Joy Press, *Stealing the Show* (New York: Atria Books, 2018), 73. "Gilmore Girls Getaway: Visit the 'Real' Stars Hollow, Connecticut," *Ctvisit.com*, 2018, http://www.ctvisit.com/getaway/gilmore-girls-getaway.

5. Brian Alexander, "What America Is Losing as Its Small Towns Struggle," *The Atlantic*, 18 October 2017, https://www.theatlantic.com/business/archive/2017/10/small-town-economies-culture/543138/.

6. Alexander, "What America Is Losing."

7. Katherine J. Cramer, "The Great American Fallout: How Small Towns Came to Resent Cities," *The Guardian*, 19 June 2017, https://www.theguardian.com/cities/2017/jun/19/americas-great-fallout-rural-areas-resent-cities-republican-democrat.

8. Press, *Stealing the Show*, 77.

9. "Gilmore Girls Getaway."

10. Johnni Macke, "The 18 Best Businesses in Stars Hollow from 'Gilmore Girls,' Ranked Once and for All," *Hellogiggles.com*, 23 April 2016, https://hellogiggles.com/lifestyle/businesses-gilmore-girls-ranked/.

11. Berrak Sarikaya, "What 'Gilmore Girls' Taught Me about Business," *Amplifyyour.biz*, 29 November 2016, http://www.amplifyyour.biz/gilmore-girls-business-lessons/.

12. "Businesses in Stars Hollow." *Reddit.com*, https://www.reddit.com/r/GilmoreGirls/comments/76tjzv/businesses_in_starshollow/.

13. Quint, "Your Friend's 'Gilmore Girls' Obsession."

14. Annie Zaleski, "'Gilmore Girls' Town Troubadour Grant-Lee Phillips Will Return to Stars Hollow: 'It Was Such a Subversive Show,'" *Salon.com*, 11 February 2016, https://www.salon.com/2016/02/10/gilmore_girls_town_troubadour_grant_lee_phillips_will_return_to_stars_hollow_it_was_such_a_subversive_show.

15. Tucker, "The Good 'Girls.'"

16. Laura Bradley, "Where You Lead: How *Gilmore Girls* Found Its Brightest Stars," *Vanity Fair*, 23 November 2016, https://www.vanityfair.com/hollywood/2016/11/gilmore-girls-lauren-graham-alexis-bledel-casting-interviews.

17. Paige Gawley, "All 62 of Kirk's Odd Jobs on 'Gilmore Girls,'" *Decider.com*, 25 March 2016.

18. Gawley, "All 62."

CONCLUSION

1. Jessica Shaw, "Mother of Reinvention: 'Gilmore Girls' Creator Amy Sherman-Palladino Explains How She Pulled Her Show out of a Slump," *Entertainment Weekly*, 11 February 2005.

2. Emily Yahr, "More 'Gilmore Girls'? Actually Netflix, We're Good," *The Washington Post*, 8 March 2017, https://www.washingtonpost.com/news/arts-and-entertainment/wp/2017/03/08/more-gilmore-girls-actually-netflix-were-good/?utm_term=.a91e3b139004.

3. Ashani Jodha, "42 Big Questions Ultimate 'Gilmore Girls' Fans Want the Netflix Revival to Answer," *Bustle.com*, 12 February 2016, https://www.bustle.com/articles/139842-42-big-questions-ultimate-gilmore-girls-fans-want-the-netflix-revival-to-answer.

4. Jodha, "42 Big Questions."

5. Yahr, "More 'Gilmore Girls'?"

6. Nicole Villeneuve, "Netflix Updates 'Gilmore Girls' Fans on the Possibility of More Episodes," *Brit + Co*, 30 July 2018, https://www.brit.co/netflix-gilmore-girls-more-episodes-update/.

7. Jethro Nededog, "Netflix's 'Gilmore Girls' Revival Is Almost Everything Fans Wanted from It," *Business Insider*, 23 November 2016, https://www.businessinsider.com/netflix-gilmore-girls-review-2016-11.

8. Mark Sweney, "Netflix and Amazon Become More Popular than Pay-TV Services," *The Guardian*, 17 July 2018, https://www.theguardian.com/media/2018/jul/18/netflix-and-amazon-become-more-popular-than-pay-tv-services.

9. Sweney, "Netflix and Amazon."

10. Lauren Graham, *Talking as Fast as I Can: From* Gilmore Girls *to* Gilmore Girls *(and Everything in Between)* (New York: Ballantine Books, 2016), 190–91.

11. Yahr, "More 'Gilmore Girls'?"

12. Constance Grady, "Gilmore Girls on Netflix: What You Need to Know about the Revival," *Vox.com*, 25 October 2016, https://www.vox.com/2016/4/13/11410986/watch-gilmore-girls-revival-netflix-cast.

13. Nededog, "Netflix's 'Gilmore Girls' Revival."

14. Patricia Garcia, "11 Things in *Gilmore Girls: A Year in the Life* That Made Absolutely No Sense," *Vogue*, 28 November 2016, https://www.vogue.com/article/gilmore-girls-a-year-in-the-life-nonsense.

15. Jennifer Maas, "'Gilmore Girls: A Year in the Life': 15 Things Still Bothering Fans a Year Later (Photos)," *The Wrap*, 25 November 2017, https://www.thewrap.com/gilmore-girls-a-year-in-the-life-anniversary-things-fans-hate/.

16. Samantha Highfill, "Gilmore Girls: Rory's Ending Explained," *Entertainment Weekly*, 28 November 2016, https://ew.com/article/2016/11/28/gilmore-girls-year-life-rory-ending/.

17. Kate Stanhope, "'Gilmore Girls' Bosses Discuss Final Four Words, Rory Criticism and Possible Future Installments," *Hollywood Reporter*, 1 December 2016, https://www.hollywoodreporter.com/live-feed/gilmore-girls-revival-creator-final-four-words-951693.

18. Shaw, "'Gilmore Girls' Creator."

19. Eleanor Bley Griffiths, "Gilmore Girls Creator Amy Sherman-Palladino Has 'Freedom' to Make More When Timing Is Right," *RadioTimes*, 10 November 2017, https://www.radiotimes.com/news/on-demand/2018-12-21/gilmore-girls-sequel/.

20. Emily Wang, "Keiko Agena Says There's Enough Story for Another *Gilmore Girls* Revival," *Glamour*, 14 September 2018, https://www.glamour.com/story/keiko-agena-another-gilmore-girls-revival.

21. Lilith Hardi Lupica, "Lauren Graham Confirms We May Never Get the Answers We Need from Gilmore Girls," *Vogu*e, 6 April 2018, https://www.vogue.com.au/culture/features/lauren-graham-confirms-we-may-never-get-the-answers-we-need-from-gilmore-girls/news-story/0286e4521ae72482

dd66bbfa4ff3a4d1.

22. Villeneuve, "Netflix Updates."

BIBLIOGRAPHY

Adichie, Chimamanda Ngozi. *We Should All Be Feminists*. New York: Anchor Books, 2014.

Ahsan, Sadaf. "'It's a Lifestyle, It's a Religion': How Gilmore Girls Has Transcended Generations, Gender and Genre." *National Post*. 24 November 2016. https://nationalpost.com/entertainment/television/its-a-lifestyle-its-a-religion-how-gilmore-girls-has-transcended-generations-gender-and-genre.

Alexander, Brian. "What America Is Losing as Its Small Towns Struggle." *The Atlantic*. 18 October 2017. https://www.theatlantic.com/business/archive/2017/10/small-town-economies-culture/543138/.

"Alexis Bledel." *Biography*. March 2003.

Baumgardner, Jennifer, and Amy Richards. *Manifesta: Young Women, Feminism, and the Future*, 10th Anniversary Edition. New York: Farrar, Straus and Giroux, 2010.

Bellafante, Ginia. "Mother and Daughter, Each Coming into Her Own." *The New York Times*. 17 May 2007.

"The Best and Worst of 2000: TV." *Time* 159, no. 25. 18 December 2000.

Bowman, Sabienna. "The One 'Gilmore Girls' Revival Series Theory about Rory's Love Life You Probably Haven't Considered." *Bustle.com*. 5 February 2016. https://www.bustle.com/articles/139829-the-one-gilmore-girls-revival-series-theory-about-rorys-love-life-you-probably-havent-considered.

———. "What Your Favorite 'Gilmore Girls' Friendship Says about You." *Bustle.com*. 26 April 2016. https://www.bustle.com/articles/156534-what-your-favorite-gilmore-girls-friendship-says-about-you.

Bradley, Laura. "Where You Lead: How *Gilmore Girls* Found Its Brightest Stars." *Vanity Fair*. 23 November 2016. https://www.vanityfair.com/hollywood/2016/11/gilmore-girls-lauren-graham-alexis-bledel-casting-interviews.

"Bringing Up Rory: Father Figures in Rory's Life." *Reddit.com*. https://www.reddit.com/r/GilmoreGirls/comments/52fm4z/bringing_up_rory_father_figures_in_rorys_life/.

Brummett, Barry. *Rhetoric in Popular Culture*, 4th ed. Los Angeles: Sage Publications, 2015.

"Businesses in Stars Hollow." *Reddit.com*. https://www.reddit.com/r/GilmoreGirls/comments/76tjzv/businesses_in_starshollow/.

Carlin, Shannon. "23 'Gilmore Girls' Pop Culture References You Totally Forgot About." *Bustle.com*. 16 November 2017. https://www.bustle.com/p/23-gilmore-girls-pop-culture-references-you-totally-forgot-about-77015.

Chase, Mary. "Gilmore Girls' Math." *AmyandMary.com*. 26 October 2018. https://amyandmary.com/2018/10/26/gilmore-girls-math/?fbclid=IwAR2ZbbPvGVKqr56-OvZsQ7s4iD
hICERHVJoLkYdy0fMgjgBpN_YOa-t4Y48.

Cramer, Katherine J. "The Great American Fallout: How Small Towns Came to Resent Cities." *The Guardian*. 19 June 2017. https://www.theguardian.com/cities/2017/jun/19/americas-great-fallout-rural-areas-resent-cities-republican-democrat.

Crusie, Jennifer. "Introduction: Speaking of the Gilmore Girls . . ." In *Coffee at Luke's: An Unauthorized* Gilmore Girls *Gabfest*, edited by Jennifer Crusie with Leah Wilson, 1–8. Dallas: Benbella Books, 2007.

Dee, Jonathan. "The Myth of '18 to 34.'" *The New York Times*. 13 October 2002.

Dibdin, Emma. "The Definitive Reading List for Each of Rory Gilmore's Boyfriends." *Elle.com*. 16 November 2016. https://www.elle.com/culture/movies-tv/news/a40817/gilmore-girls-boyfriends-reading-list/.

Ehrlich, Brenna. "11 Musical Moments That Prove 'Gilmore Girls' Was the Most Hipster Show on TV." *MTV.com*. 12 September 2014.

Elhage, Alysse. "Growing Up with a Single Mom Isn't like Life on *Gilmore Girls*." *Verily*. 4 November 2014. https://verilymag.com/2014/11/girlmore-girls-single-motherhood.

Fetto, John. "Wholesome Goodness: An Advertiser-Advocated, 'Family-Friendly' TV Show Manages Its Way into a Network's Fall Lineup." *American Demographics*. 1 August 2000.

Finkle, Jeff. "5 Reasons 'Gilmore Girls' Isn't Just for Girls." *Goodmenproject.com*. 16 December 2016. https://goodmenproject.com/arts/5-reasons-gilmore-girls-isnt-just-for-girls-dg/.

Fitzwater, Miellyn. "My Three Dads." In *Coffee at Luke's: An Unauthorized* Gilmore Girls *Gabfest*, edited by Jennifer Crusie with Leah Wilson, 69–84. Dallas: Benbella Books, 2007.

Fleegal, Stacia. "Like Mother-Daughter, Like Daughter-Mother." In *"Gilmore Girls" and the Politics of Identity: Essays on Family and Feminism in the Television Series*, edited by Ritch Calvin, 143–58. Jefferson, NC: McFarland, 2008.

Fretts, Bruce. "Happy Gilmore." *Entertainment Weekly*. 29 September 2000.

Garcia, Patricia. "11 Things in *Gilmore Girls: A Year in the Life* That Made Absolutely No Sense." *Vogue*. 28 November 2016. https://www.vogue.com/article/gilmore-girls-a-year-in-the-life-nonsense.

Gawley, Paige. "All 62 of Kirk's Odd Jobs on 'Gilmore Girls.'" *Decider.com*. 25 March 2016.

Gay, Roxane. *Bad Feminist: Essays*. New York: Harper Perennial, 2014.

Giannotta, Meghan. "'Gilmore Girls' Creator Amy Sherman-Palladino: It's Absurd to Say Show Isn't Feminist." *AMNetwork.com*. 15 November 2017. https://www.amny.com/entertainment/gilmore-girls-feminism-1.14989877.

"Gilmore Girls Getaway: Visit the 'Real' Stars Hollow, Connecticut." Connecticut Office of Tourism. *Ctvisit.com*. 2018. https://www.ctvisit.com/getaway/gilmore-girls-getaway.

Grady, Constance. "Gilmore Girls on Netflix: What You Need to Know about the Revival." *Vox.com*. 25 October 2016. https://www.vox.com/2016/4/13/11410986/watch-gilmore-girls-revival-netflix-cast.

Graham, Lauren. *Talking as Fast as I Can: From* Gilmore Girls *to* Gilmore Girls *(and Everything in Between)*. New York: Ballantine Books, 2016.

Griffiths, Eleanor Bley. "Gilmore Girls Creator Amy Sherman-Palladino Has 'Freedom' to Make More When Timing Is Right." *RadioTimes*. 10 November 2017. https://www.radiotimes.com/news/on-demand/2018-12-21/gilmore-girls-sequel/.

Heffernan, Virginia. "A Series Changes Horses, and the Ride Gets Bumpy." *The New York Times*. 7 November 2006. https://www.nytimes.com/2006/11/07/arts/television/07heff.html.

Hiddlestone, Janine. "Mothers, Daughters, and Gilmore Girls." In *Coffee at Luke's: An Unauthorized* Gilmore Girls *Gabfest*, edited by Jennifer Crusie with Leah Wilson, 31–42. Dallas: Benbella Books, 2007.

Highfill, Samantha. "Gilmore Girls: Rory's Ending Explained." *Entertainment Weekly*. 28 November 2016. https://ew.com/article/2016/11/28/gilmore-girls-year-life-rory-ending/.

Hundley, Heather L., and Sara E. Hayden, eds. *Mediated Moms: Contemporary Challenges to the Motherhood Myth*. New York: Peter Lang Publishing, 2016.

Husband, Andrew. "'Gilmore Girls' Celebrated Smart People as Celebrities When Other Shows Wouldn't." *UPROXX.com*. 23 November 2016. https://uproxx.com/tv/gilmore-girls-celebrity-cameos/.

Jacobs, A. J. *Man at His Best: Opinions "Gilmore Girls* Is the Best Show on TV for Men." *Esquire*. October 2005.

Jodha, Ashani. "42 Big Questions Ultimate 'Gilmore Girls' Fans Want the Netflix Revival to Answer." *Bustle.com*. 12 February 2016. https://www.bustle.com/articles/139842-42-big-questions-ultimate-gilmore-girls-fans-want-the-netflix-revival-to-answer.

Keveney, Bill. "Mailer's 'Gilmore Girls' Guest Shot Is a Family Affair." *USA Today*. 24 September 2004.

Kosner, Lily. "10 Musical Moments All 'Gilmore Girls' Fans Should Never Forget." *AXS.com*. 2016. https://www.axs.com/10-musical-moments-all-gilmore-girls-fans-should-never-forget-103603.

Leszkiewicz, Anna. "'People are Born Evil': The Unlikely Cynicism of Gilmore Girls Creator Amy Sherman-Palladino." *New Statesman America*. 16 November 2017. https://www.newstatesman.com/culture/tv-radio/2017/11/amy-sherman-palladino-interview-dan-gilmore-girls-marvelous-mrs-maisel.

Levy, Joe. "Gilmore Girls." *Rolling Stone*. 30 August 2001.

Littleton, Cynthia. "How Hollywood Is Racing to Catch Up with Netflix." *Variety*. August 2018. https://variety.com/2018/digital/features/media-streaming-services-netflix-disney-comcast-att-1202910463/.

Locker, Melissa. "Monkey Gone to Heaven." *Rolling Stone*. 7 May 2012. https://www.rollingstone.com/music/music-news/monkey-gone-to-heaven-87722/.

Loofbourow, Lili. "What *Gilmore Girls* Gets Right About Money and Love." *The Cut*. 3 October 2014. https://www.thecut.com/2014/10/what-gilmore-girls-shows-us-about-money-and-love.html.

———. "The Decline and Fall of the Gilmore Girls." *The Week*. 1 December 2016. https://theweek.com/articles/664566/decline-fall-gilmore-girls.

Lorre, Rose Maura. "*Gilmore Girls*' Pop-Culture References, by the Numbers." *Vulture*. 1 December 2015. https://www.vulture.com/2015/12/gilmore-girls-pop-culture-references-by-the-numbers.html.

Lupica, Lilith Hardi. "Lauren Graham Confirms We May Never Get the Answers We Need from Gilmore Girls." *Vogue*. 6 April 2018. https://www.vogue.com.au/culture/features/lauren-graham-confirms-we-may-never-get-the-answers-we-need-from-gilmore-girls/news-story/0286e4521ae72482dd66bbfa4ff3a4d1.

Maas, Jennifer. "'Gilmore Girls: A Year in the Life': 15 Things Still Bothering Fans a Year Later (Photos)." *The Wrap*. 25 November 2017. https://www.thewrap.com/gilmore-girls-a-year-in-the-life-anniversary-things-fans-hate/.

Macke, Johnni. "The 18 Best Businesses in Stars Hollow from 'Gilmore Girls,' Ranked Once and for All." *Hellogiggles.com*. 23 April 2016. https://hellogiggles.com/lifestyle/businesses-gilmore-girls-ranked/.

Manning, Jimmie. "But Luke and Lorelai Belong Together! Relationships, Social Control, and Gilmore Girls." In *Screwball Television: Critical Perspectives on "Gilmore Girls,"* edited by David Scott Diffrient with David Lavery, 302–20. Syracuse, NY: Syracuse University Press, 2010.

Marcus, Emily. "Gilmore Girls' Matt Czuchry: Fans Called Me a 'Real A-hole' for Playing Logan Huntzberger." *US Weekly*. 18 January 2018. https://www.usmagazine.com/entertainment/news/gilmore-girls-matt-czuchry-i-was-called-an-a-hole-for-playing-logan/.

McCornack, Steven. *Reflect and Relate: An Introduction to Interpersonal Communication*. Boston: Bedford/St. Martin's, 2013.

Media and Girls. Media Smarts: Canada's Centre for Digital and Media Literacy. http://mediasmarts.ca/gender-representation/women-and-girls/media-and-girls.

"Moment by Moment." *Rotten Tomatoes*. https://www.rottentomatoes.com/m/moment_by_moment.

"Movies Mentioned in the Gilmore Girls." *Listchallenges.com*. 2018. https://www.listchallenges.com/movies-mentioned-in-the-gilmore-girls.

"Music You Like That the Gilmores Hate/Music the Gilmores Like That You Hate." *Reddit.com*. https://www.reddit.com/r/GilmoreGirls/comments/7x6jv8/music_you_like_that_the_gilmores_hate_music_the.

"Musicians Mentioned on the Gilmore Girls." *Rateyourmusic.com*. 17 June 2018. https://rateyourmusic.com/board_message?message_id=349472

Nededog, Jethro. "Netflix's 'Gilmore Girls' Revival Is Almost Everything Fans Wanted from It." *Business Insider*. 23 November 2016. https://www.businessinsider.com/netflix-gilmore-girls-review-2016-11.

Nettleton, Pamela Hill. "Table for Two: *Gilmore Girls*' Lorelai and Rory Legitimize Single Mothers and Their Children as Family." *U.S. Catholic* 81, no. 12 (38–39). December 2016.

Nussbaum, Danielle. "Lauren Graham: Why Gilmore Girls Is Feminist." *Entertainment Weekly*. 8 September 2016. http://www.ew.com/article/2016/09/08/lauren-graham-gilmore-girls-feminist/.

Ochs, Meredith. "The New Pornographers, a 'Real' Supergroup." *NPR*. 25 October 2007. https://www.npr.org/templates/story/story.php?storyId=15630417.

Palczewski, Catherine Helen, Victoria Pruin DeFrancisco, and Danielle Dick McGeough. *Gender in Communication: A Critical Introduction*, 3rd ed. Los Angeles: Sage Publications, 2019.

Phan, Nathan, and Sania Syed. "Teens Aren't Fairly Portrayed in Media." *The Princeton Summer Journal*. 11 August 2014. https://princetonsummerjournal.com/2014/08/11/teens-arent-fairly-portrayed-in-media/.

Pickhardt, Carl E. "The Challenge of Mothering an Adolescent Daughter." *Psychology Today*. 6 December 2010. https://www.psychologytoday.com/us/blog/surviving-your-childs-adolescence/201012/the-challenge-mothering-adolescent-daughter.

Pittman, Allison. "Digger Stiles: A Man for One Season." *MelissaTagg.com*. 18 July 2014. http://www.melissatagg.com/giveaway/gilmore-guys-digger.

Platts, Todd K. "Locating Zombies in the Sociology of Popular Culture." *Sociology Compass* 7, no. 7 (July 2013): 547–60.

Plitt, Amy. "10 Things You Need to Know about the Revival." *Rolling Stone*. 21 November 2016. http://www.rollingstone.com/tv/news/10-things-you-need-to-know-about-gilmore-girls-revival-w449485.

Poniewozik, James. "6 DVDs Great for a Chuckle." *Time* 165, no. 23, 6 June 2005.

———. "How I Chose the List." *Time*. 6 September 2007. http://time.com/collection-post/3087799/how-i-chose-the-list/.

Poniewozik, James, and Jeanne McDowell. "Postnuclear Explosion." *Time* 156, no. 19, 6 November 2000.

Porter, Kevin. "The 15 Best Pop Culture References in 'Gilmore Girls.'" *Elle.com*. 1 November 2016. https://www.elle.com/culture/movies-tv/g29070/best-gilmore-girls-pop-culture-references/.

Press, Joy. *Stealing the Show: How Women Are Revolutionizing Television*. New York: Atria Books, 2018.

Quint, Maura. "Your Friend's 'Gilmore Girls' Obsession, Explained." *Thrillist Entertainment*. 22 November 2016. https://www.thrillist.com/entertainment/nation/gilmore-girls-why-are-your-friends-obsessed-with-an-old-wb-show.

Radish, Christina. "Amy Sherman-Palladino and Dan Palladino on the Return of 'Gilmore Girls' and the Problem with Network TV." *Collider*. 24 November 2016. http://collider.com/amy-sherman-palladino-dan-palladino-gilmore-girls-a-year-in-the-life-interview/.

Radnor, Abigail. "'It's Sunny and Safe': Why *Gilmore Girls* Is Perfect Comfort TV." *The Guardian*. 5 November 2016. https://www.theguardian.com/tv-and-radio/2016/nov/05/sunny-safe-gilmore-girls-comfort-tv.

"The Rory Gilmore Reading Challenge." *Listchallenges.com*. 2018. https://www.listchallenges.com/rory-gilmore-reading-challenge.

Ross, Sharon. "'Tough Enough': Female Friendship and Heroism in *Xena* and *Buffy*." In *Action Chicks: New Images of Tough Women in Popular Culture*, edited by Sherrie A. Inness, 231–56. New York: Palgrave Macmillan, 2004.

Saladino, Laura. "Every Movie Referenced/Watched in Gilmore Girls (Including Quotes)!" *letterboxd.com*. https://letterboxd.com/lesaladino/list/every-movie-referenced-watched-in-gilmore/.

Sarikaya, Berrak. "What 'Gilmore Girls' Taught Me about Business." *Amplifyyour.biz*. 29 November 2016. http://www.amplifyyour.biz/gilmore-girls-business-lessons/.

Sepinwall, Alan. "Best of the '00s in TV: Best Comedies." *NJ.com*. 21 December 2009. http://www.nj.com/entertainment/tv/index.ssf/2009/12/best_of_the_00s_in_tv_best_com.html.

Shaw, Jessica. "Mother of Reinvention: 'Gilmore Girls' Creator Amy Sherman-Palladino Explains How She Pulled Her Show out of a Slump." *Entertainment Weekly* 806. 11 February 2005.

Stache, Lara C. "Sexuality in Popular Culture: Is It 'All about That Bass?'" In *Contemporary Studies of Sexuality and Communication: Theoretical and Applied Perspectives*, edited by Jimmie Manning and Carey Noland, 421–32. Dubuque, IA: Kendall Hunt, 2016.

———. *"Breaking Bad": A Cultural History*. Lanham, MD: Rowman & Littlefield, 2017.

Stanhope, Kate. "'Gilmore Girls' Bosses Discuss Final Four Words, Rory Criticism and Possible Future Installments." *Hollywood Reporter*. 1 December 2016. http://www.hollywoodreporter.com/live-feed/gilmore-girls-revival-creator-final-four-words-951693.

Sweney, Mark. "Netflix and Amazon Become More Popular than Pay-TV Services." *The Guardian*. 17 July 2018. https://www.theguardian.com/media/2018/jul/18/netflix-and-amazon-become-more-popular-than-pay-tv-services.

Tucker, Ken. "A Literary Legend Pays a Visit to 'Gilmore Girls.'" *Entertainment Weekly*. 15 October 2004.

———. "Goodbye 'Girls.'" *Entertainment Weekly*. 18 May 2007.

Valenti, Lauren. "Lorelai Gilmore's 'Vicious Trollop' Lip Color Can Now Be Yours." *Marie Claire*. 3 November 2016. https://www.marieclaire.com/beauty/news/a23371/vicious-trollop-lip-color/.

VanDerWerff, Todd. "*Gilmore Girls* is Slyly Smart about Class and How Isolating Money Can Be." *Vox.com*. 1 December 2016. http://www.vox.com/culture/2016/12/1/13786732/gilmore-girls-netflix-year-life-class-money.

Villeneuve, Nicole. "Netflix Updates 'Gilmore Girls' Fans on the Possibility of More Episodes." *Brit + Co*. 30 July 2018. https://www.brit.co/netflix-gilmore-girls-more-episodes-update/.

Wang, Emily. "Keiko Agena Says There's Enough Story for Another *Gilmore Girls* Revival." *Glamour*. 14 September 2018. https://www.glamour.com/story/keiko-agena-another-gilmore-girls-revival.

Weiner, Allison Hope. "Golden Girls." *Entertainment Weekly*. 22 March 2002.

Weiss, Suzannah. "4 Problems with How We're Talking about 'Female Friendships.'" *Everyday Feminism*. 23 March 2016. https://everydayfeminism.com/2016/03/female-friendship-trope/.

Whiteside, Stephanie. "When Paris Met Rory." In *Coffee at Luke's: An Unauthorized* Gilmore Girls *Gabfest*, edited by Jennifer Crusie with Leah Wilson, 21–30. Dallas: Benbella Books, 2007.

Yahr, Emily. "More 'Gilmore Girls'? Actually Netflix, We're Good." *The Washington Post*. 8 March 2017. https://www.washingtonpost.com/news/arts-and-entertainment/wp/2017/03/08/more-gilmore-girls-actually-netflix-were-good/?utm_term=.a91e3b139004.

Zaleski, Annie. "'Gilmore Girls' Town Troubadour Grant-Lee Phillips Will Return to Stars Hollow: 'It Was Such a Subversive Show.'" *Salon.com*. 11 February 2016. http://www.salon.com/2016/02/10/gilmore_girls_town_troubadour_grant_lee_phillips_will_return_to_stars_hollow_it_was_such_a_subversive_show.

Zuckerman, Esther. "*Gilmore Girls*: A Not-So-Modest Proposal." *Entertainment Weekly*. 24 October 2014.

INDEX

ABOUT THE AUTHORS

Lara C. Stache is an assistant professor in the Division of Communication, Visual, and Performing Arts at Governors State University and writes about gender, rhetoric, and popular culture.

Rachel D. Davidson is an assistant professor in the Department of Communication at Hanover College. Go, Panthers!

Printed in the USA
CPSIA information can be obtained
at www.ICGtesting.com
LVHW091440100923
757727LV00034B/5

9 781538 112830